THE WORKS OF SRI CHINMOY

PLAYS
VOLUME II

THE WORKS OF SRI CHINMOY

PLAYS

VOLUME II

★★

THE DISCIPLE ILLUMINES THE MASTER

THE HEART OF A HOLY MAN

MOTHER, GIVE ME
THE LIGHT OF KNOWLEDGE

SUPREME SACRIFICE

THE SACRED FIRE

DESHABANDHU:
BENGAL'S BELOVED FRIEND

CHANDA AND TANDRA

LYON · OXFORD

GANAPATI PRESS

LXXXVIII

© 2018 THE SRI CHINMOY CENTRE

ISBN 978-1-911319-19-1

See appendix for notice regarding this edition.

FIRST EDITION WENT TO PRESS ON 13 APRIL 2018

PLAYS

VOLUME II

PART I

THE DISCIPLE ILLUMINES THE MASTER

THE DISCIPLE ILLUMINES THE MASTER

SRI CHINMOY

DI I. DRAMATIS PERSONÆ

MASTER
RATAN (MOST DEVOTED DISCIPLE OF THE MASTER)
ROHINI (WIFE OF RATAN, ALSO VERY DEVOTED)
RULA (THEIR DAUGHTER, AGE FIVE)
FIRST NEIGHBOUR
SECOND NEIGHBOUR
KADU (A SLIGHTLY DOUBTING DISCIPLE)
HIS WIFE
HIS SERVANT
KAVIR (SON OF KADU, AGE TWELVE)
RELATIVES AND FRIENDS OF KADU
DISCIPLE OF THE MASTER
OTHER DISCIPLES OF THE MASTER
HUSBAND AND WIFE (RICHEST DISCIPLES OF THE MASTER)
DAYAL (THEIR SON, AGE FOURTEEN)
FIRST POLICEMAN
SECOND POLICEMAN
SERGEANT
ANGEL

THE DISCIPLE ILLUMINES THE MASTER

DI 2. SCENE I

(The home of Ratan and Rohini. The Master has come to visit them and is playing with their daughter, Rula.)

MASTER   Rula, Rula, today you look so pretty. I see a necklace of pearls around your neck. You look so beautiful, so beautiful.

RATAN   Oh Master, it is all due to your grace. We had little money, little material prosperity before you came into our lives. Our wealth is all due to your grace.

ROHINI   We depend entirely on you, Master. It is your grace that has made us rich. It is your grace that has made us happy. It is your grace that will help us accomplish everything we wish to accomplish here on earth. We are so grateful to you. We shall do everything, everything, everything for you, Master.

(Master blesses the couple.)

MASTER   I am indeed proud of both of you. *(To Rohini.)* Please make me a most delicious meal today. I have not had the pleasure of eating one of your meals for a long time. You feel that I am a great Master, but I feel that I am a great eater.

ROHINI   Master, you eat our food, which takes an hour or two to prepare; but the food that you give us would have taken us centuries to get without your help. There is no comparison between your food and ours. When we eat your food, our life becomes constant gratitude to you. Where else can we get Peace, Light and Bliss if not from you?

MASTER   That is true, but we need each other. The disciple needs the Master, and the Master needs the disciple. *(To*

Ratan.) I shall go out for a walk with Rula. We will be back in half an hour. In the meantime, please help Rohini prepare the meal.

ROHINI   Master, I shall do my best to make a most delicious meal for you. If you like my food, what more do I need on earth? For my Master to say that he likes my food means that I possess Heaven right here on earth.

(Master smiles. Ratan and Rohini bow to him with folded hands. Exeunt Master and Rula.)

THE DISCIPLE ILLUMINES THE MASTER

DI 3. SCENE 2

(Master and Rula are walking in the street. Master is showing much affection to Rula and she is very happy.)

MASTER   *(suddenly)* Rula, please give me your necklace. It is so beautiful. I wish to have it. I shall give you something more beautiful than this one, much more beautiful, in return.

RULA   No, I want to keep this one. *(Pauses.)* Let me see the one you have that is better than this.

MASTER   Today you give me this one and tomorrow I shall bring you the new one.

RULA   No, I won't give it to you. Give me the better one first and then I shall give you this one.

MASTER   If you don't give it to me I shall take it away and leave you here, and you will have to go home all alone.

(Rula starts to cry.)

MASTER   Stop crying!

(Rula cries louder.)

MASTER   *(aside)* I need money badly. I could sell this necklace for thousands of rupees, but how can I get it away from this stubborn child? She is making so much noise that I shall be caught. I'll have to kill her. Then I can take the necklace and leave the city.

(As the Master grabs Rula, she starts to scream. He strangles her. When she loses consciousness, he snatches the necklace and runs away, leaving the child lying senseless on the ground. Enter two neighbours who catch the Master as he is leaving the scene.)

FIRST NEIGHBOUR   What's going on here? What's all the noise about?

(They notice the child lying on the ground and discover the necklace which the Master is trying to hide. Putting two and two together, they begin to curse the Master and strike him.)

SECOND NEIGHBOUR   Now tell us! Whose daughter is she?
MASTER   She is the child of Ratan and Rohini.
NEIGHBOURS   Take us there.

(One neighbour lifts Rula in his arms; the other holds the Master securely. Exeunt omnes.)

THE DISCIPLE ILLUMINES THE MASTER

DI 4. SCENE 3

(In front of Ratan's house. Enter neighbours with Rula and Master. Ratan rushes onstage.)

RATAN   What are you doing? This is my Guru! And why are you carrying my daughter?

FIRST NEIGHBOUR   This is your Guru? This rogue? This criminal? Look what he has done! He has killed your daughter to steal her necklace.

RATAN   *(momentarily shocked, but quickly recovering)* Don't worry. I know that my Guru has the power to revive her. See, I am touching his feet and praying to him. *(Touches Master's feet.)* Oh Guru, save my child. I am sure she is not yet dead; she is just unconscious. You have the power to revive her. Please use your power, dearest Master. Just look at her once and my Rula will be all right.

(Master looks at Rula, placing his hands on her. She revives and starts striking him.)

RULA   I hate you! You tried to steal my necklace! You hurt me!

RATAN   No, no, Rula. He was just playing a game with you. See, you are not hurt. Look at our Master's power. He has just shown you a trick.

(Exeunt Master, Ratan and Rula. Neighbours shrug as they watch them go off together.)

FIRST NEIGHBOUR   These Masters are such rogues! Had it been my daughter, I would have killed the man immediately.

SECOND NEIGHBOUR   I would have called the police and had him arrested! But this stupid Ratan has such faith in his Master, even though he's obviously the world's worst rogue. Someday something really serious will happen, and then he will learn.

(Exeunt omnes.)

THE DISCIPLE ILLUMINES THE MASTER

DI 5. SCENE 4

(The home of Kadu, another disciple. Enter Master.)

MASTER   I have come to visit you, Kadu, and I am in a mood to show some of my occult power. You can invite all your friends, relatives and spiritual brothers and sisters. Today I shall perform a miracle. I have never performed any miracles in public, but today I am going to do it since most of you people have no faith in me at all.

KADU   Master, I do have faith in you, I do have faith in you. You don't have to show me your occult power. But if you want to show it to others, then naturally I shall invite them. Everyone will be very happy and delighted to watch, I am sure.

MASTER   All right, invite them.

(Kadu calls his servant. Enter servant bowing.)

KADU   Go and invite all my friends and relatives and all my spiritual brothers and sisters. Today Master is going to perform some miracles for us. He is going to use his occult powers. Everyone is invited.

(Exit servant. Moments later, enter friends, relatives and other disciples.)

MASTER   *(to Kadu)* Where is your son, Kavir?
KADU   Oh, he is studying in his room, Master.
MASTER   Bring him here. I wish to see him.

(Exit Kadu. Re-enter Kadu, followed by Kavir with folded hands.)

MASTER Now watch. Here is Kavir. Kavir, I am going to strike you once very hard. You will definitely be knocked unconscious by my blow.
KAVIR Oh Master, I don't want to. I don't want that to happen.
MASTER Is there anybody here among my disciples who wants to participate in this miracle? After I knock the person unconscious, I will touch his head and revive him.

(Several disciples step forward to volunteer.)

ONE DISCIPLE Master, it is such an honour to be struck by you — such a joy, such a source of pride, such an honour!
OTHER DISCIPLES Please choose me!
KAVIR No! Master chose me first. I want to be struck by Master. I want to do it.
MASTER All right, Kavir. Come here.

(Master strikes him and Kavir falls down, unconscious. His mother begins to cry.)

MASTER Now I shall perform the miracle. I am touching his head. *(Places his hands on Kavir.)* Kavir, arise!

(No response from Kavir's inert body. Onlookers become alarmed.)

DISCIPLE Somebody get a doctor!
MASTER No, no! I can do it, I tell you, I can do it. Just the other day I performed this miracle at Ratan and Rohini's house. Where is Ratan? Ask him to come here. *(Exit one of the onlookers to get Ratan.)* He will tell you that I did it. He said, "Master, use your power. You have the power." And I

did it. Today I have invited everybody here to watch me, but now this power is not working.

(Enter Ratan. The women are crying. The men are terribly angry with the Master.)

RATAN Master, what is the matter? Why aren't you using your occult power? Please, please do it. I know you have the capacity. You did it for my daughter; you can do it here also. Master, Master, why are you allowing yourself to be embarrassed when you have such tremendous spiritual and occult power? *(Ratan touches Master's feet and pleads.)* Master, look at Kavir. Please touch his head. *(Master touches Kavir's head. Kavir immediately gets up and looks around.)*

KAVIR Oh Father, where was I? I seemed to be in another world. I saw my mother crying for me. I don't know where I was, but my mother and father couldn't see me. Master, I don't want to play your game any more.

SRI CHINMOY

DI 6. SCENE 5

(Master and Ratan are at the home of the Master's richest disciples.)

MASTER   *(to husband)* You are my richest disciple.
HUSBAND   Oh Master, I may be rich on the physical plane, but you are the one who is rich on the spiritual plane.
MASTER   Well, I have come to the richest person on this physical plane. It is my wish to cook for you here today. Your wife has cooked for me many times and her food is always delicious. Now I wish to cook for the two of you. And when your son comes home from school, he can join you.

(Husband and wife are overjoyed and full of gratitude. Exit Master to cook. Husband and wife set a table. After a while, enter Master.)

MASTER   Good. I am finished. Now you are the guests, so begin eating. Ratan will help me serve.
WIFE   No, no, Master. How can we allow you to serve us while we eat? Let us wait for you, and we shall all eat together.
MASTER   No, no, no. Obedience comes first in the spiritual life. Since you are my disciples, you have to obey me. We will join you later. Now you start eating.

(Master and Ratan begin serving the two disciples. After eating a few morsels of food, both husband and wife collapse onto the floor.)

MASTER   Ratan, I have put poison into their food. *(Ratan is shocked and dismayed.)* Now we can go upstairs and look for their money. I am sure that they have thousands of rupees hidden away. Let us get the money; then I shall heal them as I have healed others in the past with the help of your prayer.

THE DISCIPLE ILLUMINES THE MASTER

I know that I don't have any occult power at all. The first time, when I cured Rula, I thought it was my own power that did it. But after trying since then, I came to realise that it is only when you are there to touch my feet that I can do anything at all. It is your faith in me that cures everybody. It is from your faith that I get the capacity to perform miracles. Otherwise, I have no power at all. Now, let us go upstairs and take the money. Then you will pray to me and I shall cure them. You have helped me to do it before. I am sure we will be able to do it this time too.

(Exeunt omnes. Enter Dayal. Seeing his parents on the floor, he immediately runs to the door and shouts for the police. Enter two policemen who examine the bodies, look around, then go upstairs. Dayal sits down and buries his face in his hands. Re-enter policemen with Master and Ratan.)

FIRST POLICEMAN   You are both under arrest. Let's go.

(Exeunt policemen, Master and Ratan.)

DI 7. SCENE 6

(Ratan's house. Dayal is staying with Rohini and Rula while Ratan is in prison.)

ROHINI   Dayal, you know that my husband is completely innocent. He did not wish to kill your parents. They were always so kind to us. We were very good friends.

DAYAL   I know it. I know it, Mother Rohini. Uncle Ratan was always extremely good to me. It was because of the Guru that he did it. I do not blame you or my uncle at all. I blame the Master, that rascal! It is because of him that I have lost my parents!

ROHINI   Do not call him a rascal, my child. He is our Master. He knows the kind of experiences we need for our spiritual growth. You have lost your parents, and I have lost my two friends and my husband. I know that your loss is infinitely worse than mine. How can I console you, sweetest Dayal? Only God can comfort you, and I am sure He will. The ever-compassionate Father will certainly console you.

THE DISCIPLE ILLUMINES THE MASTER

DI 8. SCENE 7

(A few weeks later. The Master and Ratan are in the prison yard doing hard labour. The sergeant of the work gang is standing guard.)

RATAN *(to sergeant)* Please, please allow me to do two men's jobs. I don't want my Master to have to do this kind of work. I would be so grateful if you allowed me to do his work.

SERGEANT You fool! Just because of him you are now here. You are an innocent fellow. He has exploited you, you fool! He is a rogue, a real criminal! You will be freed one day, but not that shameless creature! Never!

RATAN Call me a fool, say anything you want against me, but please don't criticise my Master. He is everything to me. My heart breaks to see him here in prison, but it pains me even more to see him working like a labourer. He is not in the habit of doing this kind of work.

(Rohini, Rula and Dayal come to visit the Master and Ratan in prison. Rula runs toward her father, stretching out her little arms to him.)

RULA Father, Father, when will you come back home? Everybody says that you are innocent. Everybody says it is Master who has done wrong and got you into trouble.

RATAN Hold your tongue, Rula. He is my Master; he is my all. One more word against him and I shall thrash you. I am sure your mother has told you all this nonsense.

ROHINI *(bursting into tears)* No, no, my Lord, I have not. I told her nothing. She has been hearing about our Master from our neighbours and friends. *(Bows to the Master with folded hands and addresses him.)* Master, I do not know anything. I am an insignificant human being. I do not know what is best for us. We gave you our total surrender, and this is the result. My husband is here in jail suffering with you, and we are outside suffering for you. But I wish to keep my surrender unwavering. I am sure that what you have done is best for us. If this had not happened, perhaps something else infinitely worse would have happened. So I am grateful to you that only this has happened. But I do not know how to console Dayal, poor boy. He has lost both his parents. His loss is really severe.

DAYAL No, no, Mother Rohini. Master, last night I had a dream. My parents came to me and told me that you had done the right thing in poisoning them. They said that they were already dead, that their inner beings had already been poisoned by their money. They had thousands of rupees but did not give you anything. Their minds were corrupted; their hearts were corrupted. They loved their money more than they loved you. So, Master, they feel that you saved them from wasting many years in ignorance and bondage. In their next incarnation, they feel that you will give them more spiritual wealth and less physical wealth so that they will be able to dedicate themselves wholeheartedly to the service of God. Master, they feel that you have done the right thing, and for that they are most grateful to you. And I, too, am grateful. My parents say that they are very happy in the other world, and that makes me happy, even though I still miss them. I know that they will come to me from time to time and bless me inwardly. That will be enough. Meanwhile, my aunt Rohini will be my mother now. She is all kindness, all affection, all love. I get everything I need from her. And when my uncle comes back, he will be my father. So I shall still have a father and a mother who are your disciples.

DI 10. SCENE 9

(Ratan and Master are asleep in their prison cell. An angel appears to Ratan, who wakes up and rises to his feet.)

ANGEL   Ratan, the authorities have learned of your innocence, and they will set you free tomorrow.

RATAN   I don't want to be freed without my Master. He is everything to me. If he is not freed, I am not going to leave this prison. I will stay with him and serve him here. I won't go without him.

ANGEL   Your Master has ruined your life. He has ruined the lives of many innocent people and caused them terrible suffering. Many people had great faith in him, and now see what he has done to them. His spiritual children dare not show their faces, for his crime has been like a slur on their lives, and they are now ridiculed and mocked. Can't you recognise your stupidity?

RATAN   You call it stupidity, but I call it my oneness with my Master. This life of mine will last only for a short while. I have given it to my Master unconditionally, and I won't take it back now. I have surrendered everything to my Master. My body, vital, mind, heart and soul are all for his use only, until I die. I never want to be separated from my Master. If he is in hell, that will be my Heaven. I shall stay with him. And if he goes to Heaven, there I too shall go. I don't need earthly freedom, I don't need anybody on earth except him.

(Ratan sings.)

THE DISCIPLE ILLUMINES THE MASTER

Guruh brahma guruh vishnu
guruh devo maheshwarah
gurureva param brahma
tasmai shri gurabe namah

(Guru is Brahma, Guru is Vishnu,
Guru is the great God Shiva.
Indeed, Guru is the Brahman.
To that Divine Master I offer my obeisance.)

ANGEL   Suppose I were to give you illumination this very moment. Would you not leave your Master then, seeing that he is far inferior to you?

RATAN   No, even if you were to give me illumination I would not leave my Master. He taught me about God, he gave me the message of God, he inspired my love for God. If you gave me illumination, I would give it to my Master.

ANGEL   So you admit that your Master does not have illumination?

RATAN   I do not know whether my Master has it or not. But I feel that he has.

ANGEL   If he had illumination, how could he do such inhuman, absurd, unthinkable things? Would an illumined soul poison his own disciples in order to get their money? Those two disciples whom he poisoned have such nobility that they came to their son and told him lies in order to protect their Master's reputation and to prevent their son from losing all faith in the spiritual life. I tell you, you yourself are far superior to your Master in spirituality. Your Master is a real fake. You are deceiving yourself and placing your faith in a fraud.

RATAN   I cannot judge my Master. He knows what is best for me and for all his disciples. I am sure that whatever he has done has been for the best.

ANGEL   I shall give you some sound advice. One who has a truly illumined Master will realise God infinitely sooner than one with a false Master. Therefore, one should use discrimination and look for a genuine Master. But because of your tremendous sincerity and devotion, I am going to give you illumination anyway.

RATAN   I shall look upon the illumination you give me as a fruit. If you give me a fruit, I shall share it with my Master. If you free me, I shall take my Master with me, and if he is not allowed to leave, then I also shall stay. So whatever you give to me, you are giving equally to him.

ANGEL   The moment I touch your head, you will be illumined. Then wake your Master if you wish and touch him. You will give him illumination.

(Angel places his hands on Ratan's head. Master wakes up and watches his disciple receiving illumination. When the angel removes his hands from Ratan's head, Ratan immediately prostrates himself and touches his Master's feet. Master is illumined. Master and Ratan embrace each other, and the gate of the prison cell disappears. Exeunt Master and Ratan.)

MAITREYI

SRI CHINMOY

DI II. DRAMATIS PERSONÆ

YAGNYAVALKYA (A SAGE)
KATYAYANI, MAITREYI (HIS WIVES)

THE DISCIPLE ILLUMINES THE MASTER

DI 12. SCENE I

(Yagnyavalkya and Katyayani.)

YAGNYAVALKYA   Katyayani, I am now an old man.

KATYAYANI   My Lord, there comes a time when every human being becomes old. You are no exception.

YAGNYAVALKYA   Yes, you are right, Katyayani. Katyayani, I wish to make a simple suggestion to you. May I?

KATYAYANI   Certainly, by all means.

YAGNYAVALKYA   As you know, I have now reached a ripe old age. According to tradition, at this stage of life one must enter into the forest and offer one's life to God in prayer and meditation. It is high time for me to do that.

KATYAYANI   Who stands in your way, my Lord? Certainly I am not the one who will ever prevent you from doing the right thing.

YAGNYAVALKYA   Thank you, thank you, my dear Katyayani. Now here is the problem.

KATYAYANI   What is it? Tell me, my Lord.

YAGNYAVALKYA   Before I leave, I wish to offer you half my wealth, property and possessions, and the other half I wish to give to my other wife, Maitreyi.

KATYAYANI   That is fine with me, although it is I who take care of you most of the time. Maitreyi only wastes her time in fruitless meditation.

YAGNYAVALKYA   Katyayani, my dear, Maitreyi's meditation is not fruitless. Nor does she waste time when she meditates.

KATYAYANI   It is simply useless to tell you anything about Maitreyi. What I have said is not at all against her. I have just brought to your attention a mere fact, an undeniable fact. Anyway, since she too can claim you as her own, you may as well divide all your possessions between your darling Maitreyi and your maidservant Katyayani. I hate Maitreyi, I literally hate her! I do everything for you, and she takes all the credit. I have never seen such an irresponsible, careless and callous woman. Yet you love her dearly, more dearly than your very life. I tell you once and for all that I hate Maitreyi with all the hatred of the world at my command!

(Enter Maitreyi.)

KATYAYANI   Just think of the devil and the devil appears! Maitreyi, you have appeared unexpectedly, and I disappear deliberately!

(Exit Katyayani.)

MAITREYI   My Lord, I wish to meditate for a few minutes. Will you kindly join me?
YAGNYAVALKYA   Certainly I will.

(Yagnyavalkya and Maitreyi meditate together. Meditation over, Yagnyavalkya blesses Maitreyi.)

MAITREYI   *(thrilled and overjoyed)* My Lord, O matchless sage, I have seen, I have seen!
YAGNYAVALKYA   What have you seen, Maitreyi?
MAITREYI   I have seen your third eye wide open. Fathomless is its beauty. Measureless is its power.
YAGNYAVALKYA   I am proud of you. I am proud of your aspiration. *(Pauses.)* Maitreyi, I have something quite important to discuss with you. Do you have the time?

THE DISCIPLE ILLUMINES THE MASTER

MAITREYI Of course, my Lord, for you I have always the time. I am always at your disposal. This life of mine is ever at your express command.

YAGNYAVALKYA I knew it. I knew it. Now Maitreyi, I have already discussed the matter with Katyayani. She has fully agreed.

MAITREYI Please let me know what it is all about.

YAGNYAVALKYA Ah, of course, forgive me. The time has at last come for me to enter into the forest and spend my remaining days meditating on the Absolute, offering my existence, inner and outer, to my inner Pilot.

MAITREYI My Lord, indeed, that's a splendid idea.

YAGNYAVALKYA But listen, my divine wife. I want you to have one full half of my wealth, property and possessions, and the other half, needless to say, goes to Katyayani.

MAITREYI My Lord, do listen to me first, before I accept or reject your kind offer. You have always taught me that material wealth is of no avail. It is nothing in comparison to the inner wealth. Why, then, do you bind me with material wealth? Tell me one thing, my Lord: will this material wealth in any way add to my heart's mounting cry?

YAGNYAVALKYA Unfortunately, no.

MAITREYI Then why do you impose on me things that will take me away from the path of Truth, from the path of Divinity, from the path of Immortality? My Lord, my heart pines only for the immortal, transcendental Self. I want nothing but Immortality's Life. *Yenaham namrta syam kim aham tena kuryam.* What shall I do with the things that cannot make me immortal? Let Katyayani have all your material wealth. Let her cherish your earthly possessions, and I shall treasure your Heavenly possession — your loftiest realisation, your total oneness with the Absolute.

YAGNYAVALKYA *(while blessing Maitreyi)* Maitreyi, you are my heart's pride. You are my soul's pride. You are the pride of the absolute Supreme. Your footprints on the sands of time are indelible. Maitreyi, here is my last request: please sing a few soul-stirring songs for me.

(Maitreyi sings.)

Yenaham namrta syam
kim aham tena kuryam

(What shall I do with the things that cannot make
    me immortal?)

Hiranmayena patrena
satyasyapihitam mukham
tat tvam pusan apavrnu
satya-dharmaya drstaye

(The Face of Truth is covered with a brilliant
    golden orb.
Remove it, O Sun, so that I who am devoted to
    the Truth may behold the Truth.)

Vedaham etam purusam mahantam
aditya-varnam tamasah parastat

(I have known this Great Being, effulgent as the
    sun, beyond the boundaries of tenebrous
    gloom.)

THE DISCIPLE ILLUMINES THE MASTER

Anandadd hy eva khalv imani bhutani jayante
anandena jatani jivanti
anandam prayantyabhisam visanti

(From Delight we came into existence.
In Delight we grow.
At the end of our journey's close,
Into Delight we shall retire.)

YAGNYAVALKYA   Maitreyi, dearer than my life, to you I offer my heart's eternal gratitude. This heart of mine shall remain sempiternally with your supremely illumined heart in the direct Vision, pure Revelation and total Manifestation of the Absolute Supreme.

SAVITRI

SRI CHINMOY

DI 13. DRAMATIS PERSONÆ

KING ASHWAPATI
SAVITRI (HIS DAUGHTER)
NARADA (A SAGE)
DYUMATSEN (DETHRONED KING OF SHALVA)
SATYAVAN (SON OF DYUMATSEN; LATER, HUSBAND OF SAVITRI)
YAMARAJ (THE KING OF DEATH)

THE DISCIPLE ILLUMINES THE MASTER

DI 14. SCENE I

(King Ashwapati and his daughter Savitri.)

ASHWAPATI   My daughter, you are so beautiful.
SAVITRI   Thank you, Father.
ASHWAPATI   My daughter, you are so spiritual.
SAVITRI   Thank you, Father.
ASHWAPATI   Savitri, I love you more than I love my own life.
SAVITRI   Father, I love you, too, more than I love my own life.
ASHWAPATI   Savitri, you are my All. In you is my realisation of the Truth. In you is the Perfection of my inner life. Do you know, my daughter, why I have named you Savitri?
SAVITRI   No, Father, I do not know.
ASHWAPATI   For many years your mother and I had no child. So I prayed and prayed to the goddess Savitri to grant us a divine child. After a long time the goddess was pleased with me, and gave me the gift I longed for. And that gift is your life, your dedicated life. So it is from the goddess Savitri, my Supreme Mother, that you get your name.
SAVITRI   Father, I am so happy, so proud to hear that. From now on I shall try to identify myself with that Supreme Goddess Savitri, and I shall try to please you in every way.
ASHWAPATI   Savitri, all along you have been pleasing me. You already please me in every way. I am so proud of you. Savitri, now the time has come for you to have a partner. You need a divine consort. I have tried very hard to get a suitable husband for you, but I have not succeeded. It pains me severely, but I don't see anybody on earth who is really worthy of you.
SAVITRI   Father, forgive me, but you are mistaken.

ASHWAPATI   I will be happy if you can prove that I am mistaken. I really want to be proven wrong, for when I see that you have someone whom you love and who is really worthy of you, I will be the happiest person on earth. Please tell me, my daughter, what is the name of your future husband?

SAVITRI   Father, it is Satyavan.

ASHWAPATI   Who is he?

SAVITRI   Father, he is the son of King Dyumatsen. I am sure you have heard of Dyumatsen. He is the King of Shalva.

ASHWAPATI   Yes, my child, yes. Of course I know of Dyumatsen. But don't you know that he has been driven out of his kingdom by his enemies? He is now roaming in the forest like a beggar.

SAVITRI   Yes, Father, I know, I know. It was in the forest that I met his son, Satyavan. He has conquered my heart, Father.

ASHWAPATI   My daughter, my Savitri, to please you is to fulfil my soul. But I know that on the physical plane you will suffer much if you marry the son of a beggar. You are embracing poverty, but I am ready to offer all my wealth to make you happy and to make Satyavan's parents prosperous again. In your happiness is the fulfilment of my life and the manifestation of my soul.

SAVITRI   Father, Father, Father, I am yours. My life is yours. My life-breath is a garland of gratitude which I place at your feet.

(Enter Narada.)

ASHWAPATI   O sage Narada, do you know anything about Satyavan, the son of King Dyumatsen, who is now dethroned and roaming in the forest?

NARADA   Yes, I know, I know. Dyumatsen has now become blind. And his son — I have seen him quite a few times. He is very intelligent, very beautiful, very spiritual and divine. In every way he is a great, most promising young man.

ASHWAPATI   I am so happy, so happy to hear you say this, because my daughter wants to marry him.

NARADA   Savitri? Savitri wishes to marry Satyavan?

(Savitri looks down, embarrassed.)

SAVITRI   O sage, please tell me, what is wrong with that? What is disturbing you?

NARADA   Nothing is wrong with me, but everything is wrong with you, O Savitri.

SAVITRI   Please, please tell me what is wrong with me?

NARADA   Savitri, you have no vision of the future. But I do have that vision, and I tell you that Satyavan is going to die soon. Savitri, he will live on earth only for one fleeting year.

ASHWAPATI   Only one year, one year? And then I have to see my daughter a widow? Impossible, impossible!

SAVITRI   Father, just a few minutes ago you told me that to please me is to fulfil your soul. Now you are changing your mind. Father, real love does not care for earthly years. I love him, and that is all. I do not need anything more from my life. If my Satyavan is destined to live only for one year, I am fully prepared to accept him as my husband for that short time. If he dies, what can I do? To see him, to be with him for as long as I can, is the only thing I need in my life.

ASHWAPATI   My daughter, I am all for you. You want him; that is more than enough. I am going to speak to his father, Dyumatsen, and then we shall make arrangements for your wedding.

NARADA   Savitri, on the day you get married, start counting the days. When one year is completed, you will lose your husband. But my blessing will be with you, Savitri, because you are most devoted to him.

SAVITRI   Bless me, O sage. Satyavan, Satyavan! He is my heart's light; he is my soul's sun.

THE DISCIPLE ILLUMINES THE MASTER

DI 15. SCENE 2

(Dyumatsen, Satyavan and Savitri in the forest.)

DYUMATSEN   Savitri, my daughter, you have now been one of us for some time. My son is so fond of you, and I am so fond of you. We are all fond of one another. But my heart breaks when I see you working so hard, and when I see my son going every day to cut down trees for fuel. This life of hardship is unbearable. I was a king. I was thrown out by my enemies. Now I am in the forest, helpless. I have lost my sight, but you and my son, Satyavan — both of you are my inner eyes. My outer eyes God has taken away, but He has given me two inner eyes. One is my son; one is my Savitri. Through your eyes I see the world, and through your hearts I feel the world, O Savitri, O Satyavan.

SAVITRI   Father, we shall make you happy. Satyavan and I will make your life happy. You may not get your kingdom back, but you have us. We shall give you constant joy, constant satisfaction. We assure you, Father, at every moment we shall try to please you in your own way, according to our capacity.

DYUMATSEN   I know, I know. You and Satyavan will do everything for me. I live on earth only to feel happiness in your two dedicated lives. You are spiritual, my son is spiritual and I am spiritual. Our life of spirituality is our only consolation. Our life of spirituality is our only illumination. Our life of spirituality is God's real Pride. *(Pauses.)* You know, Savitri, Satyavan, I am happy. I am happy because my life I have dedicated to the Will of the Supreme, to the Will of God. I have no will of my own. He is now my All. He gives me inner joy, inner satisfaction. My kingdom I have lost, but I have found God inside my heart. The kingdom of falsehood has deserted me, but the Kingdom of Truth has dawned in my devoted heart.

THE DISCIPLE ILLUMINES THE MASTER

DI 16. SCENE 3

(Savitri is alone.)

SAVITRI *(thinking aloud)* Today is the last day of my husband's life. Throughout the year I have prayed to the god Surya to protect my Satyavan, but this is the fatal day. I have kept it a deep secret. Nobody knows, neither my husband nor my father-in-law.

(Enter Satyavan.)

SAVITRI *(to Satyavan)* Lord, today I would like to come with you. I would like to follow you into the thick forest where you cut down trees for fuel.

SATYAVAN Savitri, why do you want to go into the thick forest? Why? Why?

SAVITRI My Lord, since our marriage I have never made a request to you for anything. This will be my first and last request. If you fulfil my request, I will be most grateful to you. I will never ask you for another boon as long as I am on earth.

SATYAVAN Savitri, is there anything on earth that I would not do for you? My body, my vital, my mind, my heart, my soul are all for you, for you, my Savitri. Come with me.

DI 17. SCENE 4

(Savitri and Satyavan are in the thick of the forest. Satyavan has just plucked a few fruits, unripe, which they both are eating.)

SAVITRI   Do you come here every day? This place is not safe. I hear the sounds of ferocious animals. How do you come home safely?

SATYAVAN   Savitri, you have more faith in God than I have. It is God who protects me. It is God who has given me the strength to cut down the trees and make fuel. We are poor, Savitri, you know, but there was a time when we were rich and my father used to rule the Kingdom of Shalva. Now the days of outer prosperity are gone, but the days of inner prosperity have started. This last year, since you have come into my life, has been all Joy, all Love, all Delight, all Divinity. Savitri, you have transformed our inner kingdom. Before we met you, our inner kingdom was the kingdom of worries, but now it is the Kingdom of Light and Delight. Our outer kingdom was the kingdom of frustration; now it is the Kingdom of Joy and Fulfilment. *(Pauses.)* Savitri, I have finished eating. Now you observe, while I go and cut down trees.

(Savitri meditates with folded hands, silently looking at Surya, the sun god.)

SAVITRI   *(in a low voice)* O God, Lord Surya, O Sun, today is the last day of my husband's life. Protect him, protect him. Narada told me that today would be my husband's last day. I know the prophecy of the sage Narada can never prove

THE DISCIPLE ILLUMINES THE MASTER

false. But, O Lord Surya, you can save me, you can save my husband. I pray to you.

(She begins chanting Surya's name. Satyavan comes over to where she is sitting.)

SATYAVAN Savitri, I feel extremely tired. I don't know why, but I am unable to move. My hands have no strength at all. My feet have lost all strength; I can't stand up.

(Satyavan falls to the ground. Savitri takes her husband's head on her lap. Enter the King of Death, Yamaraj, tall and stout.)

SAVITRI Who are you?
YAMARAJ I am Yamaraj, the King of Death.
SAVITRI What brings you here?
YAMARAJ Your husband's life has ended.
SAVITRI I was told that it is your messengers who come to take people away. How is it that you have come yourself, O King of Death?
YAMARAJ Your husband led a most devoted, spiritual and divine life. That is why I personally have come instead of sending my messengers. Savitri, now your husband is my possession. I am taking him with me.

(Satyavan rises and follows Yamaraj, like a sleepwalker. Savitri follows Yamaraj and Satyavan.)

YAMARAJ What are you doing? Where are you going?
SAVITRI I am Satyavan's wife. Wherever my husband goes, I have to go.

YAMARAJ   Go home. You will not be able to come with us. I will not take you: your time has not come. We will walk very fast. We will disappear.

SAVITRI   O King of Death, be compassionate. I have been all devotion to my husband. I want to be with him. Now, can you not take me also? To live without my husband is impossible for me. Take me with you, please. Do me this favour. I am at your feet.

YAMARAJ   Savitri, don't be so silly. I cannot do that. But if you go home, I will give Satyavan's father back his eyesight. I will grant you that boon, if you will go home now.

SAVITRI   Thank you. I am so grateful that you will give my father-in-law back his eyesight. But I cannot leave my husband. I want to go with him.

(Savitri has been following Yamaraj for a long time. She is becoming exhausted, but she will not stop.)

YAMARAJ   Savitri, I am ready to give you any boon you want, but I tell you, I can't take you with me, nor can I give back your husband's life.

SAVITRI   O Yamaraj, either take me with you wherever you carry my husband, or give his life back to me. I will not leave him.

YAMARAJ   Savitri, your love for your husband is unique. I shall give you another boon. I shall bless you with one hundred sons. These sons will make you happy.

SAVITRI   O Yamaraj, what kind of boon are you offering me? How will I have one hundred sons without a husband? How is it possible? I have been all faithfulness, all devotion to my husband. You know, during this one year of our marriage, what kind of life I have led.

YAMARAJ   Savitri, forgive me. Forgive me.

SAVITRI   O Yamaraj, I do not want to have one hundred sons. Even if you give my husband's life back, I do not want a hundred sons. I want only my husband. My husband is all I need. Either give his life back to me so that we can go home where his old blind father is waiting for us, or allow me to go with you wherever you carry him. I shall follow your footsteps. I am tired, I am exhausted, but I am prepared to die while following my beloved husband.

YAMARAJ   Savitri, your faithfulness, your devotion, your love have pleased me. Yours is the life of love, yours is the life of devotion. Your life has taught humanity what love is, inseparable love, divine love. Your life has taught and will teach humanity what devoted oneness is. Savitri, I give you your husband.

(Yamaraj touches the forehead of Satyavan and disappears.)

SATYAVAN   Where am I, Savitri? I don't recognise this place. Where have you brought me? Where am I?

SAVITRI   Is this place new to you?

SATYAVAN   Totally new. I have never seen this place. How did you bring me here?

SAVITRI   Well, I shall tell you tomorrow how I brought you here.

SATYAVAN   I was fast asleep, Savitri. Why didn't you wake me up? True, I was exhausted, but I would have got up. I would not have been offended. Now what will Father think of us? He will think that both of us today have been very immature. Poor Father, I am sure he is thinking of us, he is missing us. Every day in the evening I come back home. Now it is already night. Father will think that, just because today we have been together in the forest, we have forgotten all about him.

SAVITRI I shall speak to your father. I shall ask him for his forgiveness and he will surely grant it.

SATYAVAN But tell me, tell me, how have I come here? How is it that we are here? This place is so unfamiliar.

SAVITRI I will tell you all about it, O Satyavan, O Lord of my life. Let us go home, let us go home. I have a sweet story to tell you. This story will give you immense joy. Let us go home. Father is waiting. He needs us desperately. Let us go home.

KALI AND KRISHNA ARE ONE

SRI CHINMOY

DI 18. DRAMATIS PERSONÆ

WIFE (A DEVOTEE OF LORD KRISHNA)
HUSBAND (A DEVOTEE OF MOTHER KALI)
THEIR SON
ANGEL

THE DISCIPLE ILLUMINES THE MASTER

DI 19. SCENE I

(The home of two devotees, husband and wife.)

WIFE   Kali, Kali, all the time Kali! What has Kali ever done for us? She has only created untold problems.

HUSBAND   Krishna, Krishna, all the time, all the time! What has Krishna done for us? He has only deceived the world, and he is deceiving you.

WIFE   Krishna has deceived the world? My Krishna has deceived the world? My Krishna is all love, all love for mankind. Your Kali is ruthless. She kills people, she destroys people. She is called destruction. I have lost my only daughter because of her. When she was seriously ill you prayed to Kali. You assured me that Kali would cure our daughter. Now we have lost our only daughter. *(Cries.)*

HUSBAND   Why didn't you pray to your Krishna? If he is so kind, so generous, so compassionate, why didn't you call on him? Why didn't you pray to him to cure our daughter?

WIFE   I didn't invoke Krishna because I did not want to conflict with your prayer. I thought that since you were praying most ardently to your Kali, your Kali would cure our dearest, sweetest daughter. We have lost our daughter because of Kali. Now if our son gets even a headache I will not allow you to pray to Kali. I will pray to Krishna, my Krishna. He will cure our son. There is no danger on earth which I cannot conquer with my prayers to Krishna. Our son will remain on earth, happy and prosperous, all by Krishna's Grace. Our son will become great, very great. And I know it is Krishna's Grace that will make him great.

HUSBAND   I also want our son to be happy and great. If you feel that your Lord Krishna will make our son happy and great, then you pray to Krishna and I shall remain silent. I shall silently pray to my Kali to give me joy, to give me peace of mind, so that I can bear your constant scoldings and insults.

WIFE   If I scold you, then you have to know that you deserve it. You are callous, useless, hopeless in every way.

HUSBAND   Let us not quarrel. Let us not fight in front of our son. I wish you to be happy; I wish my son to be happy; I wish my Kali to make me happy.

SON   How I wish I could do something so that all our problems would be solved! Father is fond of Kali; Mother is fond of Krishna. I do not know of whom I am fond. No, I *do* know of whom I am fond. But if I say I am fond of Krishna, Father will be displeased; and if I say I am fond of Kali, Mother will be displeased. So I won't say.

WIFE   All right, keep it secret.

HUSBAND   Even if you say you are fond of Krishna, I will not be displeased. You are free to choose.

WIFE   I also want to tell you, my son, that if you are fond of Kali, you must not think I will be displeased with you. You have a free choice. But it is better for you to be fond of one particular deity, to have total faith in him and love and adoration for him, You should worship only one deity, and that deity will make you really happy, great and prosperous.

THE DISCIPLE ILLUMINES THE MASTER

DI 20. SCENE 2

(Night. The son is sleeping. He suddenly awakens.)

SON   What a strange dream I had! I dreamt that I struck the statue of Kali which is in my father's room and broke it to pieces. I was so happy to inform my mother that now there is only one statue in the house. All along I have been inwardly, secretly praying to Krishna. I am fond of Krishna and not of Kali. Let me go and see if the statue is broken or not.

(Opens the door to his father's room and sees a statue of Krishna, not of Kali. He is wonder-struck.)

SON   How can it be? How can it be?

(Goes to his mother's room and looks in. Her own statue of Krishna is still there.)

SON   Now we have two statues of Krishna! But perhaps I was mistaken. Let me go again to Father's room and see. Maybe Father has replaced Kali's statue. Perhaps he has given away Kali's statue and bought a statue of Krishna so that Mother will be happy. Perhaps he does not want to quarrel with Mother any more.

(He goes to his father's room and sees that the statue of Krishna is still there. He wakes his father.)

FATHER   What are you doing here at this hour?

SON Why have you replaced Kali? Why do I see Krishna's statue?

FATHER Krishna? Krishna? How did Krishna get here? Has your mother brought her statue here and put it in my room?

SON No, the same Krishna statue is in her room. I was just there.

FATHER Let me go into your mother's room and see.

(Father and son go into the mother's room and see the same statue of Krishna there.)

MOTHER What is the matter? What are you doing here at this hour? What are you doing in my room?

SON Mother, Mother, now there is only Krishna in our family! In your room is Krishna and in Father's room is Krishna.

MOTHER What? Is it true? I can't believe my ears! That means your father has now become Krishna's devotee. I am so glad. I am so glad that at last you have replaced Kali with Krishna.

FATHER I have not done it. I don't know how Krishna's statue got into my room.

MOTHER Then how could this happen?

SON Father, this must be a miracle. Since it is a divine miracle, let us meditate together. Let the three of us meditate together and see what we can learn from within.

(They sit down to meditate. An angel appears.)

ANGEL It was your son's prayer that we heard. Your son has always been suffering from your quarrels. One of you cries for Krishna, the other is all for Kali. Although he was fond of Krishna, your son felt miserable because each of you was always fighting for his own chosen deity. In order to prove to you that Kali and Krishna are one, Kali has taken the form of Krishna. From now on there will be no quarrel between you, no dispute between husband and wife, for you know that Kali and Krishna are one. Now Krishna is in both rooms because both wife and son like Krishna. Let there be no more disputes about which deity is better. You two may worship Krishna directly, and you *(addressing the husband)* may worship Kali inside Krishna. She is most certainly there. They are one.

(The angel disappears and the whole room is flooded with light.)

SUNDA AND UPASUNDA

SRI CHINMOY

DI 21. DRAMATIS PERSONÆ

SUNDA, UPASUNDA (TWO ASURA BROTHERS)
INDRA (THE LORD OF THE COSMIC GODS)
BRAHMA (THE CREATOR)
TILOTTAMA (A GIRL CREATED BY BRAHMA)
FIRST SAINT
SECOND SAINT
THIRD SAINT
FOURTH SAINT
FOUR DANCING GIRLS

THE DISCIPLE ILLUMINES THE MASTER

DI 22. SCENE 1

(Sunda and Upasunda, two most beautiful Asura brothers, are at their palace.)

SUNDA   Upasunda, today, I don't know why or how, I am in a most powerful mood to sing.
UPASUNDA   Strangely enough, Sunda, I too am deeply inspired to sing.
SUNDA   Wonderful, then let us both sing.
UPASUNDA   You sing first, and then I shall sing.
SUNDA   Thank you, Brother.

(Sunda sings.)

What can I do?
Heaven is afraid of me.
What can I do?
I fly beyond its glee
Piercing the Blue.

UPASUNDA   *(cannot resist the temptation to interrupt Sunda)* Marvellous!

(Upasunda sings.)

What can I do?
Earth is afraid of me.
What can I do?
I fell its ignorance-tree
To plant the True.

SUNDA   Marvellous! Let me continue, Brother.

(Sunda sings.)

What can I do?
Hell is afraid of me.
What can I do?
My compassion frees its pangs
From the racking screw.

UPASUNDA   Marvellous! Let me complete the song.

(Upasunda sings.)

What can I do?
My soul is afraid of me.
What can I do?
Body's eternity
I know is due.

SUNDA   Marvellous, marvellous! No matter who composed the song, it was undoubtedly composed for us to sing. Brother, our love for each other is invincible; our beauty, unfathomable; and our power, immeasurable.

UPASUNDA   In us the world can see the supreme incarnations of authority and power. All we need now is the Life of Immortality. We have to be immortal like Indra. That's all.

SUNDA   Indra! Don't use that filthy name! He is our worst enemy. We must dethrone him. We must destroy him. We must prove to the world that he is but a speck of dust, doomed to nothingness.

UPASUNDA   Alas, he is a cosmic god. Hence he is immortal.

SUNDA   God, god? What kind of god is he? He has no sense of morality. His wild vital does not have even an iota of purity. He is a shameless creature. His life can never love the breath of Truth. It can only love the physical beauty of women.

UPASUNDA   You are not an inch from the truth. But we *have* to become immortal like Indra.

SUNDA   Indeed! Indeed!

UPASUNDA   We must start worshipping one of the principal gods in order to get a boon which will grant us Immortality.

SUNDA   Indeed! Indeed!

UPASUNDA   I personally don't care for Shiva.

SUNDA   Neither do I.

UPASUNDA   I don't care for Vishnu, either.

SUNDA   I also don't care for Vishnu.

UPASUNDA   But I love Brahma.

SUNDA   I, too.

UPASUNDA   Let us then pray to Brahma day in and day out. Let us practise austerities. Brahma's transcendental Blessing will grant us Immortality.

SUNDA   I am sure it will.

UPASUNDA   Let us leave our palace tomorrow and go to the forest to pray to and meditate on Brahma. Let us sacrifice everything for an immortal life.

SUNDA   A splendid idea, indeed!

UPASUNDA   From tomorrow on we must lead the life of true ascetics in the thick of the forest.

SUNDA   We must, without fail, we must.

DI 23. SCENE 2

(Inside two forest caves Sunda and Upasunda are chanting, praying and meditating only to please Brahma. Each one has a picture of Brahma in front of him.)

SUNDA AND UPASUNDA   *(chant together three times)*

*Hiranyagarbhaya vidmahe
veda purushaya dhimahi
tanno brahma prachodayat*

(We know Him as the Cosmic Creator.
We meditate on Him as the Purusha of the Veda.
May Brahma awaken the Supreme in us.)

SUNDA AND UPASUNDA   O Brahma, do appear before us. Do make us immortal like Indra. Everything we have, except Immortality. We don't want to remain inferior to Indra. O Brahma, O Ocean of Infinite Compassion, it is you alone who can and will fulfil our inmost desire. O Brahma, O Father of Creation, do bless us with your divine Presence supreme.

(Enter Indra secretly. Having observed the severe austerities and penances of the two Asura brothers, Indra is terribly frightened. He feels that soon these two brothers will be more powerful than he is, and then they will seize his kingdom, dethrone him and chase him out of Heaven. Indra gets an idea and exits in silence, going back to Indra Puri, the City of Indra.)

(Soon he returns to the two Asura brothers with four extremely beautiful dancing girls who, he hopes, will tempt them and ruin them. The dancers offer their superlative performances to the two brothers. In every possible way they try to lower the consciousness of the two aspiring brothers. But all their efforts are in vain. The two genuine seekers are rapt in meditation. Frustrated, disheartened and defeated, Indra leads away the four dancing girls.)

DI 24. SCENE 3

(The following day. With their eyes slightly open the two brothers are in a very high meditation. They are deeply absorbed in the transcendental consciousness of Brahma. Enter Brahma. The two aspirants immediately leave their seats and touch Brahma's feet for benedictions.)

BRAHMA Your aspiration has pleased me. Your determination has pleased me. What can I do for you?

SUNDA Lord, we want to equal the cosmic god Indra. Something more, we want to dethrone Indra and become the King of the gods.

UPASUNDA We feel that in order to fulfil our heart's desire we need only one thing, and that thing is an immortal life.

SUNDA AND UPASUNDA You have just said that you are pleased with our aspiration and determination. If what you say is true, then please, please, please grant us an immortal life so that we can conquer Indra.

BRAHMA No shadow of a doubt that I am truly pleased with you. But Indra's supreme position is well-founded. Ask for another boon.

(Sunda and Upasunda are both sunk in despair.)

SUNDA Then please give us at least the Life of Immortality. We do not want to be killed by anybody. We want our joint strength to be unparalleled in the entire history of the world.

UPASUNDA *(seeing Brahma quite hesitant)* All right. At least this much of a favour you can do: if we have to die at all, then we wish to die at the hands of each other.

BRAHMA *(blessing them together)* Tathastu. So be it.

(Exit Brahma. The two brothers embrace each other and dance with joy.)

UPASUNDA   So, we are now immortal!

SUNDA   Indeed, we are!

UPASUNDA   Brahma's loftiest vision failed to see into our future.

SUNDA   His third eye didn't function well today.

UPASUNDA   *(roaring with laughter)* How can we kill each other? Our sweetest, deepest oneness inseparable shall last through eternity!

SUNDA   *(with another roaring laugh)* How can we kill each other? Impossible! Creation has never seen and will never see such inseparable oneness.

UPASUNDA   That goes without saying. So we are now really immortal!

SUNDA   Indeed, we are. We are immortal forever!

UPASUNDA   Although Brahma says that that hostile Indra's position is well-established, I simply don't believe him. Do you?

SUNDA   Not in the least.

UPASUNDA   We know that our power is invincible.

SUNDA   Indeed, indeed!

UPASUNDA   We shall be able to conquer Indra. Look at that rascal! Even while we were practising hard austerities he had to bring down four most beautiful dancers to try to ruin our aspiration and determination.

SUNDA   You know, Brother, that Indra is a rascal of the deepest dye.

UPASUNDA   Let us first conquer all the kings on earth, and then with their added power — although we don't exactly need any more power than we already have — we shall attack

Indra, we shall dethrone Indra, and we shall chase Indra away like a cat out of Heaven!

SUNDA   How wonderful to hear that!

UPASUNDA   Let us go back to our palace. Let us wage war against all the kings immediately. Let us totally destroy their capitals. Delay is not for us. We can easily become the undisputed rulers of the whole world.

SIUNDA   Certainly we can.

UPASUNDA   No, nobody on earth will dare to question our supremacy. Once we have conquered the length and breadth of the world with our absolute power, we shall threaten, frighten, attack and dethrone Indra all at once.

SUNDA   Yes, Brother. We must do that. We must and we can. If we don't, we can't have everlasting joy.

UPASUNDA   We simply *must* do it.

SUNDA   And we easily can.

THE DISCIPLE ILLUMINES THE MASTER

DI 25. SCENE 4

(Early morning. Brahma's abode. Brahma's blessingful meditation on the world is just over. Enter four saints.)

FIRST SAINT   O Lord Brahma, save us, save the world. Sunda and Upasunda are destroying the whole world.
SECOND SAINT   O Lord Brahma, the two *Asura* brothers have conquered all the peoples of the world. These two Asuras have looted all their wealth.
THIRD SAINT   They are now fully prepared to cross swords with the cosmic gods.
FOURTH SAINT   And soon they will be ready for a ruthless attack on Indra, the King of the cosmic gods.
THE SAINTS   *(together)* O Lord Brahma, save us, save the world from these two Asuras, or very soon the human race will suffer an eternal end.
BRAHMA   *(smiling)* My sweet children, I am fully aware of the grim situation. I am fully conscious of the unspeakable misdeeds of the two Asura brothers. Do not burn with impatience. I assure you that their days are numbered.

(Brahma starts meditating. In five minutes he creates through his third eye the most beautiful girl of eighteen the universe has ever seen.)

GIRL   My Lord, my Creator, my All! My life of unconditional and eternal service I place at your feet. I am sure you have a special plan for my life. My duty, my beauty, my reality and my divinity — all I place at your feet. You are my life's soul and you are my soul's goal.

(Brahma blesses her. While being blessed she offers her soulful prayer to her creator, the Creator of the universe.)

GIRL

> My life began with duty's pride.
> My life shall live with beauty's light.
> My life shall sport with reality's soul.
> My life shall end with Divinity's Height.

BRAHMA   Tilottama, O beauty unparalleled, O beauty's perfection, descend into the world and do me a service.

TILOTTAMA   A service! This life of mine is at your express command.

BRAHMA   Go and create a terrible dispute between the two Asura brothers, Sunda and Upasunda. Go and tempt them with your beauty's mightiest power and make them kill each other while fighting for the possession of your matchless beauty.

TILOTTAMA   My Lord, my beauty is yours. My capacity is yours. My victory is yours. I am all yours.

(Exit Tilottama.)

THE FOUR SAINTS   *(together bowing down to Brahma)* We are sure that Tilottama's beauty will kill the two Asura brothers. O Lord Brahma, you have saved us, you have saved the world and you have saved the human race. To you we offer the breath of our eternal gratitude.

(Brahma smiles. Exeunt the four saints.)

THE DISCIPLE ILLUMINES THE MASTER

DI 26. SCENE 5

(The Asura brothers are in the seventh heaven of enjoyment. Lower vital music and vulgar dancing are all around. Enter Tilottama. Immediately Sunda and Upasunda are swayed by tenebrous passion.)

SUNDA   Who are you? Your body's beauty is torturing every limb of mine.

UPASUNDA   Do you need money? Do you need jewels? Do you need name and fame? I shall give you immediately anything you want. Stand beside me, please. Stay with me, please. My heart needs you badly.

TILOTTAMA   Please let me think over the matter. After all, it is quite serious.

SUNDA   O paragon of beauty, my heart can brook no delay. I love you. You are mine. You are absolutely mine.

UPASUNDA   Stop, Sunda! I can clearly see that she loves me infinitely more than she loves you. Such being the case, it is I who deserve her, and not you.

SUNDA   I am not sure. Granted, she loves you more than she loves me. But *I* love her infinitely more than *you* love her.

UPASUNDA   O beauty unparalleled, how do you declare your life on earth?

TILOTTAMA   My name is Tilottama.

SUNDA   Like your beauty, your very name is torturing my heart and soul. You make me dream, and I make the world tremble. You are in all my thoughts. I must have you. I must tell you that I love you only, and I love nobody else on earth.

UPASUNDA   Tilottama, my darling, Sunda is a stranger to truth and I am a stranger to falsehood. I love you only. I am all yours. You are all mine. The moment I saw you my heart came close to breaking with stupendous ecstasy, my darling.

SUNDA Upasunda, not once but twice, you dare to call her your darling! She is all mine. I am all hers. You rightly deserve most severe punishment from me for your unpardonable audacity.

UPASUNDA Who punishes whom? You fool, you rogue, you brute!

(Upasunda severely strikes Sunda with his naked sword. Sunda immediately crosses his own sword with Upasunda's. A terrible fight starts between the two. The fight is unbelievably fierce. In a few minutes the two brothers kill each other. Enter Brahma and Indra. Tilottama bows down to Brahma.)

TILOTTAMA O my Creator, O my Source, I was a mere instrument of yours. You have blessed the world with your divine victory supreme. Once again this world of ours shall be flooded with light and delight.

BRAHMA Tilottama, you are my greatest joy and highest pride.

INDRA Tilottama, you have saved me. You have saved my divine pride. You have saved my Kingdom's life. My heart's garland of gratitude to you I offer.

(Indra garlands Tilottama.)

RADHA AND KRISHNA ARE PURE

SRI CHINMOY

DI 27. DRAMATIS PERSONÆ

KRISHNA
RADHA (DIVINE CONSORT OF KRISHNA)
FIRST GIRL
SECOND GIRL
THIRD GIRL
OTHER DIVINE FRIENDS OF KRISHNA (MOSTLY WOMEN)

THE DISCIPLE ILLUMINES THE MASTER

DI 28. SCENE I

(Krishna sits alone. Beside him is his flute.)

KRISHNA   *(lifting his flute)* When I play on this flute, men and women, especially women, come to listen to my music. People criticise me because they feel that my association with these women is not pure. But I know how pure these women are, and I know what purity I embody. Poor Radha, she is my dearest *shakti*. She is Purity itself. But human beings, how will they understand divine Love? How will they understand divine Delight? I shall have to suffer criticism from people.

(Krishna sings.)

*Je besechhe bhalo
ei dharanire
se peyechhe shudhu byatha
parane tahar dhelechhe abani
kuruper malinata
tabu nirbhay chale sei bir
pritthvir bojha niye
ahaba ante habe upanita
prabhur charane giye*

(He who has loved this world
Has only got excruciating pangs.
The world has thrown on him all ugliness and filth
    and dirt, and impurity.
Yet the hero marches along,
Carrying the burden of the entire world.
At the end of his teeming struggles
He will go and stand at the Feet of the Lord
    Supreme.)

KRISHNA I don't mind. I am above it all. But my Radha suffers, and I feel sorry for her.

(Enter Radha.)

KRISHNA How do you feel today, Radha?

(Radha does not answer.)

KRISHNA Yesterday you were in a sulking mood. It seems today you are worse. Radha, please tell me what is going on. Yesterday I asked you what was wrong with you, and you didn't answer. Today again I am asking you. I am begging you. Now tell me what is wrong with you. Has anybody insulted you?

RADHA You are so pure, so divine. I come to you to listen to your music, to listen to your divine voice, to listen to your eternal Truth. I know you are divine, and my heart is all for you. But everybody criticises us, even my girl friends who also come here to listen to you. My girl friends are creating such gossip. It is unthinkable, unbearable.

KRISHNA Do you know why they do it? Can you tell me why they act like that?

THE DISCIPLE ILLUMINES THE MASTER

RADHA Just because you show me special attention, they can't bear it. They are jealous of me. *(Krishna smiles.)* Can you not stop their jealousy?

KRISHNA Human jealousy, Radha, is a very serious disease. I shall try to free them from jealousy. But it is a very difficult task.

RADHA Either you have to free them from jealousy, or you have to make them feel that I am pure.

KRISHNA To make them feel that you are pure — that is far easier. That I can do easily. I shall show you.

(Krishna begins playing soul-stirring music on his flute. All his divine friends come rushing to hear his music. Krishna plays for a few minutes.)

KRISHNA Today I wish to play a special game. *(Speaking to the women.)* Most of you are married. I want you to prove today that you are all chaste. I want you to prove your purity.

(When Krishna says this, some of them immediately run away.)

KRISHNA Look at this. I wanted them to prove their chastity and they have run away. You can imagine what kind of life they lead. So you people are remaining. I am so glad that you lead a chaste life. Now, here is a sieve and here is a bucket of water. One by one you come and pour the water into the sieve. If the water does not leak through when someone pours, that means that that woman is extremely pure and chaste.

(The girls line up. The first girl comes and pours water into the sieve. The water leaks through. The onlookers start laughing.)

ONLOOKERS   Oh, she is not chaste. She is not pure.

(The girl hides her face in embarrassment. The next girl starts pouring, but again the water goes through.)

ONLOOKERS   *(laughing)* She is not chaste, she is not chaste.
KRISHNA   *(to a third girl)* Now come on.

(The third girl comes and suffers the same fate. The water leaks through the sieve. Everybody starts laughing.)

THIRD GIRL   *(mockingly)* Oh, Radha should come. Let her try!
OTHERS   Yes, Radha should come. Let Radha come. Let Radha try!
SECOND GIRL   Why do you bother Radha? She is not chaste either. Have some sympathy for her. You know perfectly well what kind of life she is leading.
KRISHNA   All right, she is not leading a life of purity. But let her try anyway. Radha, please come and see. You try, Radha. Come.

(Radha comes forward and is about to pour the water. The other women immediately start laughing.)

KRISHNA   Be quiet. Let us see first.
RADHA   Look, already they are laughing and mocking and criticising me. Why should I do it?
KRISHNA   *(to the onlookers)* Don't mock. Don't laugh. This is not yet the time to laugh and criticise. You people have proved yourselves. You have proved that you are not chaste at all. You only know how to criticise and mock. Now, let Radha try. At least give her a chance.

THE DISCIPLE ILLUMINES THE MASTER

(Radha pours the water. The water does not leak through the sieve. Everybody is astonished.)

KRISHNA Now you can see who is chaste, who is pure. You people, look. You know how to criticise, how to mock. But you do not know how to lead a pure life. I am teaching you the eternal Truth. I am the Lord of the Universe. Radha comes to me for spiritual help, eternal Truth. Her love for me is divine. My love for her is also divine. Your minds are in the gutter. You remain in a filthy consciousness. You care for men, you care for earthly duties, you care for name, fame and so many things. But my Radha, I am always in her mind. She is also a married woman. She has her husband and everything else, just like you. But no matter where she goes, no matter with whom she speaks, her mind is always on my Transcendental Consciousness. She knows that I am the Lord of the Universe. *(Pauses.)* Whoever thinks of me has the purest heart on earth. Those who think of other things are not pure and can never be pure. Their purity today you observed. A day will come when the whole world will know who Radha is. The world will not only recognise her purity, but also receive from her divinity the purest delight that exists in the earth-consciousness. She is my delight; she is the delight of the Universe. Pray, meditate. All of you will one day have Radha's purity, Radha's consciousness. It will take time; it will take centuries, millennia. But it will be possible for you also to have Radha's height, Radha's consciousness, Radha's realisation.

(Radha soulfully looks at Krishna and the other girls listen quietly while the second girl sings.)

Kalo baran nai je kanu
jena kancha sona
bishwa ruper rup madhuri
jyoti diye bona
amar —
maner kali dhela pare
dekhai tare kalo
ta nahale priya je mor
sudhui ujal alo
alo andhar tahar gara
kanu bishwamoy
sabar sathe habe amar
naba parichay

(My Krishna is not black,
He is pure gold.
He Himself is woven
Into the universal Beauty, Light and Splendour.
He looks dark
Because I have spilled the ink of my mind on Him.
Otherwise, my Beloved is All-Light.
He created Light and Darkness,
He is within and without the Cosmos Vast.
With this knowledge,
I will have a new acquaintance
With the world at large.)

GANAPATI'S MARRIAGE

SRI CHINMOY

DI 29. DRAMATIS PERSONÆ

SHIVA
DURGA (WIFE OF SHIVA)
KUMARA, GANAPATI (SONS OF SHIVA AND DURGA)
NARADA (ENEMY OF KUMARA)
TWO WIVES OF GANAPATI

THE DISCIPLE ILLUMINES THE MASTER

DI 30. SCENE I

(Shiva, Kumara and Ganapati.)

KUMARA Father, I want to get married.

SHIVA Why, my son? Why do you want to get married?

KUMARA I need a woman in my life. I feel that my heart is barren. I need somebody to give me love.

GANAPATI Father, I also want to get married. I also need love from somebody, from a woman. I need it badly, Father.

SHIVA So both of you want to get married. It is a good idea. But we can't afford to have two marriages performed at the same time. One of you will have to wait.

KUMARA Father, I should get married first, since I made the proposal first.

GANAPATI No, Father, I should marry first because I am older than he is, and as you know, it is the older child that gets married first. That is our Indian tradition.

KUMARA Father, please listen to me. It is *I* who should get married first. All the time his mind remains in his books. I tell you, if you allow him to get married, he will neglect his wife. He won't take care of his wife. He will ruin her, and you will feel miserable when you see your daughter-in-law come to you shedding bitter tears. Don't allow him to get married, Father. It is I who should get married. I belong to this world. I know the ins and outs of this world. I will take care of my wife.

GANAPATI Father, Kumara knows how to talk, and I know how to act. I tell you, he talks and talks and talks, but when it is a matter of action, he will not be seen anywhere. I shall please my wife. Believe me, Father. Give me the chance. I want to get married first.

KUMARA   Father, Father, it is always said that the youngest son in the family gets the first chance in everything. I am the youngest, Father, so I should get the first chance. I should get married first.

SHIVA   All right. I will tell you what you have to do. Both of you go and travel around the world. Whoever comes back first will be given the opportunity to get married first. I will wait.

(Kumara immediately runs away. Ganapati remains.)

GANAPATI   *(to himself)* With this huge belly of mine, how am I going to run like him? Oh God, give me some wisdom. How can I outrun my brother Kumara? He is thin, swift, agile. For me even to walk, to cover a quarter-mile, is an extremely difficult task. I will die if I have to circumnavigate the world. I won't be able to do it. After I have covered two or three miles, I shall return to God instead of returning home. Let me meditate and see if I can get any ideas.

(He meditates. After some time, a brilliant idea enters his mind.)

GANAPATI   *(to himself)* My father! My father is all divinity. This world belongs to him. Naturally, if I go around him, that means I am going around the world. *(To his father.)* Father, please be seated, please be seated.

(Shiva sits down. Singing the glory of his father, Ganapati walks around him seven times.)

GANAPATI   Father, I have won.
SHIVA   How have you won?

GANAPATI   Father, I have won seven times over. You are the world. You are the Lord of the world, and you embody the world. You are the Creator; you are the creation itself. I have gone seven times around you. That means I have gone around the world seven times. Father, it is I who should get married first.

SHIVA   *(deeply pleased)* Go and call your mother. *(Ganapati goes out and returns with his mother.)*

SHIVA   *(to his wife)* Your son Ganapati has won a race against Kumara. This morning both brothers insisted on getting married. When I agreed, each of them wanted to be the first to marry. I said the first one to travel around the world would be the first to get married. Ganapati asked me to sit down. I sat down, and he walked around me seven times. Naturally he is the winner.

DURGA   I am truly happy that we have a son who is wise. The other son is strong and powerful, but he does not have wisdom, alas. He will run and run and run. God knows when he will come back. I feel sorry for that boy, and I am proud of this boy. Let us marry this son. It is my wish that this son will marry two girls at the same time.

GANAPATI   Two? Two, Mother?

DURGA   Yes, my son, two. I need two girls to help me. And who knows, when Kumara comes back, he may be disappointed, seeing that you have married first, and he may not marry at all. So the best thing is for us to get two girls for you.

GANAPATI   *(very happy)* Oh, Mother! They will help you, so you won't have to work any more. And I will be so happy and proud. Everybody else has one wife, but I will have two wives!

(Shiva smiles and blesses his son.)

SCENE 2

(Several days later, before Kumara returns home, he meets his enemy, Narada.)

NARADA   O Kumara, everything is finished.

KUMARA   What is finished?

NARADA   Finished. Your brother, Ganapati, has got married.

KUMARA   How? When? How did he reach our father before me? Has he gone around the world?

NARADA   Well, I do not know about that. But I can tell you that I have just come from your house, where I saw that he has two most beautiful girls as his wives.

KUMARA   Two? He has married two?

NARADA   Yes. Your parents are so pleased with him, so proud of him. Instead of one, they have brought him two beautiful, most beautiful girls. I don't know. When you get married, I doubt that you will get as beautiful a girl for yourself.

KUMARA   Two wives? Two beautiful wives? I can't believe you!

NARADA   If you do not believe me, you can go and see for yourself. You are very near your house.

KUMARA   Unbelievable! Unthinkable! My parents, my own parents have deceived me! Let me go and see.

THE DISCIPLE ILLUMINES THE MASTER

DI 32. SCENE 3

(Kumara, running, enters his home and sees two most beautiful girls with Ganapati and his parents. He is furious.)

KUMARA *(to his parents):* You have deceived me! You didn't even wait for me. How did he come back before me?

SHIVA My son, he knew that I am divine. He knew that I am the Creator and I am the creation. He knew that I am God and I am the world. So he went around me not once, but seven times. And you, my son, you have come only now, so late.

KUMARA No! It is all deception, all deception! I can't tolerate this. I am going into the forest. I will never, never marry in this life. I don't need women, Who cares for a woman's beauty? Beauty is, after all, only skin deep. I shall care only for the soul's beauty, the eternal beauty. Women are bondage. I don't need bondage. My brother now has double bondage: two women in his life. He was a fool to get married. Now he is stuck, but I can run towards my goal the fastest because I am free from bondage.

(Shiva blesses his son.)

SHIVA Kumara, in some cases, marriage does help; in other cases, it is an obstruction. For you, marriage would be an obstruction, a curse. You do not need a wife. You need only God. To realise Him, to fulfil Him, is your sole aim. Marriage would not allow you to think of God, to meditate on God, And I want you to realise God as soon as possible without having this added burden on your shoulders. So to remain unmarried is, for you, a real blessing. But in

Ganapati's case, marriage is a blessing, a real boon. With his marriage, he will be able to fulfil himself and God. The added strength it gives him will allow him to run the fastest in his own way. We want satisfaction, real satisfaction, from both of you. Your unmarried life the world will adore. In his case, the world will see that with a wife one can also go to God. God is both man and woman. How can you ignore the part that is woman? Ganapati will take the other half, woman, to God. Both husband and wife can go to God simultaneously to fulfil Him, which is absolutely necessary. God wants you to remain unmarried and He wants your brother to lead a married life. Your brother is fulfilling God's wish, as you will be from now on. So you please God in one way, and he pleases God in another way. Both of you are pleasing God in His own Way.

(Shiva sings.)

What is marriage?
The smile of love
That allows two souls
To soar above.

(To Kumara.)

What is marriage?
The curse of Night.
A tug-of-war.
No escape to Light.

THE DISCIPLE ILLUMINES THE MASTER

(To Ganapati.)

What is marriage?
God's fulfilment true.
In Silence and Power
His Vision's due.

DASHARATHA PROMISES
AND RAMA EXECUTES

SRI CHINMOY

DI 33. DRAMATIS PERSONÆ

MANTHARA (MAIDSERVANT OF QUEEN KAIKEYI)
QUEEN KAIKEYI, QUEEN KAUSALYA, QUEEN SUMITRA (WIVES OF
    KING DASHARATHA)
RAMA (SON OF KAUSALYA AND DASHARATHA)
KING DASHARATHA (KING OF AYODHYA)
LAKSHMANA (FIRST SON OF SUMITRA AND DASHARATHA)
SITA (WIFE OF RAMA)
BHARATA (SON OF KAIKEYI AND DASHARATHA)
SHATRUGHNA (SECOND SON OF SUMITRA AND DASHARATHA)
VASHISHTHA (A SAGE)
OFFICERS IN BHARATA'S ARMY

THE DISCIPLE ILLUMINES THE MASTER

DI 34. SCENE I

(Queen Kaikeyi and her maidservant Manthara.)

MANTHARA O Queen, do you know? Do you know what will happen tomorrow?

KAIKEYI No, I do not know. Please tell me.

MANTHARA Tomorrow Rama is going to be the *yubaraj*. He is going to become the crown prince.

KAIKEYI Oh! How delighted I am to hear that! You are the first person to give me that happy news. Take this necklace from me. *(She hands the necklace to her maidservant.)*

MANTHARA *(throws away the necklace)* O Queen I never thought that you were such a fool. I thought that God had given you some real wisdom. Don't you realise that when Rama becomes the ruler he will be all devotion to his own mother, Kausalya, and not to you? You will have no place here then. Your own son Bharata, will be like a servant. Now he and Rama are like two friends, two brothers. But the day Rama becomes King, Bharata will be nowhere.

KAIKEYI No, don't say such things. My Bharata and Kausalya's Rama are inseparable brothers. I am so happy that my Rama, who loves me more than he loves his own mother, who serves me more than he serves his own mother, is going to be the ruler of this vast kingdom. O Manthara, the news that you have given me has made my life extremely happy. You don't know how much joy I am getting now. My Rama, my own Rama will become the King.

MANTHARA O Queen, just wait and see. Kausalya's life of joy and victory will begin tomorrow. Your life of frustration and destruction will begin tomorrow.

KAIKEYI   Manthara, stop! Enough of your evil tongue. I am the Queen. I know what is best for me, best for my life. King Dasharatha has three Queens: Kausalya, Sumitra and I. But you know Dasharatha loves me most. He would not do anything which would eventually make me sad.

MANTHARA   Yes, I know he loves you most. But when Rama becomes the crown prince, instead of your son, your suffering will know no bounds. This is not my curse; it is just a bare fact. Rama will banish your son from the kingdom and he will treat you as you are treating me, your maidservant. Today you are the Queen, the most beloved Queen of Dasharatha; tomorrow you will become a maidservant like me in the service of Rama.

KAIKEYI   My love for my Rama is boundless. He is the embodiment of Truth and Light. In him I see the message of Divine Perfection. To be his maidservant is to be the great instrument of God. I am prepared to be his maidservant or whatever he wants me to be when he becomes the ruler of Ayodhya.

MANTHARA   O Queen, still there is time. Don't act like a fool. You are still the most beloved wife of Dasharatha. Have you forgotten that he once promised you that he would fulfil your desires, no matter what they were? When he was ill, you served him, you nursed him and you cured him. Because of your dedicated service he offered you two divine boons. You told him that when the time came you would ask him. Now the time has come. Do you remember how many times you have been unkind to Kausalya? When she becomes the mother of King Rama, don't you think she will pay you back?

KAIKEYI   That is true. I scolded her and insulted her many times, just because I knew I was the favourite wife of King Dasharatha. But Kausalya's heart is big. She is full of love and compassion. When her son becomes King she will not pay me back in my own coin. She will forgive me. As a matter of fact, she has already forgiven me.

MANTHARA   Wait, just wait. It is only a matter of a few hours until tomorrow, and then your sorrow begins, your suffering begins. The night of excruciating pangs begins for you, O Queen!

KAIKEYI   I am fully prepared. Whatever is going to happen will happen for my own good. My Rama will not do anything wrong to me. Kausalya will never do anything to humiliate me. Both of them are great in heart and soul.

MANTHARA   You must know that it is not for my sake that I am asking you to ask the King for the boons. My only interest in life is your joy. My life on earth is only to please you, only to make you happy. Now here is my humble suggestion. Go to the King and ask him for your two boons. Then, when he agrees to give them, ask first that Rama be exiled for fourteen years. And for the second boon, ask that your son, Bharata, be made the crown prince.

KAIKEYI   *(shocked)* I? I should ask Dasharatha for these boons?

MANTHARA   Yes, Rama has to go into the forest for fourteen years and your son Bharata has to be installed on the throne. Only then will you be happy, I tell you.

KAIKEYI   Shame, shame, unutterable shame on you, Manthara! Your advice is poison, nothing else! Leave this place immediately, before I kick you out!

MANTHARA   *(leaving)* O Queen, tomorrow you will see!

(Exit Manthara. Kaikeyi sits down and rests her chin on her hands. She is thinking.)

KAIKEYI   *(to herself)* Perhaps she is right....

DI 35. SCENE 2

(Dasharatha and Rama are together. Both are happy. Enter Kaikeyi.)

KAIKEYI Rama, my darling, I have something important to discuss with your father. Will you leave us for a moment? I shall call you back when our discussion is over.

RAMA Certainly, Mother, certainly.

(Exit Rama. Kaikeyi's expression immediately changes to one of bitter distress.)

DASHARATHA Kaikeyi, why is it that you are so distressed all of a sudden? Please tell me what is wrong with you. Are you feeling unwell? All the physicians of the world are at my disposal. Has anybody done anything wrong to you? If so, I assure you that he will be put to death. I have never seen you unhappy. Your sorrow is piercing the very depths of my soul.

KAIKEYI My King, it is easy for you to talk about your love for me, but I know you are not sincere. You try to please me daily with empty flattery and falsehoods. But do you have even an iota of love for me? No, it is all deception.

DASHARATHA *(shocked)* Kaikeyi! I can't believe my ears! Is this really you? Tell me when I have ever deceived you.

KAIKEYI You have never deceived me?

DASHARATHA Never! Never have I deceived you and never will I deceive you. You are my favourite Queen. I am all love, all sacrifice for you.

KAIKEYI Then prove it.

DASHARATHA I am at your disposal.

KAIKEYI   Send Rama into exile in the forest for fourteen years and make my son Bharata the crown prince tomorrow.

DASHARATHA   *(collapses, stunned)* Ohhh. Kaikeyi, to hear this from you! Tomorrow was to have been the happiest day of my life, and today you are giving me such a cruel blow. In one blow you have taken away all my joy, all my happiness, the very life from my heart.

KAIKEYI   I have only made a legitimate claim. Don't forget that you made a promise to me once. You granted me two boons. When you were practically dying, I nursed you back to health. You were so pleased with me that you granted me two boons, and I told you that when the time came I would ask for them. Now the time has come. Keep your promise if you are a man of truth. If not, the world will soon have a different opinion of you.

DASHARATHA   Kaikeyi, I am more dead than alive. You ruined my kingdom, you have killed me. I shall keep my promise, but do me at least one favour.

KAIKEYI   What do you want me to do?

DASHARATHA   Very simple. On my behalf you tell Rama that he has to go into the forest. On my behalf you tell your son Bharata that he will be the crown prince tomorrow. That's easy enough. *(He faints.)*

KAIKEYI   *(calls aloud)* Rama! Rama!

(Enter Rama.)

RAMA   Mother, is anything wrong with you?

KAIKEYI   Nothing is wrong, Rama. This very day you have to retire into the forest for fourteen years of exile. My son Bharata will be the King, and not you. Your father has promised.

(Seeing that his father is lying unconscious, Rama runs out and returns with Lakshmana, Kausalya, Sumitra and Sita.)

RAMA   *(to Kaikeyi)* Mother, I shall obey your command. You want me to go into the forest for fourteen years. You want my dearest brother, Bharata, to be the ruler. I am fully prepared to keep my father's promise to you. I am glad it is I who will have the opportunity to prove to the world that my father knows how to keep his promise.

(Lakshmana, Kausalya, Sumitra and Sita burst into tears.)

LAKSHMANA   Impossible! Brother, you cannot go into the forest! You cannot leave us!

SITA   My Lord, you cannot go! The world wants *you*, and not Bharata.

KAUSALYA   Rama, my darling son, don't go!

RAMA   I know, Mother, that you will miss me. I shall also miss you, I shall miss my wife Sita and I shall miss my brother Lakshmana. I shall also miss my brother Bharata and my brother Shatrughna. I shall miss all my family. But Mother, my suffering and your suffering have no meaning in my life. Only the fulfilment of my father's promise has real value for me. The world must know that my father Dasharatha has kept his promise. There is nothing so great as to keep one's promise. I want the world to be proud of my father's promise, my father's sacrifice. Mother, Sita, Lakshmana, Mother Kaikeyi, Mother Sumitra — I am leaving. It is only a matter of fourteen fleeting years. Then I shall be back with you again. Now my joy is in fulfilling my father's promise. Fourteen years from now my joy will be in living with my dear ones.

SITA   Lord, you cannot go without me.

LAKSHMANA   Rama, you cannot go without me.

RAMA   Sita, do you want to go with me into the forest? You will suffer much. How can I bear your suffering? A woman like you, who has been brought up with such care, love, affection and adoration, and all the comforts of wealth, cannot live in the forest. You must not think of going with me,

SITA   My Lord, without you my life has no meaning. To live with you in hell would give me greater joy than to live without you in Heaven. To be with you is to be in the highest plane of Delight. Wherever you are, I must be with you. I cannot remain without you. To be at your feet is my constant and eternal goal.

LAKSHMANA   Brother, to live without you is to live in ignorance, bondage and hell. I am not such a fool. This brother of yours will be your eternally devoted and dedicated slave. You are fulfilling Father's promise. Now you must also fulfil my wish and Sita's wish.

KAUSALYA   Rama, my son, take them with you. I shall remain here to look after your father. I love you more than I love my own life, but your aged father now needs my care. I do not know whether he will recover from this shock or not. But for the remaining days, the remaining hours, I want to serve him.

RAMA   Mother, you are doing absolutely the right thing. Father needs your care. He needs you badly. After fourteen years we three will come back. Mother Kaikeyi, please tell Bharata that I give him all my love, all my joy and all my blessings. Let him rule the kingdom in his own way. I am sure he will rule well. And Mother Kaikeyi, my only request to you, my last request to you, is that you will treat my mother Kausalya well.

SUMITRA   Rama, my son, you are the embodiment of truth, light and forgiveness. My heart breaks into pieces to see you and my Lakshmana leaving. But my other son, Shatrughna, is with Bharata now at his maternal uncle's home. Shatrughna will remain here. He is fond of Bharata, he is all for Bharata as Lakshmana is all for you. I shall stay here and look after your mother. I am also a Queen, but from today she will be my dearest sister. In every way I shall try to make her happy. That is my promise. That is my promise to you, my son Rama.

KAIKEYI Rama, I know that from today the world will hate me. I will be an object of contempt.

RAMA No, Mother, the world will not hate you. But even if the world hates you I will love you. You have given me the opportunity to keep my father's promise, and my mother Kausalya has given me the capacity to keep his promise. Her sacrificing heart-power has given me the capacity to keep my father's promise. Your demanding vital-power has given me the opportunity to fulfil my father's promise. I am equally grateful to you both.

THE DISCIPLE ILLUMINES THE MASTER

DI 36. SCENE 3

(Kaikeyi, Bharata and Shatrughna. Bharata is weeping bitterly.)

BHARATA Shatrughna, brother, go and bring that filthy animal Manthara. Bring that hunchbacked creature here. I shall set it all right. Bring her here.

(Shatrughna goes out and returns dragging Manthara. Bharata violently and ferociously grabs her by the ear, pulls her hair and gives her a violent kick.)

BHARATA You, you are the culprit! You are the one who inspired my mother, who instigated my mother to send Rama into exile for fourteen years. My dearest Rama, the light of my heart!

(Manthara falls to the ground unconscious.)

BHARATA *(turning to Kaikeyi, nearly in tears)* Mother, are you a human being? Have I to call you Mother? You have acted like an animal. Do you think that you have made me happy? I shall treat you ruthlessly. Every day I will make your life miserable! *(Pauses.)* No, no. You are forgiven. Rama's heart of forgiveness, his heart of compassion has forgiven you. He will be sorry if I treat you this way. But I tell you, I am Rama's brother Bharata, and not your son! My mother is Kausalya, and not you, you ingrate, you impostor! I am leaving for the forest. I will bring my brother back. It is he who will rule the kingdom. I am not only his brother, I am his devoted slave. I will not come back unless and until I have brought the brother of my heart and soul, Rama, back to Ayodhya, to his kingdom.

(Exit Bharata.)

THE DISCIPLE ILLUMINES THE MASTER

DI 37. SCENE 4

(Lakshmana, Sita and Rama in the forest of Chitrakut. Rama has started his spiritual life.)

LAKSHMANA   Look! Look, Rama! Brother Bharata's army! Bharata is invading us. Perhaps he thinks that when you go back after fourteen years you may create trouble for him. He wants to prevent any future trouble. Look at that ungrateful creature! Like mother, like son. It is his mother, Kaikeyi, who has sent you here to this life of hardship and humiliation. Now her son is coming to destroy you with his army. What else can you expect from your Bharata? After all, he is the son of Kaikeyi.

RAMA   Lakshmana, my brother, don't be so rash. How do you know that he is coming to kill me? He may be coming to take me back to the kingdom.

LAKSHMANA   *(laughing)* Brother, you are not only the embodiment of truth but also the embodiment of innocence. If he wanted to take you back he would come alone. Why has he to bring his huge army? O Brother, sometimes your innocence amazes me.

(Enter Bharata followed by officers. He prostrates himself before Rama and weeps bitterly.)

BHARATA   Brother, I am here at your feet. This army is yours. Come back! The kingdom awaits your arrival. I have not accepted my mother's foul offering to me. I have not fulfilled her foul wish. We have lost our father. Your physical absence has sent him into the other world.

(Lakshmana, Sita and Rama burst into tears.)

LAKSHMANA   Father is no more?

BHARATA   No more. He is in the world beyond. My mother Kaikeyi has ruined us all. Only your presence, Brother Rama, can bring happiness back to my life, and to our kingdom.

RAMA   Brother Bharata, it is you who have to rule the kingdom. That was Father's wish.

BHARATA   No, never! It was the wish of my cruel, brutal mother, Kaikeyi. I won't listen to you, Brother. You must come back with me. I will be your perfect slave. You are the legitimate ruler of Ayodhya, not I. Lord, come back with me, or let me stay with you here to serve you. I shall also lead an ascetic life.

RAMA   Beloved Brother Bharata, I have embraced asceticism to obey my father and my mother Kaikeyi.

BHARATA   Kaikeyi is inhuman! She is not your mother. She is God's worst mistake; she is man's worst curse. Never will I call her Mother. She has ruined our family. She has done something terribly wrong to you. I do not approve of our father's action.

RAMA   Who are you to approve or disapprove of our father? It is my bounden duty to obey him.

BHARATA   If it is your bounden duty to listen to our father, then it is my bounden duty to serve you here. I am not going back. I will not go back to the kingdom. *(Speaking to officers and to everyone present.)* My brother Rama shows no pity for me; he gives no consideration to my prayer. I shall lie down and fast unto death.

RAMA   Brother Bharata, this is not the way you should behave. You are a King, and you must face the world. You have to face the present situation with your manliness. It is I who am asking you to go back and rule the kingdom. If you wish to serve me, then you can serve me best in this way. The ocean may dry up, the sun may lose all its brilliance, but I will not be false to my father's divine promise. I shall remain in exile for fourteen years.

BHARATA   Nor can I be false to my promise. I am going to stay with you.

RAMA   Then you are disobeying me, your elder brother.

BHARATA   I am not disobeying you. I cannot live without you, that's all. You are my Lord; you are my God. I can't live without my Lord and God.

(Enter Vashistha.)

VASHISTHA   With my occult vision I have come to know what is happening here. O Rama, O Bharata, I can solve your problem.

RAMA AND BHARATA   Please, please, O Sage Vashistha, solve our problem.

VASHISTHA   Bharata, do not sit on Rama's throne. But go and be his agent. You rule on his behalf.

BHARATA   O Sage, that will not satisfy me. If he will allow me to keep his wooden sandals to represent him on the throne, then I shall go back. But I shall not go back to Ayodhya. No, I shall live in the village of Nandini which is on the outskirts of Ayodhya. From there I shall carry out Rama's orders. Brother Rama, every day I shall place your sandals on my head and on my heart before I speak to anyone. It is your sandals that will represent you on the throne and give me my authority. You are the King. I am your deputy. I shall look after your kingdom as your deputy. If you should fail to return to Ayodhya on the first day of the fifteenth year, the appointed day, you will not see your brother Bharata alive. I shall consign this body to flames, while uttering your sacred name.

RAMA   *(embraces his brother)* Brother, I assure you of my return. I shall keep my promise. I make one last request to you. Do not torture our mother Kaikeyi. Ignorance has covered her life. Let us both forgive her. Through our forgiveness her inner illumination will take place.

(Rama gives Bharata the wooden sandals from his feet.)

BHARATA   *(places the pair of wooden sandals on his heart)* This is the symbol of my loyalty to you, Rama, my brother, my father, my All. *(Embraces Lakshmana and touches the feet of Sita.)* Mother Sita, I shall do everything for you and for my brothers Rama and Lakshmana. As an anxious mother waits for her son's arrival after a long journey, as a dying man cries for a new life, I shall wait for your arrival and cry for your return.

DASHARATHA'S DREAM IS AT LAST FULFILLED

SRI CHINMOY

DI 38. DRAMATIS PERSONÆ

RAMA
BHARATA, LAKSHMANA (HALF-BROTHERS OF RAMA)
URMILA (WIFE OF LAKSHMANA)
SITA (WIFE OF RAMA)
OTHER MEMBERS OF THE ROYAL FAMILY
A LARGE CROWD OF PEOPLE

THE DISCIPLE ILLUMINES THE MASTER

DI 39. SCENE I

(Rama, Lakshmana and Sita return to Ayodhya after they have been in exile for fourteen years. Bharata receives them with boundless joy and love. There is a long procession as every person in the kingdom comes to receive them. The whole kingdom is in the seventh Heaven of delight.)

BHARATA Rama, you have come back. You have kept your promise. If you had not kept your promise, if you had broken your pledge, you would not have seen me here on earth in the land of the living. *(Touches Rama's feet.)* Here is your kingdom, Brother. Now, as before, I shall be your loving brother and slave. I submit totally to your will.

RAMA Bharata, you have shown your heart's magnanimity and your soul's nobility. You could have easily kept this kingdom for yourself. You were the King, in accordance with Father's wish.

BHARATA *(interrupting)* No, never! Father's wish was that you would be King, not I. You fulfilled Father's promise to my undivine, hostile mother. Her undivine desire compelled you to suffer much. It doomed you to fourteen years of misery, and I suffered as well. Now the darkest night is over; it is all day. The light of joy, the light of progress and achievement has dawned at last. O Rama, you have come to fulfil Father's dream. Father's lofty hopes for you will now be manifested in this kingdom on earth.

(The members of the royal family are all around. Urmila, the wife of Lakshmana, bows down to Rama and Sita, and then to her husband. While touching Lakshmana's feet, she sheds tears.)

LAKSHMANA   Urmila, why do you weep? I have come back to you. Today should be a day of enormous joy.

URMILA   My Lord, I am not weeping tears of sorrow. I am shedding tears of joy. Your body left me, but not your soul. Your soul stayed inside my heart. Now I have your body and soul together with me again.

(Urmila sings.)

Nayane nayane gopane gopane
shayane swapane madhu jagarane
jibaner dole maraner kole
taba prema-lila amar bhubane

(In secrecy supreme I see You.
You live in my eyes,
In my sleep, in my dreams,
In my sweet wakefulness.
In the stupendous mirth of life,
In the abysmal lap of death,
You I behold.
Your love-play is my world.)

URMILA   If you had remained here at the palace you would have done your human duty to me. But your soul wanted you to do your divine duty, which was to serve your dearest brother, Rama. He is all Divinity. He is the incarnation of *dharma*. You left me to be of service to him. You have come back again only to be of service to him. But your presence gives me enormous joy. I shall have you around me. I shall be with you. When it is a matter of serving, the Divine comes first and foremost. You did the right thing. You are doing the right thing. And in your sacrifice my glory looms large. In your feeling of oneness with the divine Rama, my oneness with the divine Rama shines.

RAMA Urmila, your silence when we left for the forest was deeply appreciated and admired by me. You sacrificed your husband in silence. Your life of silent sacrifice has touched the very depths of my heart. Your sacrifice springs from your divine wisdom. Your soul-stirring philosophy is absolutely correct. The Divine comes first, and not the human. I see your life of oneness with your husband, your life of inner wisdom. You are all for the cause of my divine manifestation on earth. Urmila, feel my heart's enormous delight and my soul's transcendental pride.

WHO IS THE OWNER:
THE LIFE-SAVER OR THE LIFE-TAKER?

SRI CHINMOY

DI 40. DRAMATIS PERSONÆ

PRINCE SIDDHARTHA
DEVADATTA (COUSIN OF SIDDHARTHA)
JUDGE

THE DISCIPLE ILLUMINES THE MASTER

DI 41. SCENE I

(Prince Siddhartha is walking in the garden in a contemplative mood. All of a sudden a bird falls down in front of him.)

SIDDHARTHA Ah, poor bird! My heart is bleeding for you. Who has done this? Who has hurt you? Who has aimed this arrow at you? Poor, innocent bird! Let me take the arrow out of your body. *(He removes the arrow.)* Now let me try to cure you.

(Enter Devadatta.)

DEVADATTA Siddhartha, this is my bird. What right have you to keep my bird? Give it to me!
SIDDHARTHA No, this is my bird, Devadatta.
DEVADATTA Your bird! I shot this bird. It belongs to me. This is my arrow. I aimed at the bird and it fell down here. It is mine, mine, my property, my possession.
SIDDHARTHA Devadatta, if I had not removed the arrow from the bird, it would have died by this time.
DEVADATTA The point is not whether the bird would have died or would not have died. The bird is alive, and it is my possession. It was my power, my skill, my capacity that brought the bird down to earth. You cannot have it. Everybody appreciates and admires you for your heart, for your kindness. But now let the world appreciate my capacity, my skill. You be satisfied with what you have: love. And I shall be satisfied with what I have: power. My power, my skill at archery deserves this bird, not your love.

SIDDHARTHA O Devadatta, you have the power to kill, and I have the power to love. But since I have this animal, this poor innocent bird, you shall not get it back.

DEVADATTA Siddhartha, there is a time to listen to your philosophy, and there are people to listen to your philosophy. But this is not the time, and I am not the person. You can advocate your philosophy to others who want to be like you, who want to live in the moon-world and have no practical sense. Life has to be practical. Life needs strength, life needs vigour. But your life is a life of laziness and false kindness. You should be strong. You are the Prince, and soon you will have to rule your kingdom. This kind of false attitude will not help you in any way. What I have done today, you will do millions of times more. I was about to kill a bird. You will one day kill men. At that time your philosophy will change.

SIDDHARTHA No, Devadatta, my philosophy will always remain the same. My philosophy is the philosophy of compassion, and not the philosophy of destruction.

DEVADATTA You stay with your philosophy, and let me stay with mine. My philosophy is power. Your philosophy is compassion. Well and good. Now give me my bird.

SIDDHARTHA Sorry, I will not give it to you.

DEVADATTA Are you prepared to go to the court to fight for this bird?

SIDDHARTHA Yes, I am fully prepared.

THE DISCIPLE ILLUMINES THE MASTER

DI 42. SCENE 2

(The court.)

JUDGE   Prince, why do you keep a bird which belongs to somebody else? True, you have compassion, you have love for the bird. You have love for everything. But justice says the bird belongs to Devadatta. It was he who brought the bird down to earth. It is his possession.

SIDDHARTHA   O venerable Judge, I do not know anything about justice, but my heart tells me that he who saves life is the owner, not he who takes life. My heart was bleeding for the bird and I saved it. I am prepared to give my own life for this bird.

DEVADATTA   Siddhartha, you know how to talk. You know perfectly well that no one will kill you in place of this bird. Don't show your false compassion.

JUDGE   Devadatta, I am the Judge. Let me hear more from him.

SIDDHARTHA   O sir, I feel that this bird belongs to me because I have saved its life. Devadatta practically killed the bird. Please tell me who is more important, the life-saver or the life-destroyer?

JUDGE   Prince, I agree with you. The life-saver is infinitely more important than the life-taker. You have saved the bird's life; therefore it is you who can claim this bird. The bird is yours. He who saves life or gives new life is the real owner, and not he who takes life or destroys life. Today you have offered your life for a bird. A day will come, I clearly foresee, when you will offer your life for all of humanity. Your heart will cry to save the bleeding heart of humanity. Your heart will cry to illumine the unlit mind of humanity. Your soul will cry to elevate the consciousness of humanity.

DEVADATTA   Siddhartha, today your love-power has won the victory, but a day will come when I shall conquer you with my destruction-power. You will see that power conquers love.

SIDDHARTHA   Devadatta, you are wrong. Love will always conquer, for Love is the Almighty Power.

THE BUDDHA AND ANANDA

SRI CHINMOY

DI 43. DRAMATIS PERSONÆ

THE BUDDHA
ANANDA (HIS DEAREST DISCIPLE)
A GROUP OF A FEW INTIMATE DISCIPLES

THE DISCIPLE ILLUMINES THE MASTER

DI 44. SCENE I

(The Buddha and Ananda.)

BUDDHA   Ananda, I am now an old man. I am eighty years old. Ananda, for fifty years I have been teaching and preaching. The time has come for me to depart from this world. I am weak. I am an invalid. My whole body is shattered, Ananda. This body can be of no more use here on earth.

ANANDA   *(shedding tears)* No, Master, no. You have to stay with us for quite a long time more. Your very presence is a great blessing to humanity. This *sangha* is not yet well established. This sangha needs your physical presence.

BUDDHA   Ananda, do you mean to say that the sangha expects something new from me? Do you mean to say that I have not spoken in clear terms what I have to say about this *dharma?* I have not kept anything hidden from you people. Never have I shown any sign of reticence, nor any indifference. Besides, I never thought that I would have to conduct and manage the sangha, and that it would always depend on me. So why should I stay? Why should I be involved any longer in the activities of the sangha? Ananda, from now on be self-sufficient. Have faith in yourself. Lead a spiritual life. You will realise the highest Truth. He who follows the dharma, he who takes refuge in the dharma, will alone enter into the world of Bliss, and nobody else.

ANANDA   O Lord Buddha, what you say is perfectly true, but our hearts cannot live without you. We need you. We shall eternally need you.

BUDDHA   Ananda, you need me. I need you. Again, the Truth Eternal needs us both. The Truth Eternal needs me in the world of the Beyond, and the same Truth needs you here on earth. My life has come to an end. All the experiences of the world I offer to the world. Yesterday I ate at Chunda's house. Since then I have been feeling weaker, but I wish to assure you that this weakness is not due to his food. I am suffering, true, but it is not his fault at all. He gave me food with utmost love and devotion. Nobody should blame him when I die. I offer him my deepest blessings. Before I was illumined, before I became the Enlightened One, Sujata's food helped me to live on earth. Her food made it possible for me to meditate. And now Chunda's food is helping me to enter into the highest Nirvana. I see no difference between Sujata's food and Chunda's food. Each has served a special purpose of its own.

(Enter a few intimate disciples.)

ANANDA   Look! Look! Today the Buddha's whole body is flooded with Light. This Light we have never seen around him. Such celestial Light!

THE DISCIPLES   Yes, Lord, today we see something totally new in you which we have never seen before. Your whole face is inundated with Light and Delight.

BUDDHA   Ananda, today reminds me of my days at the foot of the Bodhi tree. Just before I entered into Nirvana this body had the same Light, the same Delight. Today once again this body is flooded with Light and Delight. You are seeing it for the first time. But I am seeing it for the second time. The day ends, and my earthly sojourn ends along with it. Therefore, all of you are seeing this Light in me and around me.

(Ananda bursts into tears and is about to leave.)

THE DISCIPLE ILLUMINES THE MASTER

BUDDHA   Ananda, stay here. Don't go away. My life can now be measured in minutes. Ananda, do not cry for me. I tell all of you not to cry for me. Ananda, I have told you repeatedly that everything is transient on earth. There is nothing everlasting here. Anything that comes into life will have to give up life. You have served me, O Ananda, most devotedly, most soulfully, and for that I offer you my last blessings. Proceed on your inner strength, and you will receive liberation. You will have your liberation in due course. My spiritual journey began with renunciation and compassion, and today, at the end of my journey's close, I offer to the world the same message: renunciation and compassion. O Ananda, do not grieve.

(The Buddha dies.)

SRIBAS

SRI CHINMOY

DI 45. DRAMATIS PERSONÆ

CHAITANYA
SRIBAS (A DEAR DISCIPLE OF CHAITANYA)
A FOLLOWER OF CHAITANYA
OTHER FOLLOWERS OF CHAITANYA
WIFE OF SRIBAS
RELATIVES OF SRIBAS
SON OF SRIBAS

THE DISCIPLE ILLUMINES THE MASTER

DI 46. SCENE I

(Left stage: courtyard of Sribas' house; right stage: room adjoining the courtyard. Chaitanya is singing Hari Bol, Hari Bol *and dancing in ecstasy with his followers in the courtyard of Sribas, a dear disciple of his. All of a sudden from inside the house is heard wailing and screaming. Sribas leaves the party and runs into the house. His wife is in tears; other relatives are also weeping.)*

WIFE   Our only son! Our only son is lost forever! What can I do? What can I do?

SRIBAS   Why are you crying? Why are you weeping? What is there to cry about? His time has come. That is why he has gone to the other world. Today the Lord is dancing in our courtyard. Even the worst possible sinner will go directly to Heaven if he dies here. Since our son left the world from here, he will undoubtedly be happy. If you really love your son, then be happy, be delighted. Join us in our singing and dancing, for here, today, the Lord is with us.

WIFE   This is not the time to listen to your philosophy. We have lost our only son. I have love for our Master, Sri Chaitanya. But when one's only son dies, it is impossible to maintain the same love for the Master and the same faith in the Master.

SRIBAS   You are crying, and our relatives are crying. But our Lord is dancing in ecstasy. He is in a divine consciousness. If he hears your crying and wailing, and comes back to his normal consciousness because of it, then I shall throw myself into the Ganges. If you put an end to his ecstatic dance, then I shall put an end to my life!

(The wife calms down. Other relatives are still crying.)

SRIBAS   *(to the others)* We have lost our dearest; we have lost our only son. But my wife and I are not crying. If you have to cry, then leave our house. It is we who have suffered the loss. But to us it is no loss; it is a real gain, a real reward, because today my Lord has come to my house. Now it is not my responsibility to think of my son. My only responsibility is to think of my Master. My Master will take care of my son. So if you want to cry and weep, then all of you leave this house. This is not the place for you.

(Sribas goes back to the garden and starts singing and dancing with the others. All of a sudden, Sri Chaitanya stops singing and dancing.)

CHAITANYA   I do not know what, but something has gone wrong with me. Has anything happened at Sribas' house? *(To Sribas.)* Has any calamity taken place in your house?
SRIBAS   Lord, on the day that you have blessed my home with your divine presence, how can there be any calamity here?
ANOTHER FOLLOWER   Lord, something *has* happened.
CHAITANYA   What has happened?
FOLLOWER   Something serious has happened.
CHAITANYA   What is it?
FOLLOWER   Sribas' son has died.
CHAITANYA   When? When?
FOLLOWER   An hour ago.
CHAITANYA   Now why didn't you tell me?
FOLLOWER   You were communing with Lord Krishna, my Lord. We didn't want to put an end to your ecstatic dance. We didn't dare to do it. And why should we have done it? To us your dance is infinitely more important than this death.
SRIBAS   To me your ecstatic dance is all-important. The death of my son is of no importance in comparison.

CHAITANYA   *(starts crying)* He who can forget the loss of his only son in my presence — how can I forget his sacrifice? How can I appreciate his heart enough? How can I admire his heart enough? Sribas, you are really a man of divine sacrifice. I have never seen a man like you. Whose sacrifice can equal yours?

SRIBAS   Lord, there is no sacrifice on my part. For me there is only you. You have come to my home. Today is the happiest day of my life, the greatest day of my life.

CHAITANYA   Sribas, please go and bring the child. Let me see him.

(Exit Sribas. He returns carrying his son and followed by his wife. He places the child in front of the Master. Chaitanya looks at the child and concentrates on him.)

CHILD   Lord, it was Your wish that I should die. Who can violate Your law?

(Everyone is astonished to hear the dead child talking.)

CHILD   You brought me, Lord, into this world of Yours, and it is You who are sending me to the other world, which is equally Yours. Who is my father, who is my mother, if not You? You are the eternal Father; You are the eternal Mother. I bow to You, O Lord. I am going to Your other home.

CHAITANYA   Sribas, now your child's soul has left the body. He has gone to my other world. I have a place ready for him in Heaven. I will take care of him there as I am taking care of you, your wife and all your spiritual sisters and brothers here. Sribas, you had only one son. Now you have two sons. I am your son and my dearest disciple, Nityananda, is your son. One son has gone to the other world; two sons will take his place here.

(Sribas touches the feet of Chaitanya then dances with joy.)

WIFE *(touching Chaitanya's feet)* Lord, in You I see my child. In You I see the Heavens. In You I see the entire universe. Today I see not only Your physical presence, but Your universal Reality as well.

CHAITANYA Today you have proved to be the real counterpart of Sribas. His aspiration and your aspiration have become totally one today. I shall carry both of you deep inside my heart and lead you to the abode of Hari.

(Chaitanya blesses Sribas' wife with joy and pride.)

WHOEVER DIES TODAY AT FOUR P.M.
WILL GO TO THE HIGHEST HEAVEN

SRI CHINMOY

DI 47. DRAMATIS PERSONÆ

FIRST CITIZEN (JEWELLER)
SECOND CITIZEN
GORAKSHANATH
MATSYENDRANATH
CUSTOMER (THIEF)
CUSTOMERS FROM OTHER SHOPS
POLICEMEN
MINISTER
KING HARABHANGA
PALACE GUARDS
QUEEN
STRONG MEN

THE DISCIPLE ILLUMINES THE MASTER

DI 48. SCENE I

(Two citizens meet in the kingdom of King Harabhanga.)

FIRST CITIZEN   Unbearable, unbearable! The King is unbearable.

SECOND CITIZEN   Unpardonable, unpardonable! The King is unpardonable.

FIRST CITIZEN   He has gone crazy!

SECOND CITIZEN   He has become insane!

FIRST CITIZEN   Look at that fool! He wants his kingdom to surpass Heaven in prosperity, beauty and divinity.

SECOND CITIZEN   Look at his audacity! You say stupidity; I say stupidity plus audacity! How can his kingdom surpass Heaven?

FIRST CITIZEN   Impossible!

SECOND CITIZEN   Impossible!

FIRST CITIZEN   He has created absolute chaos in the whole kingdom. He says that everybody has to be equal, and he feels that the only way to bring this about is for everything in the market to be sold at the same price!

SECOND CITIZEN   Unthinkable! Unthinkable! How can gold and rice be sold at the same price? A seer of gold and a seer of rice! Ha! Ha! What a stupid king we have! There are things on earth which are extremely rare and there are things on earth which are extremely common. How can they be given the same price? Look at the stupidity of this king! He feels that this will make his kingdom most prosperous, and that all will become friends. Ha! Just wait and see what unimaginable things will soon happen.

FIRST CITIZEN   Well, when one loses one's brains, one does all sorts of things. The king thinks we will lead a perfectly happy life if the price of everything is equal. He is a fool, a real fool. What is worse, he is adamant in his command and we are helpless.

SECOND CITIZEN   We are helpless, true, but I abominate him — his utterance, his decree, everything he does.

FIRST CITIZEN   My friend, you hate him, and I wish to say that his very name has become anathema to me. He is despised and he will ever be despised by his entire kingdom. I am a jeweller. From now on I have to sell all my most expensive jewellery at the price of eggplants, potatoes and tomatoes.

SECOND CITIZEN   No matter, friend, how many aspersions you cast on him, you cannot change his mind. This is our fate.

FIRST CITIZEN   Fate? I don't believe in fate. I shall abrogate my fate! You will see. A day will come when Harabhanga will realise his folly and this kingdom of ours, this beautiful country, will again have real life — a life of love, a life of harmony. Once more only the right will deserve the fair. A man of knowledge will have prestige; a man of ignorance will have to work for knowledge and only then will he get prestige. People will work hard in order to achieve something and only those who deserve it will get appreciation. Two different things cannot be of the same value. A man of ignorance and a man of knowledge cannot be put on the same footing. A man of sincerity and a man of insincerity, a thief and a saint, cannot be considered equal. Just by having all eat the same food, just by selling everything at the same price, this stupid Harabhanga cannot equalise all his subjects. Impossible! His brain has reached the zenith of stupidity.

SECOND CITIZEN   And I tell you, the lion in me will not eat grass like the sheep who are the king's ministers. The king's ministers have no voice of their own. It is they who have agreed to the king's proposal. I am a lion; I shall devour the king and his sheep!

(Gorakshanath is meditating in his room. Enter Matsyendranath.)

MATSYENDRANATH   My son, are you still here? Don't you know what King Harabhanga is doing to his subjects? He has said that everything has to be sold at the same price. Gold and eggplants will be sold at the same price.

GORAKSHANATH   I know, Master. I have heard and I have read the newspaper. But I am a little amused. I am curious to see what will happen.

MATSYENDRANATH   Curious, my son! Curiosity even at this stage? You have realised God. Now why do you allow curiosity to enter into you? I know your curiosity is innocent. You are pure; your heart is all purity, all luminosity, my son. But curiosity is still a dangerous thing. Very soon this whole kingdom will be ruined. A catastrophe will take place, and I am afraid something will happen to you. I am concerned for you, and not for this kingdom. I cannot help the innocent subjects. I can only sympathise with them.

GORAKSHANATH   Master, do you know what the king said? He says his kingdom has to surpass Heaven in beauty, prosperity and divinity.

MATSYENDRANATH   *(laughing)* You know how he will make his kingdom superior to Heaven! He is an old man now. He has become senile.

GORAKSHANATH   Master, forgive me, I wish to see the end of this fun. If you allow me to stay here and see the end, I will be so grateful to you.

MATSYENDRANATH   I shall allow you to stay, but I tell you that your suffering is my suffering. If something serious happens to you, it is I who will have to help you or save you.

THE DISCIPLE ILLUMINES THE MASTER

GORAKSHANATH O Master, then I shall go away. I don't want you to suffer because of me.

MATSYENDRANATH No, no, stay here, Gorakshanath. I want you to enjoy this. I want to feed your innocent curiosity. Don't worry about me. I will be able to protect myself and I will be able to help you out, too.

GORAKSHANATH Then with your permission, Master, I shall stay.

MATSYENDRANATH Yes, you stay, with my permission. Let us see what happens.

(Exit Matsyendranath.)

SRI CHINMOY

DI 50. SCENE 3

(First citizen in his jewellery shop. Enter a customer. The customer begins looking at a beautiful ring.)

CUSTOMER   How much does this ring cost?
FIRST CITIZEN   One hundred rupees.
CUSTOMER   One hundred rupees? Why, this could not weigh much more than a few cloves of garlic! Let me go next door to the grocery store and see the price of garlic.

(Exit customer. First citizen is beside himself with rage and despair. Customer returns.)

CUSTOMER   The price of garlic is one anna. Your ring certainly does not weigh as much as a whole bulb of garlic, but I will give you one anna for it. And I won't make a report to the king against you for telling me the price was one hundred rupees. Here is one anna. Good bye.

(Customer snatches the ring and starts to leave. Jeweller begins shouting.)

CUSTOMER   If you shout I will stab you. You know it is the king's order that everything be sold at the same price.
JEWELLER   I know it is the king's order, but I refuse to sell a gold ring for one anna. It's extremely valuable!

(Customer stabs the jeweller and runs. Jeweller starts shouting.)

JEWELLER   Help, help! Somebody save me! Thief! Thief! Arrest that man!

THE DISCIPLE ILLUMINES THE MASTER

(Immediately from other shops people come in. The customer is caught and brought back in by the police.)

JEWELLER   That's the man. He has stabbed me.

DI 51. SCENE 4

(The king's palace. The king is on his throne. Enter minister.)

MINISTER   Your Majesty, the man who stabbed the jeweller was put in jail yesterday, but today he has escaped.

KING   How?

MINISTER   He was a strong man. It seems he was able to break some of the bars of the prison window, and somehow he escaped.

KING   What is to be done?

MINISTER   That is up to you. Please tell me, I am at your command.

KING   Well, if you can't find him, look for any strong young man of his size, and bring him to me.

MINISTER   Only one person?

KING   No, bring everyone. Bring all the men of his size, and I will make a selection. I will have the strongest person hanged. It is an insult to me that a prisoner can break out of my prison and escape. So the strongest man will be put to death.

THE DISCIPLE ILLUMINES THE MASTER

DI 52. SCENE 5

(Gorakshanath is meditating in his room. Enter Matsyendranath.)

MATSYENDRANATH   My son, now see, the worst calamity is about to take place. Has your curiosity been fed? Are you satisfied now? I am sure you have heard that all the strong young men in the kingdom are to be brought before the king. The king will select the strongest and have him hanged. He feels that the man who has escaped from his prison has insulted him, and he cannot brook that kind of insult. You are a very strong man. I do not know what may happen to you. Let us try to escape.

GORAKSHANATH   Master, I am at your feet. You are also strong. They may catch you as well. Although you are mature you are not yet old. I am afraid you are also in danger. Since I made the mistake, if the king sentences me to death, I am prepared. But if something happens to you, Master, I shall never forgive myself.

(Enter four guards and arrest Matsyendranath and Gorakshanath.)

SRI CHINMOY

DI 53. SCENE 6

(The King's palace. The King and Queen are sitting on their thrones. Many strong men have been brought in, including Gorakshanath and Matsyendranath, and the King is about to make a selection. The guards begin pushing the men before the King one by one.)

FIRST MAN   No, your Majesty, I didn't do it. I wasn't even there.

SECOND MAN   I was out of town.

(In this way many men are brought before the King.)

KING   Now all of you stand in a line. Instead of having you come up to me, I will go down the line. Let me see who is the strongest.

(The King goes down the line. He picks out Matsyendranath and Gorakshanath.)

KING   Undoubtedly one of you will be hanged today, but it may take me a few minutes to decide who is actually the stronger.

MATSYENDRANATH   O King, look at my health, examine my physique. I tell you, if you want to kill the stronger of us two, then it is undoubtedly I who should be killed. Look at me. Look at my arms, look at my chest, look at my feet, look at my forehead, look at any part of my body. I am far stronger than this man.

GORAKSHANATH   Do not believe him, your Majesty. Look at me, look at my body. I am obviously stronger than this man. And besides, I am younger. You wanted to have a young man, and I have young blood. He is an old man. It is clear to see. Why, he was my teacher. He may be stronger than me in some things — in knowledge or wisdom — but if you want physical strength, I am the man for you.

KING Yes, I want someone who is physically strong and not strong mentally or otherwise.

GORAKSHANATH So, King, it is I who should be killed.

MATSYENDRANATH King, believe me, I am stronger than this young man. Since you want a really strong man, it is I who should be hanged. You are such a great, compassionate king. I have never seen such a compassionate king on earth. You want to make everything in your kingdom equal to surpass Heaven in every way. I wish to say that, since I am older than he, I will not be of use to you much longer. Let the young man stay here in your kingdom to serve you. He is much younger than I, and he can serve you for many more years. Let me go to Heaven.

GORAKSHANATH King, compassion is one thing and justice is another. This man is showing his compassion. I was his student. We are like father and son. When there is danger, the father wants to embrace the danger and let his son remain safe. But there is something called a promise. King, you are most honest. Now what did you say? You said the strongest man in your kingdom would be hanged. Your Majesty, how did you become great? You became great by keeping your promises. You should continue to keep your promises, so it is I who should be killed.

KING I really can't understand it. For the first time I am seeing two men simply dying to please me. Here all are shedding bitter tears because they may have to die. If I selected them, they would be the most miserable people on earth. But here I am seeing two men fighting over the opportunity to embrace death. I have never seen anything like it.

What is the matter with you two? I want to know why you are eager to die. Is there some special reason?

MATSYENDRANATH *(pretending to be hesitant)* Well, there *is* a special cause. You think that we are very kind, nice and generous. But, O King, we are not so kind, we are not so nice, we are not so generous; our hearts are not so big. Both of us are very clever.

KING Clever? What kind of plot do you have?

MATSYENDRANATH No plot. It is only that both of us know a little bit of astrology. I am an astrologer and I taught him how to cast a horoscope. That is why he was telling you that I was his teacher.

We also meditate a little. This morning we had a vision and heard an inner voice. But King, perhaps you do not believe in visions.

KING Visions? Certainly I believe in visions. I believe in God. God has created Heaven so beautiful. It is my prayer to God that my kingdom should surpass Heaven. Now tell me, what kind of vision did you have? What did the voice tell you?

MATSYENDRANATH Both of us had the vision at the same time, and we heard the voice say that whoever dies today at four p.m. will go to the highest Heaven. That is why we are fighting for death. Otherwise, do you think that we would be so foolish?

GORAKSHANATH So, King Harabhanga, now the secret is out. It is for that purpose that I wanted to die. I wanted to go to the highest Heaven. It was not actually that I have such love for my Master. I wanted to die so that I could go to the highest Heaven.

MATSYENDRANATH It is the same with me. It was not my affection and love for my student that made me fight for the opportunity to die. I knew that I could go to the highest

Heaven immediately if I could manage to die at four p.m. in some way.

KING You think I am a fool. All the time I have been crying for Heaven, for the highest joy. Here I have pleasure, but I am not satisfied. I want something more. I know that Heaven is full of Joy and Delight. Do you think I am such a fool that I will allow one of you to go to Heaven while I remain here on this corrupt and imperfect earth? In my kingdom everybody is quarrelling and fighting all the time. That is why I wanted my kingdom to be like Heaven — even to surpass Heaven. I am so grateful that you two astrologers have told me this secret. *(Addressing his minister.)* Get ready. Invite all my subjects and all the royal family. This is my order. I am going to be hanged. I want to go immediately to Heaven. This world is corrupt. I don't see any hope for it. I wanted to bring happiness to my kingdom, but I see this will never be. It is only when I have something myself that I can give it to others. Now I am distressed, but in Heaven I shall be most happy. And from there, I will be able to send happiness down to my kingdom.

(Exit Minister.)

MATSYENDRANATH Your Majesty, I wish to say that your happiness is our happiness. If you feel that by going to Heaven immediately you will be the happiest man, then go. We shall miss you, the kingdom will miss you, but we want to be happy in your happiness.

GORAKSHANATH It is you who wanted to have the Kingdom of Heaven on earth. Now you will enter into the Kingdom of Heaven. And once you enter there, I am sure you will be able to bring down the Kingdom of Heaven into this world. In your happiness is our happiness. We wanted to go to Heaven at four p.m., but we would rather make you happy.

(The Queen starts crying bitterly.)

KING   *(to Queen)* I thought that you loved me. Now that I am going to be happy, why do you weep?
QUEEN   I *want* you to be happy, but how can I live here alone without you?
KING   Don't worry. Once I am in Heaven I will bring you there to join me. It is only a matter of time. Perhaps tomorrow I will be able to get you. When I am in the highest Heaven I will have everything, and from there I will be able to send a messenger to take you.

(The Queen smiles.)

THE DISCIPLE ILLUMINES THE MASTER

DI 54. SCENE 7

(All the subjects and the royal family are outside the palace. Suddenly four bells chime.)

CROWD   The king is dead.

(Wild shouts and cheers.)

SRI CHINMOY

DI 55. SCENE 8

(Gorakshanath and Matsyendranath are in Gorakshanath's room.)

GORAKSHANATH   O Master, I went along with you, but please tell me, why have you done this? Have we done the right thing? Oh, I know whatever you do is right, but please explain to me what we did. I want to know more from you.
MATSYENDRANATH   My son, do you feel sorry for it?
GORAKSHANATH   I do feel sorry....
MATSYENDRANATH   Why? Why do you feel sorry? You should be wise. This king was ruining the whole kingdom with his stupid laws. How can everything be of the same value? How can everybody have the same status? Is it possible? God has given some men more capacity than others. God has made some things more valuable than others. On this hand two fingers cannot be the same. They are all different. If one person prays and meditates, and another does not, naturally the former will realise God sooner than the latter. You have prayed, you have meditated and you have realised God. Equality does not come without equal merit. King Harabhanga thought that just by making the price of everything the same, all people would become equal. But that is impossible. Everything has its own value. You cannot put a lion and a sheep together, feed them the same food and expect them to become the same. The sheep will remain a sheep, and the lion will remain a lion. Spiritual people will be spiritual, and ordinary people will be ordinary. God's Kingdom is vast and everybody has his own place. One cannot mix with those who are of a different standard and expect them to become equal. Now once again this kingdom will have a sane life. A new king will take Harabhanga's

place — perhaps his own son — and you will see that, like other kingdoms, this kingdom will have prosperity. It will have judgement, peace and divine glory, for everything will have its proper value according to its capacity and according to its merit. My son, you and I have done a great service for the Supreme.

GORAKSHANATH   Master, I have understood your philosophy. I am always at your feet and at your command. To please you, to be unconditionally yours, is the sole object of my life.

(Gorakshanath sings.)

Taba sri charan mama aradhan
taba darashan mama harashan
taba parashan mama naba man
taba alodhan mama niketan

(My supreme adoration is Your Feet.
Your very sight is my delight.
Your very touch is my new mind, and Your Light
    of infinite Wealth is my true home.)

PART II

THE HEART OF A HOLY MAN

THE HEART OF A HOLY MAN

SRI CHINMOY

HH I. DRAMATIS PERSONÆ

MASTER
FIRST DISCIPLE
SECOND DISCIPLE
THIRD DISCIPLE

THE HEART OF A HOLY MAN

HH 2. SCENE 1

(A spiritual teacher with his three disciples.)

MASTER Can you tell me, my children, what is the largest thing on earth?

FIRST DISCIPLE Oh, earth itself is the largest thing, Master.

SECOND DISCIPLE No, the sky is the largest.

THIRD DISCIPLE No, no, the nether world is the largest.

MASTER *(to the first disciple)* You are right; earth is the largest thing. *(To the second disciple.)* You are right; the sky is the largest thing. *(To the third disciple.)* You are right; the nether world is the largest thing. Now, do you know the story of Lord Vishnu?

DISCIPLES We don't know. Please tell us.

MASTER With one foot, Lord Vishnu covered the earth, the sky and the nether world. But the heart of a holy man is so big that it can contain both of Vishnu's feet. If you want to have a heart as vast as the heart of a holy man, then you have to be totally pure.

FIRST DISCIPLE Master, how can we make ourselves pure? I feel that my body and my vital are very impure.

MASTER If you feel that your body and vital are impure, then do this. Take a shower at least twice a day to keep your body outwardly clean and pure. And to keep your vital pure, do not compete with anybody. No rivalry, no competition: feel that you will reach your Goal at God's choice Hour. If you have that feeling, God will take you to Himself. You pray and meditate. Make your best effort, but feel that I will take you to your destination according to the Will of the Supreme, at His choice Hour. Then you will have purity in the vital.

SECOND DISCIPLE   Master, I know my mind is very impure. What can I do?

MASTER   In your case, you have to unlearn most of the things that your mind has taught you.

SECOND DISCIPLE   Master, I do not know what the things are that my mind has taught me. Please tell me.

MASTER   Your mind has taught you how to doubt, how to suspect, how to criticise. Learn to stop doubting, stop suspecting and stop criticising others. Then your mind will become pure.

THIRD DISCIPLE   Master, my heart is impure. How can I make my heart pure?

MASTER   From now on, every day try to be always ready to open your heart's door for me. I knock at your heart's door early every morning. Do not block the door with your desires, for then I cannot come in and pierce the veil of darkness within you. Open your heart's door and allow me to enter into you. There I shall play with someone who is inside your heart, a most beautiful child, your soul. Watch how we play with immense joy and inner love for each other. When you watch us playing, your heart is bound to become pure. A day will come when we shall gladly invite you to take part in our game, to be one of us. Then you will feel that your heart is of us, your heart is for us: that your heart is made of aspiration, and your life is made for our manifestation.

ARUNI

SRI CHINMOY

HH 3. DRAMATIS PERSONÆ

AYODADHOMMYA (A SAGE)
ARUNI (HIS DISCIPLE)
WIFE OF AYODADHOMMYA

THE HEART OF A HOLY MAN

HH 4. SCENE I

(The cottage of the sage Ayodadhommya.)

AYODADHOMMYA   Aruni, my son, you are fond of me; I am proud of you. You have pleased me in every possible way, and I am proud of you at every moment.

ARUNI   Father, O Father of my heart and soul, O Father of my earthly existence, O Father of my Heavenly Delight, it is all due to your Grace that I am able to serve you.

AYODADHOMMYA   *(giving him a smile)* My son, today I am in serious difficulty. I do not have a servant. I cannot afford a servant.

ARUNI   Father, why do you need a servant? This servant of yours will do anything for you. You know that. He may not do it according to your satisfaction, but he will do it gladly, cheerfully, wholeheartedly and unconditionally.

AYODADHOMMYA   Aruni, I know. I know you will do everything for me. To please me you came into the world. But, Aruni, this is a difficult task.

ARUNI   Please tell me. I shall do it to the best of my ability. I am at your command.

AYODADHOMMYA   If you think you can help me out, then go to my paddy-field, Aruni. You will see that the water is flowing out of the field through one levee which has given way. I tried my best to fix it but could not succeed. Water is passing through the levee. And if no water remains in the paddy-field, then we shall not have a good crop this season. A paddy-field needs much water.

ARUNI   Father, I shall fix it for you. Don't worry.

(Exit Aruni.)

AYODADHOMMYA   *(to himself)* I have never seen such a devoted, dedicated disciple. But, poor fellow, how will it be possible for him to stop the water from flowing out of the paddy-field? We need a servant, a strong man to fix the levee. Anyway, let me see what my dedicated spiritual son can do for me.

(Enter Ayodadhommya's wife.)

WIFE   Is Aruni here?
AYODADHOMMYA   I have just sent him to the paddy-field to fix the levee.
WIFE   I have just come from there. I did not see him on the way.
AYODADHOMMYA   Perhaps he is going by some other route.
WIFE   Anyway, do you really think he will be able to fix it?
AYODADHOMMYA   I do hope so.
WIFE   I know he would give his life for you, for us. But if it is a task beyond his capacity, poor boy, what will he do?
AYODADHOMMYA   Let us see.

HH 5. SCENE 2

(The sage's cottage. Evening has set in.)

WIFE Look, it is dark now, and poor Aruni is still in the fields. Let us go and see what he is doing. Poor boy, he is still working very hard. We have to do something for him. Let us go and help him. I am sure he has not been successful. That's why he is still there.

AYODADHOMMYA You stay home and make a meal for us. Let me go and bring him back. If he has not been successful, tomorrow we shall try to find somebody else to do the job.

(Exit Ayodadhommya.)

SRI CHINMOY

HH 6. SCENE 3

(Ayodadhommya comes near the paddy-field. It is dark. He cannot see anything. He shouts aloud.)

AYODADHOMMYA   Aruni, Aruni, where are you?

ARUNI   Father, I am here.

AYODADHOMMYA   Where are you? I can't see you. What are you doing there? Come here, I can't see you.

ARUNI   Father, please tell me which command of yours I should follow: the morning command or the evening command?

AYODADHOMMYA   What do you mean?

ARUNI   In the morning you commanded me, Father, to come and fix the levee, so that the water would not run out of the paddy-field. I tried my best in every way, but I failed. Then, as a last resort, I lay down on the levee, and thus I prevented water from flowing out of the paddy-field. I have been lying here most of the day. If I get up from this place according to your second command, then the water will flow out again.

AYODADHOMMYA   Aruni, listen to my second command. Come here. *(Aruni leaves the bank and comes. He stands in front of his Master. His whole body is soaked and covered with mud. He is shivering all over.)*

AYODADHOMMYA   *(blessing him)* Aruni, you have pleased me beyond your imagination. You have pleased me beyond my expectation. I write down this deed of yours in my heart, with my joy, with my love, with my gratitude. Also, I write down in gold letters on the tablet of your heart, my joy, my pride, my gratitude. Aruni, today I give you a new name, a name which will do justice to your sacrifice for me, your love for me, your devotion to me, your service to me. Your name will be Uddalak. *(Chants.)* Aum. Uddalak. U-D-D-A-L-A-K. Today you were a human dike, protecting my field with your body. Tomorrow you will be Uddalak, the divine dike, protecting humanity with your unparalleled devotion and sacrifice.

DON'T ENCOURAGE THE UNDESERVING ONES

SRI CHINMOY

HH 7. DRAMATIS PERSONÆ

SAGE
DOG
LEOPARD
TIGER
ELEPHANT
LION
ANGEL

THE HEART OF A HOLY MAN

HH 8. SCENE I

(A cave deep in the forest. A Sage is meditating and his dog is lying on the floor next to him. The dog gets up and goes out for a minute. Soon the dog re-enters, running.)

DOG   Master, save me, save me, save me! I have been attacked by a leopard, which is chasing me. It wants to kill me.
SAGE   Don't worry, my little friend. I have occult power. I shall turn you into a leopard, so that you won't have to be afraid of him.

(He turns the dog into a leopard. It is now very happy and secure.)

LEOPARD   Master, I am hungry. I am going out to eat but I shall come back soon.

(Exit leopard. The Sage meditates. Soon the leopard re-enters, running.)

LEOPARD   Master, a tiger! A tiger is chasing me! Save me! Save me!
SAGE   A tiger? Don't worry. What can a tiger do to you? I shall turn you into a tiger.

(The leopard becomes a tiger.)

TIGER   Oh, now I am really powerful. I am so grateful to you, Master. Now I don't have to be afraid of anything. I am very hungry. Let me go out and eat since there is no food here. I will soon come back to guard you.

(Exit tiger. The Sage smiles and continues meditating. Re-enter tiger running.)

TIGER   Master, an elephant! An elephant is trying to kill me! Save me, save me, O Sage!

SAGE   Don't worry. What can an elephant do? I am here to save and protect you. Let me turn you into an elephant.

(The tiger becomes an elephant. It is now full of confidence.)

ELEPHANT   Now I am really hungry. What I have eaten since morning is not nearly enough to support this bulk. Let me go and get food from somewhere. I shall come back to you soon.

SAGE   Yes, go with my blessings.

(Exit elephant. The Sage continues meditating. Soon the elephant comes back running.)

ELEPHANT   Oh, a lion! A lion wants to kill me now! How is it that God has not made me as powerful as the lion? I have to bow down to the lion. Save me, save me! Please, Master, this time make me as powerful as the lion.

SAGE   Don't worry. I have the power to stop the lion from killing you. I shall turn you into a lion.

(The elephant turns into a lion.)

LION   Ah! Now I am really powerful. Now I don't have to worry about anything. I can destroy anything; I can kill everything. When I want to eat, I can eat whatever I choose. Now I am the king of the animals. Let me take a little rest. Nobody will dare to come and bother me now. You meditate.

(The Sage gives the lion a smile and starts meditating. He chants from the Vedas, the Upanishads and the Gita.)

LION   O Sage, I am hungry. There is no food here and I am hungry.

SAGE   Then go out and look for some food. I am a poor man. I have no food to give you.

LION   No, I won't go out to look for food. Why should I? I don't have to. I am the strongest of all. I can kill you. I can eat you. I don't have to go out at all. What can you do about it?

(The lion comes near the Sage menacingly. The Sage immediately turns it back into a dog. The dog humbly tries to come near the Sage and sit at his feet.)

SAGE   No, I will not allow you, you ungrateful creature! Get away from me! You were a dog, and out of my infinite compassion I turned you into a lion. Then you wanted to devour me. Get away from here.

(The Sage turns the dog out into the forest and continues meditating. After a while he starts thinking aloud.)

SAGE   Have I done the right thing? The poor dog is helpless. I have turned it away in this thick forest.

(An angel appears.)

ANGEL   You have done the right thing, O Sage. In this world you have to be careful that when you give something to someone, that person deserves it and is ready to receive it. For only when a person has receptivity will you be able to bring down infinite Peace, Love and Light from above and manifest the Supreme in him. If he cannot receive your blessingful gift properly, he will misuse it. He may be so ungrateful that he will even use it against you. In the spiritual life, many spiritual Masters have taken their disciples right from the gutter, from lives of darkness and impurity. With their love, affection and concern they have given these disciples new life. Solely by their grace, they have lifted these disciples from darkest ignorance to Light and Delight. But the disciples are such ungrateful people. They feel that it is their own effort or their own merit that has brought them so high. When other disciples come later and gain favour with the Master, they feel that the Master is unjust, undivine. They criticise and insult the Master in every way and leave him.

So, Sage, in this world do not encourage the undeserving. If you help people indiscriminately, they will not appreciate the blessings of your Divinity. You will see happen to them what you have seen happen to your dog. You helped the dog in order to protect it. You transformed it into a leopard, then into a tiger, then into an elephant and finally into a lion. Then you saw what happened. When the lion became hungry, it was ready to kill you. In the spiritual life also, when people become really hungry for more name, more fame, more favour, more satisfaction, more power to lord it over others, they will stand against their Master and be ready to ruin his mission.

So be wise, O Sage. Only help those who deserve your love, affection and blessings. Only help those who are ready to be under your guidance with utmost humility all the time, from the day they accept you right up to the day they receive their illumination from you. When a disciple becomes great, divinely great, he has to feel that it is by your grace and not by his personal effort. What little effort he made was due to your grace, for it was you who inspired him to cry for a better life. Your disciples have to know and feel that from darkest inconscience your grace brought them into Light.

LIGHT IS THE ONLY WEALTH WORTH HAVING

SRI CHINMOY

HH 9. DRAMATIS PERSONÆ

THIEF
KING
QUEEN
PRINCESS
PRIME MINISTER
A GROUP OF SPIRITUAL SEEKERS
ROYAL RETINUE
AN ANGEL

THE HEART OF A HOLY MAN

HH 10. SCENE 1

(A room of the royal palace late at night. A thief enters and is quietly moving around when the King and Queen enter, talking. The thief quickly hides.)

KING   I think the time has come for our second daughter to get married. But this time we shall not make the same mistake that we made with our first daughter. We married her to a military man. We thought that this man, who held a high post in the military, would bring her joy. But alas, there is no joy, no peace in her life. It is all constant fighting, constant battle. This time let us not ask for name and fame. Let us look for a simple man, very simple. Let us look for a religious man for this daughter of ours, for she is also very religious and spiritual.

QUEEN   My Lord, I fully agree with you. Our daughter is extremely spiritual. She should have a saintly person as her husband. She will then be happy, and we shall be happy. You are the King. We have abundant wealth. We have name and fame. All we need now is peace and joy. This daughter of ours will have peace and joy and she will give it to us.

KING   Where can we find a saintly person?

QUEEN   Well, there are always saintly people praying and meditating on the banks of the Ganges. I see them quite often. I think it would be a nice idea if we chose one of those saintly people who meditate every morning watching the sun rise over the Ganges. They are sincere people, simple people. How I wish our daughter could marry one of them!

KING   Ah, that is a splendid idea! I, too, thought of it. Tomorrow morning let us ask our Prime Minister to go and see if there is one saint there who is really suitable for our daughter.

HH II. SCENE 2

(The next day. The King and Queen are speaking to their daughter.)

QUEEN   My child, you will be really happy and you will make us really happy if you marry a saintly, simple, religious person. You can see your elder sister's fate, how miserable she is with her military husband. Although he holds a high post, there is no joy, no peace in their life together. If you live with a simple, innocent, aspiring person, then your life will be all joy.

PRINCESS   Mother, you are right, absolutely right. I really want to have a person like that as my partner, someone who is simple, religious and spiritual.

(Enter Prime Minister.)

KING   Prime Minister, I wish you to go and mingle with the saints and sincere seekers who are praying to God on the banks of the Ganges. I wish you to see if any of them would like to marry my daughter. Then you select a husband for her.

QUEEN   It is beneath our dignity, it is beneath our daughter's dignity, to ask if anybody would like to marry her. Is there anybody on earth who wouldn't marry our daughter? She is so charming, so beautiful, so loving. Is there anybody who would dare to say that he would not marry my daughter?

KING   Dearest wife, I am not sure. These religious people do not care for earthly beauty, name and fame. But if we find one, I will be so proud and happy.

PRIME MINISTER   Your Majesty, let me try at least. Let me see what I can do for our Princess. I am sure I will be successful.

PRINCESS   I feel shy. I do not wish to come with you.
PRIME MINISTER   It is not necessary at all, since this is the first time. Let me go alone and see what actually happens. You come next time.

THE HEART OF A HOLY MAN

HH 12. SCENE 3

(The bank of the Ganges. The thief who had overheard the King and Queen's conversation is wearing an ochre cloth and meditating with the religious people. He is chanting most devoutly, crying for God's Grace and nothing else. He wants to show that he is the most religious person on earth. Enter the Prime Minister. He goes to these religious people and asks several of them, one by one, if they would like to marry the Princess. They all refuse.)

PRIME MINISTER *(to another seeker)* Would you like to marry the Princess?

SEEKER What do you mean? We are crying for divine Light, Peace and Power. Do you think we will be satisfied with a human being?

PRIME MINISTER Don't argue with me! Don't you know that I am the Prime Minister? I can easily take you to the palace and compel you to marry the Princess. If you don't obey me, I can put you into jail.

A SECOND SEEKER You can put us into jail, you can even kill us, but we are not going to marry the Princess, no matter how beautiful she is, no matter how wealthy her parents are. We want only the infinite riches of God, not human wealth. Do anything you want with us, but we shall not marry the Princess.

PRIME MINISTER *(turning to the thief, who has kept silent all this time)* It seems to me that you would agree to my request. Are you interested in marrying the Princess?

(The thief remains silent.)

A THIRD SEEKER   Shame, shame, shame! Look at this fellow. He has cast a slur on us. We are all spiritual people crying for God's Peace, Light and Bliss, and he meditates with us. Now he is silent because he wants to marry an earthly woman. He wants to enjoy earthly pleasure. Shame, shame! Get away from here! We don't want you with us!

THIEF   You hypocrites! You liars! Outwardly you are acting like saints, but inwardly you are really animals. Outwardly you are saying you don't want women, but inwardly you are crying for earthly wealth and pleasure, and inwardly you are enjoying vital pleasure. I can see clearly that you people are all impure, impure, impure! I am sincere. I want God. But at the same time I still have not transcended the pleasures of the human senses. I shall marry her. And I shall realise God much sooner than you by gradually transcending my desires instead of suppressing them as you people are doing.

PRIME MINISTER   All right, tomorrow I shall come to you with the Princess and we shall take you to the Palace.

(Exit Prime Minister.)

THIRD SEEKER   *(to the thief)* It is beneath our dignity to sit beside you. You are an earthly man, whereas we are all crying to be Heavenly beings. We would not marry any woman. We know we would fall if we did. Marriage is frustration. Frustration is destruction. Meditation on God is Illumination, and Illumination is transcendental Delight. This is what we have come to realise.

(Exeunt all the seekers.)

THE HEART OF A HOLY MAN

HH 13. SCENE 4

(The banks of the Ganges the following morning. All the seekers have left the place where they were meditating the day before and are meditating in another place. The thief, in his ochre cloth, is praying and meditating all alone in the same spot as on the previous day. Enter Prime Minister with Princess and retinue.)

PRIME MINISTER   Look, I have brought the Princess here.

THIEF   O Prime Minister, I have changed my mind. I know she is beautiful. I know she is rich. I know she has everything that the world longs for. But I am not really a religious person; I am a thief. I overheard a conversation between the King and the Queen. They said they wanted their daughter to marry a religious person, and I thought that if I could marry the Princess I would be the happiest and the richest person on earth. Therefore I put on this ochre cloth and started meditating with the saints and seekers. Yesterday you saw, Prime Minister, how much they hate me. I fought with them, I insulted them, saying that they were all insincere people. But today a new light has dawned on me. Today I see that if I can get the boundless wealth of the world and this paragon of beauty by being false, just by telling lies, then if I tell the truth, if I meditate on the Truth, I will naturally get something far more satisfying than the wealth of the King and the beauty of the Princess. The Princess has beauty; this I don't deny. Her father has wealth; that I don't deny. But my sincere cry for God, who is all-Beauty, who is all-Wealth, will give me real joy, real satisfaction. There are many, many kings, many queens, many princesses on earth, but they do not have happiness. I need happiness. I used to steal people's money; I used to tell lies and accomplish quite a few things, but there was no happiness for me. Today I am determined never again to swerve from the path of Truth. I shall only follow the path of Truth, and grow into the Highest, Eternal Truth.

(An angel appears and blesses the thief.)

ANGEL   I am most pleased with you, my son. Take the inner wealth I give to you: boundless Peace, Love and Bliss. I want you to marry this girl. You will not fall from the Truth. I have given you the wealth of the Spirit; now with this spiritual wealth I wish you to enter into material wealth, to control and guide the material wealth. I wish you to manifest the divinity of your inner wealth on earth through your outer wealth. I am blessing you. Your life's inner cry has reached its highest height. Now, manifest that highest height here on earth. Your acceptance of this Princess, your acceptance of this material wealth, will please me. Use this material wealth to serve the inner wealth which you already have. Here I unite you *(addressing the thief)*, the spirit of the inner world, and you *(addressing the Princess)*, the matter of the outer world. Now I make you one.

(To the Princess.)

It is here on earth, in you and with you, that your husband will manifest God. It is with your help, your conscious help, that your husband will manifest God on earth. Without your help he cannot do it. And it is with him, with his help, that you will realise God, the Highest Absolute. Your realisation depends on him; his manifestation depends on you. I make both of you one to please the Supreme with your realisation and manifestation. By realising the Supreme and by manifesting the Supreme you will fulfil the Supreme.

(The thief and the Princess bow down to the angel.)

SARASWATI

SRI CHINMOY

HH 14. DRAMATIS PERSONÆ

BRAHMA
VISHWAMITRA (A GREAT KING WHO BECAME A SAGE)
SARASWATI (GODDESS OF KNOWLEDGE AND WISDOM)
VASHISHTHA (A GREAT SAGE)
FIRST PILGRIM
SECOND PILGRIM
THIRD PILGRIM
SHIVA

THE HEART OF A HOLY MAN

HH 15. SCENE 1

(Vishwamitra is meditating in his forest hermitage. Enter Brahma.)

BRAHMA   Vishwamitra, you have been humiliated by Vashishtha.
VISHWAMITRA   Brahma, at last! At last you have come! You have listened to my prayers. I have prayed to you for so many years. Today you have come to me.
BRAHMA   Yes, I have come to fulfil your desire. I have come to give you the knowledge of Brahman. Today you equal Vashishtha.

(Vishwamitra bursts into joyous laughter.)

VISHWAMITRA   Ah! Today at last I have equalled Vashishtha. That Vashishtha, who smashed my pride, whose cow Nandini smashed my pride! Now I equal him in the knowledge of Brahman. *(Touching Brahma's feet.)* Oh Lord Brahma, I am so grateful to you. You have given me the knowledge of Brahman today.

(Brahma blesses Vishwamitra. Exit Brahma.)

VISHWAMITRA   Now I have got the knowledge of Brahman. I have equalled Vashishtha. Now I am not inferior in the knowledge of God and Truth. But still, I want to take revenge on him. He humiliated me like anything. I am on this side of the river Saraswati, and he is on the other side. Let me invoke the presiding deity of Saraswati.

(He invokes Saraswati, the presiding deity. Saraswati appears.)

VISHWAMITRA   Saraswati, I want you to do me a favour. Go to the other side of the river and bring Vashishtha here. If you do not do this, I shall annihilate you.
SARASWATI   O Sage, certainly I shall do it.

HH 16. SCENE 2

(Vashishtha is meditating, deep in trance. Enter Saraswati.)

VASHISHTHA   Can I be of any service to you?

SARASWATI   Yes, O Sage of the highest magnitude. Please come with me. Come, I shall take you to the other side of the river in a special boat, my boat. Vishwamitra needs your presence.

VASHISHTHA   Vishwamitra? What for?

SARASWATI   I do not know. But if I cannot take you to him, I am sure he will destroy me. You have more compassion than any human being on earth; your compassion is boundless. I know you will come with me. If I come to you with Vishwamitra's message, I know this message of mine will not irritate you. You will not kill me with your occult power. You have the capacity to destroy but you are all forgiveness, you are all compassion. But if I don't bring you, Vishwamitra will certainly destroy me.

VASHISHTHA   Saraswati, do not worry. I will come with you.

HH 17. SCENE 3

(Vishwamitra's forest hermitage. Enter Saraswati and Vashishtha.)

VISHWAMITRA   Ah, Saraswati. You have done your job well. Any boon you ask for I shall fulfil. But first I am going to get a weapon to kill Vashishtha here and now.

(Exit Vishwamitra.)

SARASWATI   *(grabbing Vashishtha)* Come! Come! Come! Let us go!

(Exeunt Saraswati and Vashishtha.)

HH 18. SCENE 4

(Vashishtha's side of the river. Enter Saraswati and Vashishtha.)

VASHISHTHA What a divine *Lila* — you take me and you bring me back.

SARASWATI If I hadn't taken you, he would have killed me. So I took you, and then he wanted to kill you. But I don't want him to kill you. It is better for me to be killed. You have done no harm to him. You are all forgiveness, you are all compassion. Since I won't be able to fulfil his desire, since I won't be able to bring....

VASHISHTHA Why not? You can take me. You *did* take me.

SARASWATI Yes, you went, and you are ready to go again. You are most kind to me. But I don't want you to be killed by him. You are a Brahmin. He is a Kshatriya. For a Kshatriya to kill a Brahmin is very bad. I will not allow it. No, I shall not. If he invokes me, I shall go to him and say that I am ready to be killed by him.

(Vashishtha blesses Saraswati. Exit Saraswati.)

SRI CHINMOY

HH 19. SCENE 5

(Vishwamitra is invoking Saraswati. Enter Saraswati.)

VISHWAMITRA Saraswati, you have deceived me. You have deceived me! Now you deserve punishment. I shall destroy you. No. Just by destroying you I won't get enough satisfaction. I shall degrade you. I shall dishonour you. Everybody says your water is extremely pure. Everybody drinks your water. I am going to turn your water into blood. Nobody will ever drink your water again. It will be disgusting — all red.

SARASWATI My water, my existence, will be all red?

VISHWAMITRA Yes, everybody will loathe you. Nobody will come near you. Nobody will dare to touch your water. Nobody will ever want to look at you.

THE HEART OF A HOLY MAN

HH 20. SCENE 6

(A group of pilgrims come to the river Saraswati which is all red.)

FIRST PILGRIM   This Saraswati was once upon a time such a beautiful river. It had such clear, pure water.
SECOND PILGRIM   Everybody drank, everybody swam here. It gave everybody such joy, such fun, such comfort, such delight.
THIRD PILGRIM   Now the river Saraswati has become an object of fear and disgust. Let us pray for its restoration.

(They sit down and pray to Lord Shiva. Shiva descends.)

SHIVA   I have heard your prayer. I am making Saraswati once again clear and pure for you to use, for everybody to use. Long ago, Vishwamitra did not have the knowledge of Brahman. Because he didn't have the knowledge of Brahman, Vashishtha and Vashishtha's divine cow defeated him. Now he has got the knowledge of Brahman from Brahma. Now he has equalled Vashishtha. But nature's transformation is a different matter. God-realisation is one thing. Vishwamitra didn't have it before. Now he has it. But for God-manifestation, one needs the transformation of human nature. Vishwamitra lacks this transformation of nature. Vashishtha has it. Unless and until Vishwamitra has changed his nature, he will not be able to manifest God on earth. Vashishtha is all love, all compassion for mankind. He has transformed his nature and is manifesting God on earth. Vashishtha still remains unparalleled, infinitely superior to Vishwamitra.

THE SAINT AND THE KING

SRI CHINMOY

HH 21. DRAMATIS PERSONÆ

SAINT
KING (A DISCIPLE OF THE SAINT)
A SERVANT OF THE KING

THE HEART OF A HOLY MAN

HH 22. SCENE I

(The saint and the king are together.)

KING   O Guru of my heart and soul, please tell me how I can please you most.

SAINT   You can please me most, my son, by allowing me to sit at the foot of a mango tree in your garden. There is a particular mango tree where I wish to sit every day and meditate without interruption for hours and hours. I do not want to be in your palace. It is so full of noise, so full of clamour. I feel I will be infinitely happier alone. To tell the truth, I will only be really happy if I am left alone to meditate under that particular mango tree. And every day you may come and see me, once in the morning, and once in the evening.

(The king touches his Guru's feet.)

KING   Yes, O Guru, I shall do it. Every day I shall come in the morning and in the evening to have your darshan. And I shall send food for you three times a day. Please call me whenever you want to. I am always at your command, O Guru.

SRI CHINMOY

HH 23. SCENE 2

(The saint is meditating under the mango tree. The tree is full of ripe mangoes. One of the servants of the king is tempted to have some mangoes, so he throws stones at the tree. Some of the stones strike the saint and some mangoes drop on the saint, and he is hurt. The servant takes away the mangoes hurriedly.)

THE HEART OF A HOLY MAN

HH 24. SCENE 3

(Soon the king comes and sees that his Master's arms and legs are bruised. He is shocked to see this, and bursts into tears.)

KING   O Master, why didn't you call me? How could this happen? How could you suffer so much? Who threw stones at you? Who could have done this kind of thing to my Master? It must have been one of my servants. Please tell me. Do you know the person? I shall kill him.

SAINT   No. I know the person, but I won't tell you who he is.

KING   Why not? Why not?

SAINT   He threw stones at the mangoes, not at me. The mangoes are the children of the tree, but the tree has forgiven him. Look, the tree is still here: it did not fall on him. The tree has forgiven him, although he took away quite a few mangoes. If a tree has the capacity to forgive a man, since I am a religious man, a superior being, I should also have that capacity.

KING   O Guru, if you forgive this servant of mine, he will go on with his wrongdoing. Is it fair, please tell me, to allow a criminal to go without punishment?

SAINT   You call him a criminal, but I call him an ignorant fellow. And again, it is I who sat here while your servant was throwing stones at the mangoes. I could have moved away.

KING   You? Why should you? You are my Master, you are my All. I am at your feet. What kind of audacity did he have to throw stones at the mangoes while you were sitting at the foot of the tree? I shall now go back to the palace and order all my servants to come here. And the one who did this will have to make a confession. If he does not make a confession, then I shall find out by some other means who the real culprit is.

SAINT   The real culprit is your Guru. He allowed this ignorance. He allowed this man to throw stones. If I had told him to stop, he would have gone away. But he was hungry; he was tempted to have a few delicious mangoes, and I did not stop him. I could have asked him to climb up the tree and take some mangoes, or I could have moved away, but I did neither. If you want to say that it is his mistake, I wish to say, no, it is my mistake. It was I who allowed him to throw stones at the mangoes. And the result is that I am hurt. So, O King, do not blame him; it is I who am the real culprit. If you feel that I have done the right thing by forgiving him, which you should, then I wish to tell you that this quality of forgiveness I learnt from this tree. And I impart this quality of forgiveness to you, King. Forgive your servant. It is through forgiveness, mutual forgiveness, that we live on earth. There can be nothing superior to forgiveness. If it is a matter of crime, then forgiveness is the only cure. And if it is a matter of experience, then I wish to tell you that through this servant I have experienced hunger, temptation and wrong action. From this servant's ignorance, I got one experience. And from the forgiveness of this tree, I got a divine experience. Ignorance teaches us; knowledge and forgiveness teach us. Ignorance teaches us how to destroy ourselves; knowledge and forgiveness teach us how to build ourselves, how to place ourselves within everyone, how to become one with everyone, how to become universally one.

(The king touches his Master's feet with a new light, a new vision.)

THE SEEKER AND THE THIEF

SRI CHINMOY

HH 25. DRAMATIS PERSONÆ

SEEKER
THIEF

THE HEART OF A HOLY MAN

HH 26. SCENE 1

(The cottage of an advanced seeker. A thief is rummaging around. Enter the seeker. The thief begins to run away.)

SEEKER   A thief!

(As the thief runs away, he drops a watch and a mango. The seeker picks them up and begins to chase the thief.)

SEEKER   Oh thief! Oh thief!

(The thief stops and turns around.)

THIEF   You fool, why do you bother me? I have returned your things. I am not taking away your watch or your mango. I have dropped them. Why are you chasing me? You cannot say that I have stolen anything. I am going now. Don't bother me.

SEEKER   I want you to take this mango. I want you to take this watch.

THIEF   Why?

SEEKER   You must need them more than I do. That's why you were taking them away. You need this watch and this mango, but I need something else. I need *amrita,* the divine nectar. I want to drink amrita, and not eat mangoes. By drinking amrita I will become immortal. I do not need this watch; I need eternal time. I want to live in eternal time. The things that I need most I shall pray for. But you need this most delicious mango to eat, and you need this watch so that you will know at what time you should go out to steal and when you are supposed to come back. You need them more than I do, and I am glad that I am in a position to fulfil your needs.

THIEF   And who is going to fulfil your needs? I am grateful to you for fulfilling my needs. I need a mango, true, and I need this watch. But I certainly can't fulfil your needs.

SEEKER   My friend, since I have fulfilled your needs, there will be someone on earth to fulfil my needs, too. The time has come for your desires to be fulfilled, and God has chosen me to fulfil them. A time will also come when my needs will be fulfilled. My aspiration will bear fruit at God's choice Hour. At that time, He will send someone into my life whose very touch will give me my realisation, my liberation. I am waiting for that person to come into my life.

THIEF   You are great indeed, and now I will also become good. Because of your inspiration, I will lead a better life. Will you bless me? *(The seeker blesses him.)* From now on I shall be a good man. I shall eat this mango, and I shall sow the seed in my garden. One day the seed will germinate. It will grow into a plant, and then it will become a tree. And at the foot of that tree I shall sit and meditate. You have given me a watch, but I shall not use it to tell me when to go out stealing and when to come back. I will use it only to see the hour at which I must meditate. Early every morning I will get up and meditate at a certain time. When I have the mango tree, I will meditate at the foot of the tree. But until then I shall meditate in my room, and your watch will make me punctual.

SEEKER   Those are both excellent ideas. Use this watch to see that you get up early every morning to meditate. After five or six years, you will be able to sit at the foot of the mango tree and meditate. You will see, as the mango tree bears thousands of mangoes, your aspiration also will bear fruit. You will have Peace, Light and Bliss in boundless measure.

GAUTAMI

SRI CHINMOY

HH 27. DRAMATIS PERSONÆ

GAUTAMI
HER SON
SNAKE
HUNTER
YAMARAJ (THE KING OF DEATH)
TIME

THE HEART OF A HOLY MAN

HH 28. SCENE I

(Gautami and her son in the forest.)

GAUTAMI   My son, you and I have come to the forest to meditate on God. You are dearer to me than my life. I have nobody on earth except you. Your father left us two years ago. He is now with God. One day we two will also go to God and be with your father there in Heaven. My son, in you I have everything.

SON   Mother, you are my everything. You are my everything, Mother.

GAUTAMI   My son, I wish you to sing me a most soulful song. While you are singing, I shall meditate. And when your singing is over, you also join me in meditation.

SON   Certainly I shall do so. Do you want me to sing any particular song, Mother?

GAUTAMI   I wish you to sing that song which you sing so soulfully, *Nayam atma bala-hinena labhyo* [This soul cannot be won by the weakling.]

SON   Yes, Mother, I shall sing that song to please you.

(The son sings the song most soulfully. Gautami meditates with her eyes closed. Suddenly a snake comes and bites the son. He screams and Gautami's meditation is disturbed. She sees the snake. The son's face becomes pale. He faints, then dies in front of his mother.)

GAUTAMI   O snake, you have killed my son! O God, there was no doctor here; there was nobody to save my son's life. My son is no more. O Lord, You know what is best. Let Thy Will be done, O Lord.

(Enter a hunter.)

HUNTER   O venerable lady, is this your child?

GAUTAMI   My only son. He has been bitten by a snake.

HUNTER   Your only son has been bitten by a snake, and he is dead? Let me kill the snake. And after I have killed it, shall I destroy it by burning it or shall I cut it into pieces? Tell me how I can please you.

GAUTAMI   I do not want you to kill the snake.

HUNTER   Why not? Your only son is no more, and you don't want me to kill the culprit? Why?

GAUTAMI   If you kill the snake, do you think that I will get my son's life back?

HUNTER   No, you won't get your son's life back. But the snake deserves punishment. The snake has killed him, and I have the capacity to kill the snake.

GAUTAMI   No, I don't want you to kill the snake. The time had come for my son to leave this body. The snake was just an instrument. It was an innocent instrument, and I really don't want you to kill it.

(The snake lifts up its hood.)

SNAKE   Mother Gautami, I didn't want to bite your son, but the King of Death, Yamaraj, sent me to bite him. So I have bitten him, and he is now dead. But it is not my fault.

HUNTER   Whose fault is it, then? This boy was such a young child. Now he is dead. What did he do? Why should Yamaraj want to kill an innocent, beautiful, divine boy? Yamaraj sent you. True, it was his crime; he did the wrong thing. But it was you who executed his order; it was you who killed the boy. Your crime is more serious, so it is you who deserve my punishment.

SNAKE   O hunter, you are a wise man. When you wish to perform religious sacrifices, when you wish to perform *pujas*, you appoint a priest, and the priest prays and meditates for you. He adores and worships God for you. Then you get the benefit, you get the merit, you get the result of the *puja*. The priest does everything for you, but since you are the employer, you get the benefit. The priest does not get it. I was employed by the King of Death. I have only worked for him. The consequences of my acts belong to him.

(Enter Yamaraj.)

SNAKE   Master, I listened to you. You asked me to bite the boy, and I did. Now he is dead, and they blame me. I just executed your will and they blame me. They want to kill me — at least this hunter wants to kill me.
GAUTAMI   I don't want to kill you. I want the hunter to let you go.
HUNTER   I want to kill you. I *will* kill you. *(To Yamaraj.)* Why are you so cruel? You sent this snake to kill this young boy who was so beautiful, so divine.
YAMARAJ   Look, hunter, I am not responsible. Time, Eternal Time, ordered me to send the snake to bite this young boy. I am under the express command of Time.

(Enter Time.)

TIME   What is this all about?
YAMARAJ   O Time, I executed your order, and now they are blaming me. Is it my fault that I asked the snake to come and bite this boy? It was your order. We are all at your feet, O Time.

TIME It is not your fault; it is not my fault. It is nobody's fault. In his previous incarnation this boy did something wrong, and this is the result. He is paying the penalty for his action in his previous incarnation.

GAUTAMI O hunter, go away. I knew this; I felt it. Everything here on earth is caused by God's Will. O Yamaraj, go back to your home. O Time, go back to your abode. Please allow me to pray to my God. He will give me strength; He will console my heart; He will illumine my life. My son is with God and my husband is with God. As long as God wants me to stay on earth to work for Him, I shall stay. And when He wants me to go back to Him in Heaven, with my heart's deepest joy I shall go back. I have no son, I have no husband. In my outer life I am alone; but in my inner life I am never alone. God is within me, guiding me, protecting me and illumining me. I need only one Person on earth and in Heaven: that is my God. In Him I see my husband, my son, my Everything. God is my All, my only One.

KURU

SRI CHINMOY

HH 29. DRAMATIS PERSONÆ

KING KURU
MINISTER
INDRA

THE HEART OF A HOLY MAN

HH 30. SCENE I

(King Kuru and his minister.)

KURU Minister, come with me. Follow me. *(Minister follows him for a good distance.)* This is a vast plot of land. I want this land to be cultivated, and I want a bumper crop from this land very soon.

MINISTER That is a wonderful idea, your Majesty. I shall appoint some farmers to cultivate this land.

(Enter Indra.)

INDRA O King, on this land hundreds of sages have meditated and prayed. Here they have performed sacrifices. Here they have performed their rituals; they have meditated on God. This is soil of sacrifice, soil of aspiration and realisation. O King, don't destroy this hallowed land.

KURU I don't believe in all that spirituality — meditation and sacrifice and all that. I need this land. I don't want it to remain uncultivated. I am a man of principle, a man of wisdom. Don't fool with me. This is my kingdom. This is my land.

(Indra disappears, then enters in the form of a Brahmin.)

INDRA Your Majesty, this is your kingdom, this is your property. I have no right to advise you, but I wish to say that the gods will be happy in Heaven if you leave it as it is.

KURU Then pray to God. I will allow this land to remain uncultivated provided you pray to God that whoever dies in this place will go to God immediately. It is said that whoever dies in Kashi (Benares) goes to Heaven. I want this place also to be as sacred as Benares. No matter who he is, if he is a thief, a murderer, a man of the worst possible principles, whoever dies here must go to Heaven immediately. If this desire of mine can be fulfilled, then I shall leave this place uncultivated.

(The Brahmin immediately changes back to Indra.)

INDRA   I fulfil your desire. This will be one of the most sacred places in India. Just because the sages prayed and meditated here, just because of my presence, just because of your surrender to my will, everybody who dies here — even if he is the worst possible man — will go to Heaven. And I wish to say that here also the battle of life will take place. The Divine and the undivine will fight. The Divine will eventually conquer the undivine and manifest and fulfil God on earth. On the physical plane, the undivine will be swallowed up by the one Divine Compassion-Light. But on the inner plane, on the spiritual plane, the undivine will enter into the Divine and be transformed, perfected and fulfilled. Once conquered by the Divine, once surrendered to the Will of the Divine, the undivine will become part and parcel of the Divine and will be utilised for the Divine. It will feel boundless joy and delight. It will see the difference between pleasure, which it once had, and joy, which it now has. The undivine will be lost in the Divine and will become Divine itself, and here it will find its real fulfilment.

UDPANTIRTHA

SRI CHINMOY

HH 31. DRAMATIS PERSONÆ

TRITA, EKATA, DWITA (SONS OF THE SAGE GAUTAMA)
BEAR
COSMIC GOD
GAUTAMA
THE SUPREME GOD

THE HEART OF A HOLY MAN

HH 32. SCENE I

(The home of the sage Gautama, who has recently died. His three sons are together.)

TRITA   *(to his two brothers)* Now that our father is not with us, we have to be very clever and wise.

EKATA   Certainly we have to. What do you think we should do?

TRITA   Let us go to our father's disciples. Father had quite a few rich disciples. They will sympathise with us; they will give us gifts, all sorts of gifts. They will give us their cows, and we will be able to sell milk. With their gifts we shall be able to stay on earth without working.

DWITA   That is a splendid idea. Let us go and get all we can, whatever wealth his disciples give us. This is our opportunity. Right now they are mourning, they are crying for their Master. This is the time when they will be very large-hearted and sympathetic towards us.

(Exeunt omnes.)

HH 33. SCENE 2

(The three brothers have gone to the homes of the disciples. Each disciple has offered them gifts. They are returning home with many cows and expensive things. Ekata and Dwita are behind the cows and Trita is ahead of the cows. Suddenly Trita sees a bear and runs away. While running, he falls into a very deep well. The bear does not disturb the other two brothers. It just leaves the place. Trita cannot get up out of the well. He shouts for his brothers.)

EKATA *(to Dwita)* Dwita, this is our opportunity to go home with all the cows and the money. We shall share it only with each other.

DWITA Trita is the cleverest and the most learned. He always manages to get the most of everything. This is the time for us to share with each other and not have him in our family any more.

(Exeunt Ekata and Dwita.)

TRITA O God, come and save me. My two brothers are so inhuman. They have heard me crying, but they are not coming to my rescue. Save me, God, please save me.

(Enter a cosmic god.)

TRITA Please help me out of this well.

COSMIC GOD With my occult power, I am filling the well with water again. The water will raise you to the top of the well. Then you will be able to get out.

THE HEART OF A HOLY MAN

(Trita soon climbs out of the well.)

TRITA   Since you are so kind to me, please grant me another boon.
COSMIC GOD   What is the boon?
TRITA   That whoever touches the water of this well will be purified. No matter what kind of sin he has committed, he will be forgiven if he touches the water of this well.
COSMIC GOD   Granted.
TRITA   Now, give me a third boon.
COSMIC GOD   What is your boon?
TRITA   I will be so grateful if you grant me the boon that any desire of mine will be fulfilled.
COSMIC GOD   You will have to pray and meditate to get that boon. Stay here; pray and meditate. If you please me, that boon also I will one day grant. You pray and meditate here. When the time comes, I shall come and bless you, and your wish will be fulfilled.
TRITA   Thank you, O Lord. I shall do nothing but pray and meditate until you come back again.

SRI CHINMOY

HH 34. SCENE 3

(In Heaven.)

GAUTAMA   O Lord Supreme, I have hundreds of disciples, but it is only my own sons who are quarrelling and fighting. Look at this. Two sons did not come to save the third. A cosmic god went and helped him. Now he is meditating to get a boon from the cosmic god that all his desires will be fulfilled. Look at these three sons of mine! I am ashamed of them. How is it that my sons behave this way when I was so spiritual? By Your Grace I realised You. How is it that my own sons are unspiritual? How did it happen?

SUPREME GOD   Gautama, the physical sons are not your children, it is the spiritual sons who will realise you. They cry inwardly. They need spirituality, they need God, they need Love, they need Light, they need Truth. Your physical sons do not care for these things. Whoever cries for Truth, Love and Light will get them. Look at Krishna. Krishna's own children were not spiritual at all. In your case, also, it is the same. But Krishna's devotees, like Arjuna and Vidura, realised Me. So don't worry. Your real sons are those who think of Me and meditate on Me. Your physical sons, from now on, are only part of My creation. Do not expect anything from them. Expect everything from your spiritual children who are thinking of you, meditating on you and praying to you and to Me. They will attain realisation. As you know, we are dealing with Infinity, and Eternity. One day your physical sons will also realise Me. But right now, I wish you to consider only those who cry for Light and Truth as your real sons.

THE HEART OF A HOLY MAN

GAUTAMA   I understand, O Lord, that my real sons are those who think of You and meditate on You, those who need Light and want to live constantly in Light and for Light.

HH 35. SCENE 4

(Trita is meditating by the well. The cosmic god comes to him and blesses him.)

COSMIC GOD   Trita, I am most pleased with your prayer and meditation. I shall grant you any boon you want.
TRITA   O god, I want the boon that all desires of mine will be fulfilled by you immediately.
COSMIC GOD   Granted.

(Trita bows to the cosmic god, who then disappears.)

THE HEART OF A HOLY MAN

HH 36. SCENE 5

(The home of Gautama. Trita's brothers are happy and prosperous.)

(Enter Trita.)

TRITA You two rogues! You unnatural brothers! You didn't care to save me from the well.

EKATA We didn't know where you had gone. We looked for you.

DWITA We thought that you had been killed by the bear.

EKATA I shouted so loudly. I shouted myself hoarse for you. I didn't hear any reply. I wept and cried because I thought that you had been killed.

DWITA I searched for you everywhere, but I did not see you anywhere. I searched and searched but you were nowhere to be found. Finally I came to the conclusion that you had been killed.

EKATA I also thought that you had been killed. That's why I cried and wept so bitterly. We didn't hear you calling us.

TRITA You rogues! You people were talking loudly, both of you. You said how happy both of you were that you would be able to keep all of Father's property and all the gifts and cows that we got from his disciples. You wanted to share only between yourselves. I heard you saying it. You didn't hear me? You liars! I heard you talking in normal voices, while I was shouting and screaming from the well. You didn't hear me? Oh no, certainly not!

EKATA Believe me. I didn't hear you.

DWITA Believe me, I didn't hear you either.

TRITA All right, both of you did not hear me. But I have come out of the well anyway. A god came because he was pleased with me. Now, I have meditated, and I have occult powers. With my occult vision I see clearly that you heard me.

EKATA AND DWITA *(together)* We don't deny that you have occult powers, but we didn't hear you.

TRITA More lies? Still? Now listen. If you really did not hear me crying for help, you will remain on earth as you are now. Both of you will enjoy Father's property, and I will have my own life: a life of spirituality, a life of renunciation. I shall have my own followers, and I shall live without you. But if you did hear, then at this moment I curse you. Both of you will turn into bears.

(Immediately both brothers turn into bears and run away into the forest. Trita walks away from the wealth left behind by his two brothers. He wants to lead a life of renunciation.)

THE DISCOVERY OF SHOES AND UMBRELLA

SRI CHINMOY

HH 37. DRAMATIS PERSONÆ

JAMADAGNI (A SAGE)
RENUKA (HIS WIFE)
SURYA (THE SUN GOD)

THE HEART OF A HOLY MAN

HH 38. SCENE I

(Jamadagni and Renuka are outside their house.)

JAMADAGNI Renuka, my dear, I am extremely eager to do something.

RENUKA My Lord, what is it? Tell me.

JAMADAGNI I need your help, Renuka, in this matter.

RENUKA Lord, to please you, to fulfil you, I came into the world.

JAMADAGNI I am so proud of you, Renuka. I want to practise archery. In my childhood and adolescence I was fond of it, and now, in my ripe old age I am growing fond of it again. Even though I am a spiritual man, a sage, and many people worship me, I am still fond of this game. I want to practise my aim at archery. I will shoot at a particular target, and you will bring the arrows back to me.

RENUKA Nothing will give me greater joy than to do this for you.

JAMADAGNI But I would like to spend the whole day practising. It is not a matter of a few minutes or a few hours.

RENUKA If you want to practise all day, I have no objection. On the contrary, I will get immense joy from watching and helping you.

HH 39. SCENE 2

(Jamadagni is in a field, shooting arrow after arrow at a target. Renuka brings the arrows back to him. Hours pass.)

JAMADAGNI   Renuka, why are you no longer bringing the arrows back so quickly? Are you tired?

RENUKA   I am really tired. I am exhausted.

JAMADAGNI   Why? Why are you so tired?

RENUKA   Lord, you can see how bright the sun is. It is like a furnace. My head is aching and my feet are burning from this scorching heat.

JAMADAGNI   I have the power to curse the sun, to punish him. You know that I have tremendous occult power.

RENUKA   Yes, my Lord, I know it.

JAMADAGNI   Then right now I shall look at the sun and punish him.

(Enter Surya in the guise of a Brahmin.)

JAMADAGNI   What can I do for you? Do you want anything special from me?

SURYA   No, I have not come here for a favour. I saw from a distance that you were practising archery, and your wife was bringing your arrows back. I was really amused and inspired. I got tremendous joy from watching you play this game, so I came to observe it from close by.

JAMADAGNI   All right, wait and see what I am going to do. I am now going to destroy the sun with my occult power. The sun is ruining our game. Because of the heat, my wife is not able to bring the arrows back to me so quickly. There is no joy in the game if I have to wait such a long time for her to bring back the arrows. So I am now going to threaten the sun, and see what the sun says.

SURYA May I give you some advice?

JAMADAGNI Advice! Do I need advice from any human being after having realised God? I don't need any advice. But anyway, tell me, what is your advice?

SURYA If your wife could have a pair of shoes and an umbrella....

JAMADAGNI Shoes? What are shoes? And what is an umbrella? I have never heard of these things. Brahmin, it seems you are talking nonsense.

SURYA No, no, O Sage. *(He brings out from his robe a pair of shoes and an umbrella.)* This is called an umbrella and these are called shoes.

RENUKA Shoes? What are they for?

SURYA To protect your feet.

RENUKA And the umbrella, what is it for?

SURYA To protect your head, to protect your whole body.

RENUKA But I don't know how to use them. I have never seen them before.

SURYA Come, I will show you. *(He puts the shoes on Renuka's feet and opens the umbrella for her.)* This is how you use them. When it is very hot, when the sun is unbearably bright, your head will be protected by the umbrella's shade, and your feet will be protected by the shoes. *(Turning to Jamadagni.)* O Jamadagni, O Sage, protection is needed from below and from above. When one has protection from above, one can rise, one can go up to the highest, one can realise the highest; and when one has protection from below then one can manifest the deepest. You have realised God; that is true. But in the field of realisation, there is no end. You have realised a portion of the Truth; the Transcendental Truth you have not realised. You have touched the foot of the tree —

that is your realisation. But there is a realisation which is infinitely superior. That realisation you will have when you can climb up to the top of the tree, bring the fruit down to the ground and distribute it to others who do not know how to climb. This is the highest type of realisation. What you have realised within also has to be manifested without. For that you need protection. If you are not protected here on earth, you cannot manifest the Divine. Shoes and umbrella will protect your wife from the forces of the outer world, and will remind you of the protection which you need in the inner world in order to reach the highest Goal.

(The Brahmin changes into Lord Surya. With his effulgent Light, he looks at Jamadagni and Renuka. They bow at his feet.)

JAMADAGNI AND RENUKA   *(together)* O Lord Surya, you came to us in the garb of a Brahmin, and offered us protection. Your outer protection will comfort our outer lives and your inner protection will immortalise our inner lives.

THE MASTER WITH HIS FOUR DISCIPLES

SRI CHINMOY

HH 40. DRAMATIS PERSONÆ

THE MASTER
INSINCERITY
IMPURITY
JEALOUSY
INSECURITY

THE HEART OF A HOLY MAN

HH 41. SCENE I

(The Master is with two male disciples, Insincerity and Impurity, and two female disciples, Jealousy and Insecurity.)

MASTER   Insincerity, you are killing me. Impurity, you are killing me. Jealousy, you are killing me. Insecurity, you are killing me.

INSINCERITY   Master, I know that I am insincere, but please tell me how I can become sincere.

MASTER   Fast for one day. Fast today for the whole day, and tomorrow come and see me.

IMPURITY   Master, I know I am impure, but please tell me how I can be pure.

MASTER   Fast today. Don't eat anything. Come back tomorrow.

JEALOUSY   Master, I know I am jealous. But how can I get rid of my jealousy? Please tell me.

MASTER   Fast today. Eat nothing at all. Tomorrow come and see me.

INSECURITY   Master, I know I am insecure. At every moment I am insecure. Please tell me how I can be secure, how I can have confidence in my life.

MASTER   Don't eat anything today. Fast. Don't have even a glass of water. Come back tomorrow and I shall tell you how you can have a life of security. All of you go home and come back to me tomorrow. I shall tell you *(to the boys)* how you can be sincere and pure, and how you *(to the girls)* can get rid of jealousy and insecurity.

SRI CHINMOY

HH 42. SCENE 2

(The following day the four disciples return to their Master together.)

MASTER   Insincerity, how do you feel today?

INSINCERITY   Master, I feel very, very weak. Yesterday I didn't eat anything. That's why I feel so weak.

MASTER   See, you have become sincere today. Yesterday you didn't eat and that's why you are weak. So your sincerity has spoken through you. You are no longer insincere. But now, how can you maintain your sincerity? From now on, see two persons in your life. There are two types of people: one is inferior to you and one is superior to you. When you see someone inferior then immediately say inwardly to yourself: "It is beneath my dignity to lie to this person who is inferior to me. Why should I be afraid of him? Let me speak out freely and say what I think." And when you see someone who you feel is superior, then say to yourself, "Oh, he is my superior. Today or tomorrow he will catch my lies, and I will be punished. So why should I lie to him? Punishment and embarrassment will be my fate." You can conquer your insincerity in this way. By telling the truth to both inferiors and superiors, you can bring Perfection into your life. *(To Impurity.)* Impurity, how do you feel today?

IMPURITY   Oh, I feel much purer today. I feel really pure today.

MASTER   Once a month you should fast, and drink only water and juice. Don't eat solid food one day each month. That will help you in your purity. But in order to maintain inner purity all the time, early every morning, breathe in and out at least fifty times. Each time you breathe in, feel that you are breathing in not air, but purity. And each time you breathe out, feel that you are breathing out only impurity.

And in the evening, feel that you are breathing in Light and breathing out gratitude to God. This way you will have purity every day, every hour, every second in your life. *(To Jealousy.)* Jealousy, how do you feel today?

JEALOUSY   I feel quite fine. I feel that I am lighter today. Yesterday I didn't eat at all, and today I feel lighter.

MASTER   For only one day you have not eaten, and already you feel light. Now feel that the food that you did not take yesterday was ignorance. For one day you did not eat ignorance. For one day you did not allow this food to enter into you. That's why you feel light. So feel, Jealousy, that there is a kind of food which is ignorance. If you eat it, you become heavier. If you don't eat it, you become lighter. From now on, do not allow yourself to be tempted by this food called jealousy. When you don't eat it, you will feel light; then you can run the fastest towards your Goal. What do you want? You want to reach your Goal, the sooner the better. So don't eat this ignorance-food, which is jealousy. *(To Insecurity.)* Insecurity, how do you feel today?

INSECURITY   Master, I feel very weak today. It seems to me that my insecurity has increased today along with my physical weakness.

MASTER   It is true. Insecurity is already spiritual weakness, and when you do not eat, you become physically weak as well. When physical weakness is added to weakness in your inner life, naturally you will be even more helpless than you were before. First make yourself physically strong. You can make yourself physically strong by eating normal food every day. And you can make yourself spiritually strong, confident, by feeling that God needs you and wants to have you in His Heart, because He wants to be complete; He wants to be universal. Always feel that He whom you need, God, also needs you in order to be all-pervading. You feel that God is very great and He can easily do without you. Yes, He can do without you, but He cannot be perfect unless and until He has made you perfect. Since He is for all, He can be all-perfect only by making you perfect. So try to have confidence. This is your security. Give to God what you have: ignorance. Don't hold it for yourself; give it gladly, cheerfully, constantly to Him. And feel that since you have played your part, then it is His Duty to give you what He has: Light. Devotedly, confidently give Him your ignorance, and receive devotedly and confidently His Light. In this way you will always remain secure and confident.

(The four disciples bow down to their Master with utmost gratitude. They sing together.)

> *Khama karo khama karo ei sheshbar*
> *samarpiba jaya malya charane tomar*
> *ami taba asimer mauna barabhay*
> *tumi sindhu ami bindhu mor parichai*

(Forgive me, forgive me, this is the last time, forgive me.
I shall offer to You at Your Feet the garland of Victory.
I am the silent compassion of Your Infinity.
You are the Ocean, I am the tiniest drop.
This is my only identification.)

PART III

MOTHER, GIVE ME
THE LIGHT OF KNOWLEDGE

MOTHER, GIVE ME
THE LIGHT OF KNOWLEDGE,
THE LIGHT OF DISCRIMINATION
AND THE LIGHT OF RENUNCIATION

SRI CHINMOY

LK I. DRAMATIS PERSONÆ

NAREN (VIVEKANANDA)
SRI RAMAKRISHNA
DISCIPLES OF SRI RAMAKRISHNA

MOTHER, GIVE ME THE LIGHT OF KNOWLEDGE

LK 2. SCENE I

(It is night. Inside the Kali Temple, Naren is meditating. After a while, he prostrates himself before the statue of Mother Kali.)

NAREN   *Jnana viveka vairagya de ma.* Mother, give me the Light of Knowledge, the Light of Discrimination and the Light of Renunciation, so that I can always see you.

(Enter Sri Ramakrishna hurriedly.)

SRI RAMAKRISHNA   Naren, have you asked Mother Kali for money for your family? What have you been doing?
NAREN   What a surprise! I forgot all about it.
SRI RAMAKRISHNA   No harm. I shall give you another chance. Ask her for money, for material wealth. Mother will give it to you.

(Naren turns to the statue and begins meditating again.)

NAREN   Mother, give me the Light of Knowledge, the Light of Discrimination and the Light of Renunciation. Mother, Mother of mine, Mother of my heart and soul.
SRI RAMAKRISHNA   Again the same thing? Why do you forget that your mother and brothers and sisters are all starving? Ask the Mother to save your family from poverty. This is the only time that you can ask the Mother for that. I will not be able to give you the same opportunity every day. I am ready to give it to you any time. But Mother will not allow it. Today I have promised you because Mother has told me that she will fulfil your prayers today, no matter what you ask of her. Now you have lost your second chance.

But I wish to give you another chance. Please, my son, this time don't forget. Remember, you must ask the Mother for material wealth. That is what you need. Right now you don't need spiritual wealth.

NAREN   No, I won't take any more chances. I do not need material wealth. I want nectar from the Mother, and not anything else. For gourds and pumpkins I will not ask. I can ask only for the nectar-fruit.

SRI RAMAKRISHNA   Since you cannot ask the Mother for material wealth and prosperity, then I wish to say that you will never have a comfortable life. But from now on you will be able to manage. You and your family will not starve. You will be able to live at least from hand to mouth. Mother will do that much for you. *(He shouts)* Come, all those who are here! No matter where you are! Come! All my disciples, come!

(Enter disciples.)

SRI RAMAKRISHNA   You people have told me that my Naren has become an atheist. Look! He could not ask for material wealth from my Mother. Do you know that he starves? His mother and his sisters and brothers have no food at home. Yet he could not ask Mother Kali for material wealth. Nowhere on earth will you find anyone who can equal my Naren. He is your leader. He will lead and guide you. He will preserve you. This body of mine is completing its role. Soon I will belong to the other world. *(To Vivekananda.)* Naren, my child, sing a song. I shall meditate while you sing.

(Naren sings. Sri Ramakrishna meditates in deep trance.)

MOTHER, GIVE ME THE LIGHT OF KNOWLEDGE

Sundara hate sundara tumi
nandana bana majhe
nishidin jena antare mor
tomari murati raje
tumi chhara mor nayan andhar
sakali mithya sakali asar
chaudike mor bishwa bhubane
bedanar sur baje
pabo kigo dekha nimesher tare
ei jibaner majhe

(You are beautiful, more beautiful, most beautiful,
Beauty unparalleled in the garden of Eden.
Day and night may Thy image abide in the very
    depths of my heart.
Without You my eyes have no vision,
Everything is an illusion, everything is barren.
All around me, within and without,
The melody of tenebrous pangs I hear.
My world is filled with excruciating pangs.
O Lord, O my beautiful Lord,
O my Lord of beauty, in this lifetime, even for a
    fleeting second,
May I be blessed with the boon to see Thy Face.)

VISHWAMITRA

SRI CHINMOY

LK 3. DRAMATIS PERSONÆ

VISHWAMITRA (A POWERFUL KING)
ATTENDANTS AND ADMIRERS OF VISHWAMITRA
VASHISTHA (A GREAT SAGE)
NANDINI (COW OF VASHISTHA)
ARMY OF VISHWAMITRA
ARMY OF NANDINI
MESSENGER FROM THE SUPREME

MOTHER, GIVE ME THE LIGHT OF KNOWLEDGE

LK 4. SCENE I

(King Vishwamitra and a group of attendants and admirers are in the forest. They are returning to the palace after hunting. On their way they see the cottage of the great sage Vashistha and decide to pay him a short visit. Vashistha welcomes the King and his party.)

VASHISTHA   Your Majesty, you are tired. You are exhausted. You are thirsty. You are hungry.

VISHWAMITRA   O sage, you are perfectly right. But this is not the place where I could expect anything, let alone food. Your poverty beggars description.

VASHISTHA   I see, Your Majesty, I see.

(Vashistha enters into his hermitage and comes back with a large quantity of milk. The King and his attendants are wonder-struck.)

VASHISTHA   Let me serve the King. You all serve yourselves, please.

VISHWAMITRA   *(after drinking)* Ah, my thirst is quenched. The milk is most delicious. O sage, where did you get this milk?

VASHISTHA   *(smiling)* King, I shall tell you later on.

(The sage enters into his hermitage and comes out with a most delicious meal — a variety of dishes. The King and his attendants are simply amazed.)

VASHISTHA   Your Majesty, let me serve you. *(To the others.)* You all serve yourselves, please.

(While all are eating, Vashistha chants.)

*Aum
Purnam adah purnam idam
purnat purnam udacyate
purnasya purnam adaya
purnam evavashisyate*

(Infinity is that.
Infinity is this.
From Infinity, Infinity has come into existence.
From Infinity, when Infinity is taken away, Infinity
    remains.)

VISHWAMITRA   O sage, God made a mistake. He didn't give me an ear for music. But he has made me a really practical man. Please tell me the source of your milk and all the food that you have offered us just now.

VASHISTHA   Ah, don't you know the source, my source, my only source?

VISHWAMITRA   I am all curiosity. For God's sake, do not exploit my patience!

VASHISTHA   Your Majesty, yonder you see my Nandini.

VISHWAMITRA   That cow?

VASHISTHA   Yes. To you she is just an ordinary cow. But to me, my Nandini is my all. She gives me everything I need. She is my protection. She is my salvation. She is my perfection.

VISHWAMITRA   O sage, you may stop now. Everybody knows that Vashistha is a wise sage. I wish you to be wiser. And it is I who can make you so.

VASHISTHA   O King, do make me wiser. I really want to be wiser than I am now.

VISHWAMITRA   I can make you infinitely wiser, this very day. Look, you are pure, but poor. You are pure, but obscure. Vashistha, you love your cow. The cow is your daughter. Now, don't you want the entire world to appreciate and admire your child? I am the mightiest King on earth. Thousands and thousands of people come to my palace. They all will adore your Nandini. And you need not feel sorry, for I shall give you one thousand cows in return. Only let me have your Nandini.

VASHISTHA Impossible.

VISHWAMITRA I shall give you anything you want: money, property, name, fame, whatever you want, in the twinkling of an eye. Just let me have your cow.

VASHISTHA Impossible.

VISHWAMITRA Sage, you are a fool! Enough of your audacity. Don't exploit my patience. Don't exploit my compassion. Must I unseal your ears so that you can hear from others about my powers? Don't you know that there is no human being on earth who is not at my express command? How dare you defy me! You don't deserve my earnest request. You deserve, rightly deserve, my lofty contempt. Your audacity knows no bounds. Therefore I shall give you nothing, absolutely nothing! Vashistha, I am taking your cow away!

VASHISTHA Impossible.

(Vishwamitra commands his attendants to seize the cow. Nandini charges Vishwamitra's men with such force that they all run for their lives.)

VISHWAMITRA I am disappointed, I am disheartened.

VASHISTHA And badly defeated.

VISHWAMITRA Defeat! No defeat. Vishwamitra never accepts defeat. Victory, here, there, everywhere: that is my name! I am going back to my palace. Soon I shall be back with my indomitable force, and then I shall take your Nandini away.

VASHISTHA Impossible.

VISHWAMITRA   You fool! You are the worst fool I have met in this incarnation. *(Addressing the heavens.)* God, this fool has no equal on earth. Anyway, Vashistha, I shall be back soon. In the meantime drink milk from your Nandini to your heart's content, for this will undoubtedly be the last chance for you to enjoy her milk.

VASHISTHA   Impossible.

VISHWAMITRA   The entire world knows that I am a man of action, immediate action. Your vast ignorance does not permit you to recognise who I am. I don't blame you, but I *do* blame your ignorance.

(Vishwamitra hurriedly leaves the hermitage, followed by his attendants.)

LK 5. SCENE 2

(Vashistha and Nandini.)

VASHISTHA Nandini, your mother is Kamadhenu, the cow that fulfils all desires, earthly and heavenly. She has blessed you with her infinite capacities. You are now blessing me. You fulfil all my wishes. You are my everything.

NANDINI Master, my Lord, you are my all. To serve you, to please you, to fulfil you, I came into the world. Your aspiration and realisation are fulfilling the Supreme in a unique manner. You are His chosen son. You are His colossal pride.

VASHISTHA Nandini, the King will soon come back with a very large force. And then, God alone knows.

NANDINI O greatest sage, like God, you and I know perfectly well that I am going to defeat the King easily. I shall produce an army infinitely more powerful than the army of King Vishwamitra. I shall smash his pride. He has told you that this time he will take me away. I assure you that I shall make him touch your hallowed feet. He must and he will.

(Enter suddenly Vishwamitra with a very large army.)

VISHWAMITRA Vashistha, so — are you ready? Death is inviting you and your cow!

(Immediately Nandini produces a most powerful army. A battle ensues in which the whole army of King Vishwamitra is destroyed by Nandini's army. Only the King is left alive.)

VISHWAMITRA   Forgive me, O sage, forgive me. You are my life's only haven. My army is gone. Helpless, hopeless and meaningless my life now is. Once again I implore your loftiest bounty.

(Vishwamitra prostrates himself before Vashistha. Vashistha places his right palm on Vishwamitra's devoted head.)

VASHISTHA   O King, I forgive you. My Nandini forgives you. Ask for any boon; I shall grant it immediately.

VISHWAMITRA   What need have I for any boon from you right now? Once I was the mightiest King and now, without my army, I am nothing. My life is worse than useless. Glory gone. Pride gone. What remains is a sea of tears.

VASHISTHA   Nothing is gone. I give you all back.

(Vashistha sprinkles sacred water on the dead bodies of Vishwamitra's soldiers. Life is restored. Once again they are ready to fight against Nandini's soldiers. Vishwamitra's joy and pride now know no bounds. Once more he challenges Nandini. In a few minutes' time Nandini again destroys Vishwamitra's whole army. Vishwamitra's life is at her mercy.)

VISHWAMITRA   *(to Vashistha)* You have conquered me with your spiritual power. Our physical strength and military strength are no match for your spiritual strength. But listen, Vashistha, listen. I tell you I shall utterly smash your pride before long. I shall launch into the life of spirituality. I shall give up my palace, my kingdom and all that I have. I shall practise austerities. I shall meditate day in and day out until I have reached my Transcendental Goal. I shall transcend your highest height. I, Vishwamitra, accept no permanent defeat. God in Heaven is my witness!

VASHISTHA Vishwamitra, in the realm of the Spirit, rivalry cannot live. If or when you transcend my spiritual height I shall garland you. I shall adore you. I shall worship you.

VISHWAMITRA Action, action! I am a man of action. I don't talk, I don't preach, I just act. Today I touched your feet. Tomorrow I shall make you touch my feet. I shall cross the sea of ignorance-dream. I shall face the One Absolute alone. And then I shall see you, Vashistha, kissing the dust of my feet.

VASHISTHA *(raising his right hand in the form of benediction)* Tathastu [so be it].

(Nandini bursts into roaring laughter. Exit Vishwamitra.)

VASHISTHA Nandini, my child, Vishwamitra has at last left us. What shall we do now? Shall we eat or shall we meditate?

NANDINI My Lord, let us meditate first and then eat.

VASHISTHA Fine, my child, that's a splendid idea.

(Both Vashistha and Nandini start meditating. Light and delight are sporting in their eyes. Enter a divine messenger from the Supreme.)

MESSENGER O peerless sage, the Supreme has sent me to you with a most special message: Vishwamitra in the distant future will become a sage. But your highest height he will never be able to transcend. The Supreme treasures your life on earth. You are His best instrument on earth. With you and through you He is manifesting His Divinity's Height and Immortality's Light on earth. *(Turning to Nandini.)* Nandini, the Supreme is highly pleased with you. With His infinite Love, Infinite Joy and infinite Pride, He unites the breath of your most devoted service to the life of your master's dedicated surrender.

SRI CHINMOY

(Exit messenger. Nandini sings.)

Tumi amai diyechha aj
samarpaner bani
ami tomai sapechhi mor
kusum hriday khani
andhar rate ashru sathe
moher karar ajanate
simar gehe thakbona ar
jani ami jani
tumi amar jenechhi ma
chirantaner rani

(Today You have given me the message of surren-
    der.
I have offered to You my very flower-heart.
In the dark night with tears,
In the unknown prison-cell of illusion,
In the house of the finite,
No longer shall I abide.
I know You are mine.
I have known this, Mother,
O Queen of the Eternal.)

DHRUVA

SRI CHINMOY

LK 6. DRAMATIS PERSONÆ

KING UTTANPADA
UTTAMA, DHRUVA (HIS SONS)
SURUCHI (MOTHER OF UTTAMA)
SUNITI (MOTHER OF DHRUVA)
A VAST AUDIENCE AT THE PALACE
FIRST SAGE
SECOND SAGE
THIRD SAGE
FOURTH SAGE
FIFTH SAGE
SIXTH SAGE
SEVENTH SAGE (THE LEADER OF THE SAGES)
INDRA (THE LORD OF THE GODS)
YAMA (THE KING OF DEATH)
DEMONS AND RAKSHASAS
LORD VISHNU

MOTHER, GIVE ME THE LIGHT OF KNOWLEDGE

LK 7. SCENE I

NARRATOR   There was once a great king whose name was Uttanpada. He had two sons, Dhruva and Uttama. Uttama's mother was Suruchi, and Dhruva's mother was Suniti. Suruchi happened to be the favourite wife of Uttanpada. Naturally, her son Uttama became Uttanpada's favourite son.

(King Uttanpada's palace. The King is seated on his golden throne. Around him is a vast audience. Suruchi's son, Uttama, comes and sits on his father's lap. Uttanpada begins to caress him. Seeing this from a distance, Dhruva comes running to sit on his father's lap, too. But he is caught and held back by his stepmother, Suruchi.)

SURUCHI   Dhruva, stop! You are such a fool! Don't you know that you are Suniti's son and not mine? How dare you approach your father? It is only *my* son who is permitted to sit on his lap. You must never dare to approach your father for kindness, affection or love. Only *my* son, Uttama, will have everything that your father has and is. You stay away from the King, Dhruva. I give you a last warning.

(King Uttanpada is totally indifferent to the situation. The audience is terribly shocked. Dhruva begins shedding bitter tears.)

SURUCHI   Dhruva, now get away from here. I don't want to see you any more. You must know that it is my Uttama who is going to inherit his father's regal throne and not you! Never! Go and stay with your mother and don't come here. Don't bother us!

LK 8. SCENE 2

(Dhruva enters his mother's room. He is shaking with anger and, at the same time, crying with sorrow. His mother is all concern for him.)

DHRUVA   Mother, Suruchi has badly scolded and insulted me. I was going to my father, but she held me back. She said I had no right to approach my father for affection and love because I am your son. She has insulted me and scolded me. She said it is *her* son who is going to inherit my father's throne and not me. She showed me such contempt, Mother, I can't tell you! She was so mean. She asked me to leave the place, and not to come near my father any more. There were many, many people who saw me being insulted, but my father did not care at all. He did not say a word in my favour. Mother, what am I going to do with such a father and such a mean, cruel, nasty stepmother?

SUNITI   *(fondling her son)* Dhruva, my child, don't cry, don't weep, don't feel sad and miserable. God knows what is best for us. He will one day make us happy. He will really give us what we need most. You pray to God. Today you have been insulted by your stepmother. Well, I have been insulted by her since she came into your father's life. She insults me at every moment — mercilessly, without any cause. I too suffer, I cry within. And now that you have also been insulted, my dearest son, I feel my heart is broken. But what can I do? What can you do? Only God, the ever-compassionate Father, can put an end to our suffering. Let us pray to Him to give us joy and inner illumination. We shall see that our inner joy will infinitely surpass Suruchi's pleasure. Let us not enter into the world of competition, my son. I have been praying to God every day and, beginning today, I wish you to join me.

DHRUVA   Mother, I want to pray, I want to meditate, but I don't know how. I don't know anything about it.

SUNITI   My son, yonder is a forest. Go there and look around. You will find people praying and meditating. Ask them how to pray, how to meditate, how to invoke God — His Love and Light. They will teach you.

DHRUVA   Mother, is it true?

SUNITI   Yes, my son.

DHRUVA   Mother, I am off. I shall come back only when I have brought for you Joy, Delight and Blessings, all from God.

(Exit Dhruva. Suniti sheds soulful tears, while her only son leaves for the forest to pray to God.)

SRI CHINMOY

LK 9. SCENE 3

(Dhruva is wandering in the forest all alone, looking for some spiritual people. He sings.)

*Dake amai dake
dake akash dake batash
dake shashi tara
dake shyamal nibir kanan
dake jharna dhara
hasi dake ashru dake
dake kshina sur
dake prabhat sandhya dake
dakichhe dupur
sabai khunje khelar sathi
dake amai ai
charidike ekiy dhwani
bela baye jai
dake amai dake*

(The sky calls me,
The wind calls me,
The moon and the stars call me.
The green and the dense groves call me,
The dance of the fountain calls me,
Smiles call me, tears call me.
A faint melody calls me.
The morn, noon and eve call me.
Everyone is searching for a playmate,
Everyone is calling me, "Come, come!"
One voice, one sound, all around.
Alas, the Boat of Time sails on.)

MOTHER, GIVE ME THE LIGHT OF KNOWLEDGE

(Finally Dhruva comes to a spot where he sees seven sages meditating together. Most humbly he bows down before them.)

DHRUVA   Dear sirs, please help me. I am looking for someone to teach me to pray and meditate.

FIRST SAGE   We shall help you, we shall teach you. But before that, tell us who you are and what brings you here.

DHRUVA   My name is Dhruva. My father is King Uttanpada and my mother is Suniti. This morning my stepmother, Suruchi, insulted me so cruelly, so brutally, so unbearably. She said that my brother, Uttama, will inherit the throne.

SECOND SAGE   So you want to inherit your father's throne. Is that your prayer? Is that why you have come into the forest?

DHRUVA   No, certainly not! I don't want my father's throne. I want to have joy and inner happiness that will forever last. I want to share with my mother that kind of joy. My mother has taught me that earthly possessions have no value. Let Uttama have my father's throne; let him have everything from his kingdom. I do not need earthly possessions to make me happy. I wish only to see the Feet of God; I wish to realise Him. I wish to be eternally happy, divinely happy, supremely happy.

THIRD SAGE   We are so pleased with you, Dhruva. We shall help you.

FOURTH SAGE   You have to pray from now on to Lord Vishnu. It is he who will be able to grant you the boon. He will be able to make you the happiest man on earth and your mother the happiest woman on earth.

FIFTH SAGE   We shall teach you how to pray to him, how to meditate on him.

SIXTH SAGE Your sincerity, your inner cry for God, your true love of God, have given us tremendous joy and we offer you our blessingful pride.

DHRUVA *(again bowing down to the seven sages with deepest gratitude)* O divine sages, then please teach me how to pray and how to meditate.

LEADER OF THE SAGES Come and sit in front of me, Dhruva. Dhruva, this is how you will pray. You will pray to the Lord Vishnu: "O Lord Vishnu, I wish to please you, I wish to serve you, I wish to become totally, unconditionally yours." And this is how you will meditate: you will not allow any thought to enter into your mind; you will keep your mind absolutely free from thoughts and ideas. Only try to feel all the time within your heart the lotus-feet of Lord Vishnu. This is how you should pray and how you should meditate. Your prayer and your meditation will undoubtedly bring Lord Vishnu right before you. He will bless you with his infinite affection, with his infinite compassion, love, joy and pride. If you pray and meditate, in the near future you are bound to see him and your desire, your aspiration, is sure to be fulfilled. You are a young boy. You have been mistreated by your stepmother, your father has been indifferent to you, your mother has been suffering for a long time and you are dissatisfied with this world. When your aspiration is fulfilled your whole being will be flooded with joy, eternal joy. You and your mother will be the perfect instruments of God on earth. With our blessings go to pray and meditate over there. That place is called *Madhuvana,* the honey-forest. You pray and meditate there and from here we shall keep our conscious concern on you. We shall think of you and meditate on your divine, supreme success. Now go and pray over there. *Madhuvana* is most beautiful and most inspiring.

(Dhruva bows to the leader of the sages, then to the other six sages with utmost humility and gratitude.)

DHRUVA   O sages, O seekers of the highest magnitude, O greatest lovers of God, my whole existence is grateful to you.

(All the sages bless Dhruva with utmost joy and pride and Dhruva departs.)

SRI CHINMOY

LK 10. SCENE 4

(Dhruva is now in the Madhuvana practising severe austerities. He is determined not to eat anything until he sees the lotus-feet of Lord Vishnu. As his aspiration is increasing, his inner strength is increasing too. The mountains and meadows are shaking before him with reverential awe. His power of meditation is frightening. The earth itself it wonder-struck. The dwellers in Heaven are all extremely worried. They feel that if this is the way Dhruva prays and meditates, then his power will soon far exceed their own. Indra and Yama meet together. They want to put an end to Dhruva's penance, his austere life, his overwhelming power of meditation. They want to play a trick on Dhruva. With their occult power they take the form of Dhruva's mother, Suniti, and enter into the grove of Madhuvana. Dhruva is in deep trance.)

"SUNITI": My son, I have found you at last. I am totally lost without you. It was your presence that gave me joy; it was your presence that made my life worth living on earth. In your absence I have no one to think of me, no one to protect me, no one to care for me. Feel your mother's heart, Dhruva. I need you. Come back with me, my son. Now that you know how to pray and meditate, come back to the palace with me. You can meditate there.

("Suniti" sings.)

Madhuman me parayanam
madhumat punarayanam

(Sweet be my departure from home.
Sweet be my return.)

"SUNITI": At home you can do everything you want to do. You will see the feet of Lord Vishnu. Dhruva, my darling, come. Come with me.

(Dhruva is in deep trance. He does not hear a word of his "mother's" affectionate, loving, commanding voice. Exit "Suniti".)

(Enter Indra and Yama. Since Indra and Yama failed in their first attempt, they bring all kinds of evil spirits and demons to destroy Dhruva totally. Enter demons and rakshasas. They attack Dhruva.)

INDRA AND YAMA Eat him up, eat him up! Kill him! Destroy him, destroy him! He will surpass us — a mortal, an insignificant creature! He will surpass us if we don't stop him from praying and meditating!

(Dhruva, still in deep trance, does not budge an inch. His gaze passes beyond, far beyond, into the very breath of the demons and rakshasas who leave in fear, frustration and disappointment.)

LK II. SCENE 5

(Indra and Yama come before Lord Vishnu. They bow down to him.)

INDRA AND YAMA O Lord, how is it that you are not fulfilling Dhruva's desire? Can you not grant his boon? His power of meditation will soon surpass all our spiritual power. We pray to you to save us. If you don't want to grant his boon, let us grant it. Let us go on your behalf. Let us go and please him.

LORD VISHNU O Indra, O Yama, it is not so easy. You cannot fulfil Dhruva's aspiration; you cannot feel his heart. He is great, he is supremely great. But I shall fulfil him, and I shall fulfil your desires as well. I shall go and ask him to stop praying and meditating. Then you will be pleased. You will still have your enormous light and power, but my Dhruva will have a life, a world of his own.

INDRA O Lord Vishnu, as long as he does not surpass me, I will be most grateful to you. I want nobody to surpass me; I want to be the Lord of the gods, the cosmic gods. I want to remain the most powerful one here in Heaven and there on earth.

(Lord Vishnu gives Indra a delicate, soulful, blessingful and compassionate smile. Exeunt Indra and Yama.)

MOTHER, GIVE ME THE LIGHT OF KNOWLEDGE

LK 12. SCENE 6

(Dhruva is in deep meditation. His whole being is meditating on the lotus-feet of Lord Vishnu. His inner being is surcharged with supernatural power. Enter Lord Vishnu with his discus, Sudarshan Chakra, his mace and his conch, a diadem on his brow. He comes with his infinite glory and stands in front of Dhruva, his dearest and greatest devotee. He places his hands on Dhruva's devoted head. Dhruva opens his eyes with supreme astonishment. Immediately he touches the feet of Lord Vishnu.)

LORD VISHNU   My dearest, my fondest child Dhruva, I am the object of your prayer, I am the object of your meditation. I am most pleased with you; I am most proud of you. I have come here to fulfil your desires and your aspirations.

DHRUVA   My Lord, if you are really pleased with me, then you know what I want. I want only to be all the time at your lotus-feet. I am your child; I want to serve you.

(Lord Vishnu touches Dhruva's forehead with his conch. Immediately Dhruva receives inner illumination. All the supernal qualities, the infinite divine Light, Peace and Bliss of Lord Vishnu enter into him.)

LORD VISHNU   Dhruva, my Dhruva, ask me for any boon. Immediately I shall grant it.

DHRUVA   O my Lord, my eternal Lord, you have given me everything I wanted. You have given me all that I wanted and beyond, far beyond my imagination's flight. What more do I need?

VISHNU   No, Dhruva, I want to give you something more. I want to give you a particular place of your own. Yours will be a divine station far above the earthly world. You will become one with the real Dhruva: *Dhruva Tara,* the pole-star. You will sustain all the stars and other planets in their course. You will guide the aspiring, seeking, struggling world. You will show the earth the world of Light and Delight. You will be the guiding light, the pole-star. It is with you that the earth-consciousness will enter into my life of infinite Peace, Light and Bliss. Dhruva, I bring your mother back into your heart. It was she who advised you to pray to God; it was she who inspired you to come into the forest and meditate. Today all her sufferings have come to an end. In you your mother will have her supreme glory and satisfaction. Also, I bring before you the seven sages who inspired you, who helped you, who taught you how to pray and meditate. Dhruva, you have far surpassed them now. They will be all joy, all pride for you because they want someone on earth to be supremely divine, supremely unconditional, supremely great. They want someone to be my most perfect instrument, and they will now see in you my supreme manifestation.

(Enter Suniti who, seeing her dearest son, is overwhelmed with delight. She touches Lord Vishnu's feet, then sits beside her son with enormous joy and pride, shedding tears of gratitude to Lord Vishnu.)

SUNITI   O Lord Vishnu, you have heard my son's prayers. You are our own, our very own. Each breath of ours, each heartbeat of ours is for you.

(Vishnu offers her his brightest smile. Then the seven sages enter. Seeing Dhruva, they are overwhelmed with joy, delight and pride. One by one they touch the feet of Lord Vishnu and Dhruva.)

ALL THE SAGES   Dhruva, long, long before you were born we were praying to Lord Vishnu to see his lotus-feet. It is you who have brought down into the world before us his presence, our cherished Goal. It is because of you that we are seeing the chosen object of our adoration today. It is your prayer and meditation that has brought our Lord Vishnu here. If not for you, centuries would have passed by and we would not have seen the lotus-feet of our Lord Supreme. It is because of you that today we can kiss the golden feet of our Lord Vishnu, the eternal Lord. Dhruva, Dhruva, our hearts are all gratitude, our lives are all gratitude, our realisation is all gratitude to you, to you, to you.

TWO DIVINE LIARS: ARE THEY REALLY SO?

SRI CHINMOY

LK 13. DRAMATIS PERSONÆ

KRISHNA
SATYAVAMA (HIS WIFE)
DURVASHA (A GREAT SAGE VERY DEVOTED TO KRISHNA)

MOTHER, GIVE ME THE LIGHT OF KNOWLEDGE

LK 14. SCENE I

(Krishna's palace. Krishna and Satyavama are together.)

SATYAVAMA   How is it that people think you are full of compassion? I see that you have no compassion at all. Look at your greatest devotee. He is repeating your name so devotedly and so soulfully! But you don't care for him. All he eats is a blade of grass now and then, because there is nobody to feed him.

KRISHNA   What do you want me to do?

SATYAVAMA   Why don't you ask someone to look after him? You have so many admirers and devotees. Why don't you ask someone to bring food to Durvasha every day, so that he can continue his meditating and still have proper food to eat.

KRISHNA   He does not need that kind of food.

SATYAVAMA   *(becoming angry)* He does need it, but you don't supply it.

KRISHNA   No, no. His food is different, entirely different.

SATYAVAMA   I am sure that if I take him some proper food, delicious food, right now, he will eat voraciously.

KRISHNA   Well, perhaps you are right. You can try it. Go to him on the other side of the Jamuna, and then come back and tell me what he says about the food.

LK 15. SCENE 2

(Satyavama, having prepared a most delicious meal, goes to the River Jamuna, and tries to cross it. The Jamuna is a tiny river that is usually knee deep, but when there is a flood or a storm, it has to be crossed in a ferryboat. Satyavama sees that the water is raging like the surges of the sea. The boatman refuses to take her across because of the danger. Satyavama, depressed and angry, returns to the palace.)

SATYAVAMA   Krishna, I went to cross the river to take food to your dearest disciple, but the river was hostile to me. Do something!

KRISHNA   All right. Go and say this to the river: "If my Lord Krishna has not seen the face of any woman other than me, then calm down."

SATYAVAMA   How can I say this? I know how many women friends you have. I cannot say to Jamuna that you have never seen the face of any woman but me. It is all lies! Jamuna will never calm down. You have seen the faces of millions of women. To say that you have only seen my face is ridiculous!

KRISHNA   Go. Go and say what I have told you to Jamuna and see what happens.

MOTHER, GIVE ME THE LIGHT OF KNOWLEDGE

LK 16. SCENE 3

(Satyavama stands at the edge of the raging river.)

SATYAVAMA   O Jamuna, if my Lord Krishna has not seen the face of any woman but me, then please calm down so that I may cross.

(The river subsides and she crosses.)

SATYAVAMA   *(thinking aloud)* I am sure the Jamuna has allowed me to cross just to please Krishna.

(She comes to the place where Durvasha is meditating. He is in a high trance, but slowly opens his eyes when she approaches him.)

SATYAVAMA   O Durvasha, I have observed that for many weeks now you have been repeating my Lord's name with deepest devotion, and you have taken almost no food. Today, I have brought you food which I myself have prepared for you.
DURVASHA   *(still in a meditative mood, touches the feet of Satyavama)* Mother, your compassion is food enough for me. Yet I am supremely grateful that you have thought of me and brought me food.

(Satyavama has to feed Durvasha herself as he is still in a trance-like state. When he has finished the food, Durvasha bows and touches Satyavama's feet.)

SATYAVAMA   Now I am going home. I am happy that you are pleased with my meal.

(Exit Satyavama. Durvasha resumes his deep meditation, and a little later Satyavama returns.)

SATYAVAMA   O Durvasha, please do something for me. There is no boatman at the river and my Lord is on the other side. I cannot cross because of the storm. While I was coming here it was also stormy, but my Lord made the river subside. But now my Lord is not here. Please tell me what I should do.

DURVASHA   This is very easy, Mother. I will tell you. Go and say this to the river: "If Durvasha has not eaten anything but a few blades of grass for many years, then you must calm down, O Jamuna."

SATYAVAMA   You fool! You liar! I have just fed you a most delicious meal with my own hands, and now you are asking me to say this!

DURVASHA   Mother, please tell the river what I have told you. I will come with you.

(Exeunt Durvasha and Satyavama.)

LK 17. SCENE 4

(Satyavama and Durvasha at the river.)

SATYAVAMA *(sarcastically, to the river)* If Durvasha hasn't taken anything to eat for several years except a few blades of grass, then please, Jamuna, calm down. *(The waters subside. Satyavama is surprised and angry.)* Durvasha, your Lord is a liar and you are a liar! I am caught between two liars. But at least I am able to go home.

(Exit Satyavama.)

LK 18. SCENE 5

(Krishna's palace.)

SATYAVAMA   Krishna, you are a liar and you have taught your dearest disciple also how to tell lies.

KRISHNA   What lies have we told?

SATYAVAMA   You said that you have never looked at any woman's face in your life except mine. How can it be? Millions of women you have seen. We have so many relatives, including your own mother, your sister and many others around us. So how can you say that you have not seen any other woman's face?

KRISHNA   Satyavama, you don't understand my spiritual knowledge. You are my dearest. You and I are one. When I look at any woman, immediately I see your face in that person. All women to me are represented by you. When I look at any woman's face, physically it is different, but according to my inner wisdom, inner light, I see that it is you who are that particular person. You are the Divine Mother and I am the Divine Father. So I see my female part, you, inside everyone. How, then, can I say that I am seeing somebody else? It is you I see in different forms, in different shapes.

SATYAVAMA   *(satisfied)* I see. You are dealing with your universal consciousness. You are the Lord and I am your divine *Shakti*. But what about this liar Durvasha? He is your devotee. I fed him a delicious meal with my own hands. And immediately afterwards he said that he had not eaten anything but a few blades of grass for several years!

KRISHNA   Dearest Satyavama, all the while you were feeding him, Durvasha was in trance. He always remains in trance. And in trance what he eats is delight, ecstasy. That is his only food. He has practically lost all outer consciousness. On rare occasions he comes down to the earth-consciousness. Most of the time he is in his highest transcendental Consciousness, where he is communing with me. I feed him Peace, Light and Bliss. When he told you that he had taken only blades of grass, he was speaking the truth. He ate your food, true, but he didn't get any taste from the food you gave him. He was only drinking my divine nectar all the time. Before he entered into this rigorous discipline, this austere life, he decided that he would eat only blades of grass after beginning serious meditation. That particular idea is still in his mind, and he still thinks that he is eating only grass and nothing else, for he is not aware of outer things, earthly things. He has lost the consciousness of the outer world. So if you give him delicious earthly food, he gets no more taste from your meal than he gets from grass. That is why he could say that he had not eaten anything other than a few blades of grass for many years.

SATYAVAMA You have convinced me, my Lord. I am most grateful to you. I withdraw my charges.

(Krishna smiles.)

O WORLD-RENOUNCER, BE CAREFUL!

SRI CHINMOY

LK 19. DRAMATIS PERSONÆ

CHAITANYA
A GROUP OF HIS DISCIPLES
THE YOUNGER HARIDAS (A DISCIPLE)
GOVINDA, A DISCIPLE

MOTHER, GIVE ME THE LIGHT OF KNOWLEDGE

LK 20. SCENE I

(Chaitanya and a group of disciples. Enter the younger Haridas.)

CHAITANYA   Haridas, I understand that you have brought rice from Madhavi?
HARIDAS   Yes, my Lord.
CHAITANYA   You have brought rice to me from a woman?
HARIDAS   Yes, my Lord.
CHAITANYA   From a beautiful woman?
HARIDAS   Yes, my Lord.
CHAITANYA   You have drunk her beauty?
HARIDAS   *(embarrassed)* Yes, my Lord.
CHAITANYA   I shall never see your face again! Never! You have renounced the world, but you have looked at her face. How many times have I told you not to look at women's faces, but to look at their feet? I told you to bring food for me. But you didn't have to bring food from a beautiful woman. You have looked at her face and drunk her beauty to your heart's content. Haridas, you have betrayed your spiritual life. I can't have you with me any more.

(Haridas touches the Master's feet, weeping bitterly.)

CHAITANYA   Haridas, enough. In this life I shall not see your face any more. *(Calls.)* Govinda, Govinda! Take him away! Take Haridas away.

(Enter Govinda.)

GOVINDA   *(quietly to Haridas)* Haridas, Haridas, don't worry. Lord Chaitanya will forgive you one day. Right now he is just punishing you, but you know that his love is for everyone. His love is boundless, and it is for everybody,

(Exeunt Haridas and Govinda. A few minutes later, enter Haridas crying and touches Chaitanya's feet. When Chaitanya ignores him he starts singing, imploringly.)

Khama karo khama karo ei sheshbar
samarpiba jaya malya charane tomar
ami taba asimer mauna barabhay
tumi sindhu ami bindhu mor parichai

(Forgive me, forgive me, this is the last time, forgive me.
I shall offer to You at Your Feet the garland of Victory.
I am the silent compassion of Your Infinity.
You are the Ocean, I am the tiniest drop.
This is my only identification.)

CHAITANYA No, Haridas, no more. I won't look at your face. You deserve this punishment. You should know not to look even at a wooden statue of a woman. Even the sages are tempted by women. Your renunciation was no renunciation. It was all a show — a farce! You deserve your punishment. In this lifetime I shall not see you any more. Do whatever you want with your life.

HARIDAS Lord, I shall wait and see for a few months. If you do not accept me again, then I shall commit suicide. I shall cast this body, this life, into the Ganges.

CHAITANYA Don't threaten me, Haridas. Do anything you want with your life. Die today if you want to. I don't need you. You have cast a slur on the life of renunciation. Householders can do anything. My householder disciples have received instructions from me about how they can lead a regulated vital life, about how they can control their vital life. In your case, you accepted the life of renunciation. After that, how can you enter into the world of mental and vital enjoyment, Haridas? I am ashamed of you. A world-renouncer does not behave as you have behaved. Leave the path of the *sannyasin*. Who asked you to offer your life entirely? Who asked you to pretend? Who asked you to deceive the world? Leave this place for good.

HARIDAS Lord, since you will not see me any more, my life is useless. I shall enter into the other world. From there I shall serve you. This life without you is death, and I embrace death in order to offer you my dedicated service from Heaven. In Heaven also you have your divine existence. You have appreciated my voice many times, my singing capacity and my chanting. From Heaven, I shall sing through my soul and please you here, my Lord.

CHAITANYA Haridas, leave me.

(Haridas touches the feet of his Master for the last time and leaves.)

CHAITANYA *(to the others)* I know he will take his life. But I have to show the world that the life of renunciation is not a joke. He who accepts the life of renunciation must not mix with women, wealth or worldly possessions. This path is arduous. This life is most difficult. Its goal is the Goal of Goals. I tell you, to commit suicide is the worst possible sin. But if one gets the inner assurance from his spiritual Master that the Master approves, the Master can compassionately relieve him of the sin of committing suicide. Then he will not suffer from it. Haridas is getting my inner assurance. I shall permit him to commit suicide, and I shall free him from that sin. He will be able to serve me in Heaven. From Heaven he will be able to sing inwardly, and please me with his divine voice. But I wish to warn you people, only on very rare occasions do spiritual Masters tolerate suicide. In his case, I shall tolerate it and forgive him. But this is an exception. Don't commit suicide, thinking that you will be able to come down into the world again and make better progress. On the contrary, when you commit suicide, you take a wrong turn and go backwards. Not only do you lose your potentialities and destroy all your possibilities, but you start your spiritual journey over again from the very beginning. You are lost, totally lost. You delay your progress immeasurably. So, my children, never commit suicide. Be brave. Fight the world. Face your inner weaknesses and conquer them. Strengthen your inner life; strengthen your outer life. Act like a hero. Be the master of yourself. God has to be pleased in this world. Temptation has to be conquered; illumination has to take place on earth, in you, in each individual in the entire world.

JAJATI

SRI CHINMOY

LK 21. DRAMATIS PERSONÆ

JAJATI (A KING)
SUKRACHARYA (FATHER-IN-LAW OF JAJATI)
DEVAJANI (DAUGHTER OF SUKRACHARYA AND WIFE OF JAJATI)
JADU (ELDER SON OF JAJATI AND DEVAJANI)
TURBASU (YOUNGER SON OF JAJATI AND DEVAJANI)
SHARMISHTHA (OTHER WIFE OF JAJATI)
DRUHYU (ELDEST SON OF JAJATI AND SHARMISHTHA)
ANU (MIDDLE SON OF JAJATI AND SHARMISHTHA)
PURU (YOUNGEST SON OF JAJATI AND SHARMISHTHA)

MOTHER, GIVE ME THE LIGHT OF KNOWLEDGE

LK 22. SCENE I

(Sukracharya and Jajati are together.)

SUKRACHARYA   Jajati, you have deceived my daughter, and you have deceived me. While you were married to my daughter, Devajani, you also got married to Sharmishtha secretly, and she has given you three sons. You have deceived us badly. Without my knowledge, without my daughter's knowledge, you did all this. You deserve severe punishment from me. I curse you. You will be paralysed. You will not be able to move at all from now on. The end of your life has come. *(Jajati falls to the ground and cannot move at all.)* Old age will enter into you immediately. *(Jajati's whole face changes.)*

JAJATI   Forgive me, forgive me, Father I have done a terrible thing to your daughter and to you. Is there any way I can be forgiven?

SUKRACHARYA   No forgiveness for a rascal like you! But I can tell you only this, that if anybody is willing to take your paralysis on himself, and to take on your old age, he can do so, and you will be freed. Then, eventually, if you want to take these sufferings back again, you can. If nobody agrees, if nobody will take on your paralysis and your dotage, then you will have to suffer in this condition until the end of your life.

JAJATI   Oh, I am so grateful to you! I have so many devoted sons. I am sure one of them will do this for me. I have two sons by your daughter, Devajani, and three sons by Sharmishtha. I am sure one of them at least will gladly listen to me. Why only one? All of them will listen. Everybody will be eager to fulfil my desire. I am always so kind to them;

they are so affectionate to me. I am so proud of them; they are so fond of me. I am grateful to you, Father.

(Exit Sukracharya.)

MOTHER, GIVE ME THE LIGHT OF KNOWLEDGE

LK 23. SCENE 2

(Jajati is lying down. Beside him are his two wives and his five sons.)

DEVAJANI   What have I done? I made a mistake by complaining to my father. His curse is more severe than your crime. Ah, what is to be done?

(Both of his wives feel sorry. They are nursing their husband.)

JAJATI   *(to his sons)* Don't feel sorry for me, my children. Don't feel sorry, my wives. My father-in-law, Devajani's father, is still kind to me. He has told me that if anybody wants to take on himself my paralysis and my old age, he can do so. You know, my children, I have been so kind to you, so affectionate to you. I have helped you in every way. You are all young. You will allow me to live on earth for a few more years with joy, enthusiasm, energy and vitality. And then when I die you will regain your health, your strength, your vitality, your energy, everything. And mind you, whoever does this for me will be King. Whoever takes on my old age, my paralysis, my disease, will be King. *(To Jadu.)* Jadu, look how I am suffering, my son, my eldest son. Now do me this favour. Take this incapacity from me. Just for a few years I shall enjoy life, and then I shall give you my throne.

JADU   Father, forgive me. Even for a moment I could not bear to have that kind of disease. I want to enjoy the world. You have done much for me and I am grateful to you. But I cannot take away your disease.

JAJATI   *(to his second son)* Turbasu, will you accept my disease for a few years?

TURBASU   Father, forgive me. Old age is a very serious type of disease. One loses one's brain. When the brain is gone, everything is gone. Father, I am grateful to you for what you have done, and I shall ever remain grateful. But I can't take on your paralysis and your old age.

JAJATI   Devajani's sons have disappointed me. Now let me try Sharmishtha's sons. *(To Druhyu)* Druhyu, you know how I am incapacitated. I can't speak well, I can't move. You have love for me. Do me the favour — take my disease.

DRUHYU   Father, forgive me, forgive me, forgive me. This life of mine is only for joy and pleasure. This life is to see people, mix with people and get joy from the world — nothing else. Father, I can't. I cannot do it. You are suffering outwardly, and I shall suffer inwardly for you. But I cannot suffer both inwardly and outwardly for you, Father. Forgive me, but I am ready to suffer only inwardly for you.

JAJATI   *(to Anu)* Anu, Anu, will you not take on yourself my disease?

ANU   Father, forgive me. I want to live a pure life. I know that if I take your disease on myself I will suffer and I will not be able to pray to God. I won't remain pure, Father. I want to realise God as soon as possible, so I cannot think of your disease. I feel sorry for you, but I am helpless. Forgive me.

JAJATI   *(to Puru)* Puru....

PURU   Father, you don't have to ask me. I shall take your disease.

(Puru touches the feet of his father and immediately falls to the ground. His whole face is changed. His body becomes the body of an old man. He is totally paralysed. Sharmishtha begins shedding tears.)

SHARMISHTHA   *(to Jajati)* Look! Look! Look what you have done! You are an old man. You have already enjoyed the world. And now you have ruined my son, my youngest and dearest son. He could have enjoyed the world. He could have done much for the world. You have ruined his life!

PURU Mother, don't scold my father. Let him enjoy the world for as many years as he wants to. Then, when he is satisfied, he will take his disease back. Even if he does not want to, if he wants to enjoy the world to the end of his life, let him enjoy. I shall enjoy his suffering. Let him enjoy the pleasures of the world.

(Jajati sheds tears of gratitude.)

JAJATI *(to Puru)* Just a few years, a few fleeting years I shall enjoy, and then I shall take my disease back and you will be King. I shall make you King. *(To his other sons.)* You ungrateful creatures! I will have nothing more to do with you. Get out of my kingdom! Get out! It is I who could have made you happy and prosperous. I did so much for you, but you have disappointed me bitterly, and my punishment is severe. You four are banished from my kingdom.

LK 24. SCENE 3

(Many years have passed. Jajati enters Puru's room. Puru is lying on his bed, asleep, and is not awakened by Jajati's entrance.)

JAJATI   *(to himself)* Ah, I have seen the world, I have enjoyed the world. I have been mixing with friends, having parties, living an ordinary life, but there is no joy, no satisfaction in it. I have seen that money cannot make me happy, women cannot make me happy, earthly possessions cannot make me happy. What can make me happy? Only God.

(Jajati sings.)

Amar katha bhabi kebal tai parane byatha
kemane hai hasbe mane madhur nirabata
bhabi kebal manda amai amiy amar ari
nemi hiyay tomai prabhu nitya jena smari

(I always think about myself,
That is why my heart is full of pangs.
Alas, how can sweet silence smile in my mind?
I always think ill of myself.
I am my only enemy.
With sanctified heart, may I always remember You,
   my Lord Supreme.)

JAJATI   The life of pleasure can never satisfy any human being. What man needs is a life of joy and fulfilment. In order to have joy and fulfilment we must swim across the sea of desire and enter into the sea of aspiration. In me the life of desire has totally ended, and now the life of aspiration slowly begins. *(He calls aloud.)* Puru! Puru!

(Puru wakes up. Jajati goes and touches him.)

JAJATI   Puru, I wish to take back my disease from you. My son, you become King now. Let me take my punishment. I shall pray to God in this state and try to realise God through my prayers and meditation. You have pleased me most, my son, and you have my blessingful love, joy and gratitude. My kingdom is yours. Everything I have is yours.

(Jajati falls down. His body is paralysed. His face becomes aged and wrinkled.)

PURU   *(gets up as a young man again)* Father, I am glad and proud that I have pleased you in your own way. Now, in your life of aspiration, in your life of love for God, I wish God to fulfil you.

SIDDHARTHA BECOMES THE BUDDHA

SRI CHINMOY

LK 25. DRAMATIS PERSONÆ

SIDDHARTHA (LATER, THE BUDDHA)
SUJATA (A DEVOTEE)
FIRST ASCETIC
SECOND ASCETIC
THIRD ASCETIC
FOURTH ASCETIC
FIFTH ASCETIC

MOTHER, GIVE ME THE LIGHT OF KNOWLEDGE

LK 26. SCENE I

(Siddhartha is sitting under a tree in high meditation. Enter five ascetics.)

FIRST ASCETIC   O Siddhartha! Siddhartha! Look at Siddhartha!

SECOND ASCETIC   I am sure he will soon realise the highest Truth.

THIRD ASCETIC   Without fail.

FOURTH ASCETIC   We have also been crying for our realisation. We have been praying to God and working so hard in our inner life. But still the realisation of God is a far cry for us. I am happy that at least one person will realise God.

FIFTH ASCETIC   At least Siddhartha will reach the highest Truth. It does not matter who reaches the Truth first; I want people to be free from ignorance.

FIRST ASCETIC   Let us not disturb him. He is in deep meditation, in trance. Let us not disturb poor Siddhartha. May God bless him. He has not been eating at all. He drinks only water. He is so weak, so weak. Poor fellow! Such a hard, austere life! I am sure God will soon grant him illumination.

SECOND ASCETIC   He could have enjoyed all the pleasures of the world. He was the Prince, and in every way he could have lived a life of pleasure.

THIRD ASCETIC   He knows that the life of pleasure cannot give him abiding satisfaction.

FOURTH ASCETIC   But it is very difficult to overcome vital movements, vital pleasure.

FIFTH ASCETIC   God has something special to do with Siddhartha's life. I can clearly see it.

(Enter Sujata, who bows down to Siddhartha and places before him a bowl of sweetmeats. Siddhartha opens his eyes and accepts food from Sujata.)

SUJATA O Sage, I am so grateful to you that you have accepted my food. For days you have not eaten anything. Your body has become so weak, so thin. Now I shall bring food for you regularly. You pray to God; I shall serve you. I am so glad, so grateful that you will accept my devoted service.

SIDDHARTHA I have come to understand that starvation is not right. The extreme path is not the right way. The middle path is by far the best. To reach the highest Truth one need not stop eating altogether. One has to eat a moderate amount of food. The food that is necessary for health, to keep the body fit, one must eat. But at the same time one must not be a voracious eater. When I realise the highest Truth, mine will be the middle path.

FIRST ASCETIC Shame, shame! Look at Siddhartha! He is eating food!

SECOND ASCETIC Look who is serving him! Such a beautiful girl!

THIRD ASCETIC Well, what can you expect? How long can one control his vital life?

FOURTH ASCETIC Alas, Siddhartha has fallen.

FIFTH ASCETIC He does not deserve our appreciation and admiration. He has taken sweetmeats from such a beautiful girl. He is serving his senses and he is feeding his body. See, the life of pleasure has already started. A woman is enough to destroy a man's aspiration no matter how sincere, how devoted he is. One beautiful woman is enough to take even such a great aspirant from the path of Truth. Let us go.

FIRST ASCETIC Whom to blame? The girl or Siddhartha?

SECOND ASCETIC   I blame the girl. She has ruined Siddhartha's aspiration.
THIRD ASCETIC   I blame Siddhartha. Who asked him to be so weak? If he had been strong in his mind he could have rejected her.
FOURTH ASCETIC   Well, we must remember that it is a difficult task to conquer the wrong movements of the vital.
FIFTH ASCETIC   It is difficult also to pray to God, to meditate on Truth.
FOURTH ASCETIC   But since he made an attempt to realise the Highest, he should have continued.
FIFTH ASCETIC   I feel sorry for him. At the same time I feel that he can be of no use to us now. I thought that he would illumine us as soon as he got his own illumination.
THIRD ASCETIC   I thought the same. But now it is impossible. Let us leave, let us leave. Siddhartha has failed, Siddhartha has fallen.

(Exeunt the five ascetics. All this time Sujata is feeding Siddhartha and showing her loving, soulful gratitude to him. Tears of gratitude are flowing from her eyes.)

SIDDHARTHA   Sujata, don't pay any attention to them. They are ignorant people. From ignorant people we can expect only ignorance. You have come to feed me, and I am grateful to you. My blessingful joy you will always feel.
SUJATA   O Sage, I don't pay any attention to those ascetics. They are fools. They do not see your utmost sincerity. They do not see your burning cry for Truth, for God. It will take them thousands of years to realise God, but I clearly see that very soon you will reach your goal. I see that the day of your realisation is fast approaching.

SIDDHARTHA They came, and now they have left. They saw something in me, and that is why they wanted to stay. But when they saw me take food from you, they left. They left just because their minds are still impure; just because their vitals need more purification; just because they could not identify their lives with my aspiring consciousness and your dedicated consciousness. Your dedication knew and felt the depth of my aspiration. And my aspiration feels the depth of your dedication. Sujata, I bless you with all my heart and soul. Here I shall sit, here at the foot of the Bodhi tree. Here I shall realise the Truth. I shall not move from this spot any more. Even if I suffer from cold or hunger or thirst, or from anything else, I shall not move. Here at this very place my Illumination must take place. And I shall put an end to sorrow.

(Sujata bows to Siddhartha and leaves. Siddhartha sings.)

Hihasane shushyatu me shariram
twagasthi mangsam pralayancha jatu
aprapya bodhing vahukalpa durlabham
naivasanat kayamatah chalishye

(Here on this seat may wither my body;
Skin, bone and flesh may be destroyed.
Without getting the supreme Wisdom
Attainable only with difficulty
In myriad aeons,
Definitely I shall not move from this seat.)

MOTHER, GIVE ME THE LIGHT OF KNOWLEDGE

(Siddhartha meditates. He is having visions of life. The life of pleasure, vital movements, sex forces — all are trying to enter into him.)

SIDDHARTHA Ah, these lower vital movements are trying to enter into me. No, I shall not permit them. I have my inner strength, indomitable strength. I shall fight against them.

(Siddhartha meditates with tremendous determination. Suddenly his whole being is flooded with Light. He starts to sing.)

> *No more my heart shall sob or grieve.*
> *My days and nights dissolve in God's own Light.*
> *Above the toil of life my soul*
> *Is a Bird of Fire winging the Infinite.*
> *I have known the One and His secret Play;*
> *And passed beyond the sea of ignorance-Dream.*
> *In tune with Him, I sport and sing,*
> *I own the golden Eye of the Supreme.*
> *Drunk deep of Immortality,*
> *I am the root and boughs of a teeming vast.*
> *My Form I have known, and realised,*
> *The Supreme and I are one — all we outlast.*

(All of a sudden his body begins radiating a golden Light and Siddhartha becomes the Enlightened One, the Buddha.)

BUDDHA I know, at last I know the Truth! I know the way. I know the way to end sorrow, to exterminate the tree of suffering. From today I shall serve humanity with my inner Light. I have seen the Truth, and this Truth every human being on earth will achieve. My Truth is for all. My Love is for all. My Realisation is for all. I am for all. This life of mine, this dedicated life of mine, is for humanity's use.

Now that I have the Transcendental Light within me, I shall go out into the world to teach others.

(Exit the Buddha.)

MOTHER, GIVE ME THE LIGHT OF KNOWLEDGE

LK 27. SCENE 2

(The five ascetics are meditating. Enter the Buddha.)

BUDDHA   Now I have come to Benares, a sacred place. *(He sees the five ascetics.)* Ahhh! Here are the five ascetics who came to me and left me.
FIRST ASCETIC   Look, here is Siddhartha again.
SECOND ASCETIC   But this time he cannot fool us.
THIRD ASCETIC   Certainly not. He cannot fool us any more.
FOURTH ASCETIC   But look at him. He looks different.
FIFTH ASCETIC   I see something in him, something strange.
FIRST ASCETIC   Well, I seem to see some Light in him.
THIRD ASCETIC   His whole face is glowing.
FOURTH ASCETIC   His face? His entire body is glowing!
FIFTH ASCETIC   He is illumined, totally illumined!

(The Buddha approaches them. One by one they touch the Buddha's feet. The Buddha, with his compassionate smile, blesses them.)

SECOND ASCETIC   Siddhartha, you are no more Siddhartha.
THIRD ASCETIC   You are the Enlightened One.
FIRST ASCETIC   O Buddha, we are bathing in the sea of your Light.
FOURTH ASCETIC   O Buddha, we are your first disciples.
ALL TOGETHER   With us the journey of your manifestation begins. With us the manifestation of your mission begins.

(The Buddha gives them a smile of compassion, joy and pride.)

BUDDHA   You have my Compassion. You have my Light. You have my Bliss, my children, my sweet children.

SARIPUTRA, YOU ARE A FOOL

SRI CHINMOY

LK 28. DRAMATIS PERSONÆ

THE BUDDHA
SARIPUTRA (A DISCIPLE)

MOTHER, GIVE ME THE LIGHT OF KNOWLEDGE

LK 29. SCENE I

(The Buddha and his disciple Sariputra.)

SARIPUTRA O Lord Buddha, I am sure that you are the greatest of all spiritual Masters. Nobody before you attained to your height, and nobody after you will be able to equal you. You are unparalleled. You will always remain unparalleled. Nobody has come near your realisation, and nobody will ever come near your realisation.

BUDDHA Sariputra, how do you know that nobody before me has ever attained to what I have attained? And how do you know that nobody will surpass me in the future? How can you make this kind of utterance? Do you know anything of the past? Do you know anything of the future?

SARIPUTRA O Lord, I do not know anything about the past or the future, but I know everything about you.

BUDDHA Sariputra, you are a fool. You know very little about me. A spiritual Master of my calibre cannot be known totally by anybody on earth. You see my outer history, my outer life. But my inner life you do not see, you cannot see. In my outer life I do perhaps ten things a day. In my inner life I am doing millions of things daily. The inner life of a spiritual Master will always remain a mystery. The outer life of the Master may be observed, but it will not always be understood. Very often it will be misunderstood. So, Sariputra, about my outer life you know practically nothing, and about my inner life you know nothing at all.

SARIPUTRA I know nothing, true. But I know who you are. You are my liberation and you are my All.

BUDDHA Sariputra, do not think of the past. Do not think of the future. Think only of the present. The past we have left behind. The future has not yet arrived. To think of things that we have left behind is useless, and to think of things that have not yet happened is equally useless. Forget about the past. Forget about the future. Think only of the present. It is today that you have to aspire. It is today that you have to realise. It is today that you have to manifest. It is today that you have to conquer all your desires. It is today that you have to bring to the fore all your aspiration. It is today that you have to become what you inwardly are, the Light. It is today that you have to give to the world at large what you are, the Light.

TWO DISCIPLES

SRI CHINMOY

LK 30. DRAMATIS PERSONÆ

FIRST DISCIPLE
SECOND DISCIPLE
MASTER

MOTHER, GIVE ME THE LIGHT OF KNOWLEDGE

LK 31. SCENE 1

(Two disciples in a room in their Master's ashram.)

FIRST DISCIPLE   I told you, I told you, I told you!

SECOND DISCIPLE   What did you tell me?

FIRST DISCIPLE   I told you that our Master has nothing. Nothing! He has no spiritual power. He has no occult power. He knows only how to talk. He talks about transcendental Reality and universal Consciousness and all about what he can do with his occult power. But it is all lies. He knows how to talk and we know how to listen to him. But he has nothing, nothing. Look, he has been suffering from his rheumatism for the last three months. If he had even an iota of occult power, he could have cured himself.

SECOND DISCIPLE   My heart tells me that he has the capacity to cure himself, but that God is asking him to have this experience.

FIRST DISCIPLE   He says he is taking on our *karma*, but we have done nothing. I have done nothing wrong. You and the other disciples have done nothing wrong. What happens is that he blames us when *he* does something wrong. Who knows what he has done wrong in the inner world? That's why he gets punishment. And outwardly he blames us.

SECOND DISCIPLE   He never blames us. And I believe him when he says he is taking our karma.

FIRST DISCIPLE   You believe him? Then believe him. Remain with him and suffer. Die with him.

SECOND DISCIPLE   I shall die with him. Not only shall I die with him, but I shall die for him.

FIRST DISCIPLE   God created two types of people on earth: one type to deceive, another type to be deceived. One type to be rogues, the other type to be taken advantage of.

(Enter the Master. The first disciple begins to edge away. The second disciple touches the Master's feet.)

MASTER   *(to the first disciple)* So you know that I have no capacity, that I just brag? I am not the right Master for you. You will do the best thing by going to some other Master, or waiting for the right Master to come to you. Leave me. Go home and live peacefully. *(To the second disciple.)* You believe in me. It is my duty to help you, to guide you. Now tell me, do you really feel that I take your ignorance, your imperfection into my body? Or do you just say it because you have studied my philosophy and books written by others? You have read about Ramakrishna, who took away the impurity, imperfection and ignorance of his disciples and suffered so much. Many, many spiritual Masters have said they have done the same. Do you think that I am just saying it because so many of them have said it? Do you think I am only talking, or do you think I actually take these things from you?

SECOND DISCIPLE   Master, I know what you take from me. Every day you take from me insincerity, obscurity, impurity, jealousy, doubt, insecurity and many other imperfections. Where do they go? I give them to you; they come to you. If there is nobody else on earth who believes it, I don't mind. Even if you tell me that you don't take it, that it is your own karma, I will not believe you. I know that God is giving you this experience for my sake. If I had gone through this particular experience, perhaps I would have died.

MOTHER, GIVE ME THE LIGHT OF KNOWLEDGE

MASTER   My child, there are two reasons why I suffer. One reason is that I really take upon myself the burdens, the imperfections, the undivine qualities of my close disciples. That is what the Supreme wants me to do. There are two ways to take this karma. One way is to take it on oneself and suffer, and the other way is to throw the imperfections of the disciples into the Cosmic Consciousness. But the easier way, infinitely easier, is to take it on oneself. It is a direct way. You are suffering, and directly I touch you and take away your suffering. The other way is like carrying you to a different place, to the Universal Consciousness. The Cosmic Consciousness can be seen as a refuse heap. I take your impurities and imperfections and make them into a bundle. Then I have to carry that bundle there and throw it away. But the other way I just touch you and, like a magnet, I take away your sufferings, your pains, your undivine qualities. That way is easier and that's why I do it. God wants me to do this. I say to God, "God, my children love me so much and I do not love them, I don't please them." Then God says to me, "Look how you suffer for them. Look at your own love, My son — how sincerely, how devotedly you love them. You feel that in your children's perfection is your perfection, which is absolutely true. They love you just because they feel that if they can possess you, they will possess everything. They love you to have you; you love them so that you can bring them to Me. You love them because you feel that if you can bring them to Me, then you have played your part. By loving you for themselves, they feel that they have played their part. And when you love them, when you bring them to Me, to your Highest, then you feel that you have played your part." *(Pauses.)* Also, God has given me another reason to suffer. Many people come to me with only desire, desire, desire. They come to me only to fulfil their desires. But when they see that I am paralysed with pain, that I am also subject to suffering and disease, that I am as weak as they are, they say, "He is an invalid, he is helpless. How can he help us in any way? How is he better than us?" They feel the best thing is for them to go to somebody else who can help them, and many leave. But the truth of the matter is that God wants these people to leave me. This is the only way He can throw them out of my spiritual family. When they leave, my boat becomes lighter and can then go much faster towards the Goal. God wants desiring people, unaspiring people, to leave their Master and make the Master's boat lighter. So these are the reasons I suffer. When a sincere disciple sees that I am suffering for him, he says, "If I really love my Master, then I should give him only joy." So the disciple makes a promise, an inner promise: "I want him to be constantly proud of me. Nothing will give me greater joy than to see that my Master is always proud of me." So the disciple does not make any more mistakes and the Master becomes happy and proud.

(The first disciple touches the Master's feet.)

FIRST DISCIPLE Master, for so long I was a faithless, inhuman creature. From today on I shall be your faithful, devoted disciple.

SECOND DISCIPLE Master, I have been your devoted, faithful disciple for so long. Today you have told me the secret of your suffering. From today on I consider myself an important, conscious part of you. I consider myself an arm of yours. Master, your compassion is my life's only salvation.

FIRST DISCIPLE Master, your forgiveness is my life's only salvation.

MOTHER, GIVE ME THE LIGHT OF KNOWLEDGE

MASTER *(to the first disciple)* By recognising your stupidity, your ignorance, you have brought your divinity to the fore. *(To the second disciple.)* By recognising me, my spiritual Truth, you have manifested God's Divinity on earth. You have manifested God's Will on earth.

AKBAR, TANSEN AND HARIDAS

SRI CHINMOY

LK 32. DRAMATIS PERSONÆ

THE EMPEROR AKBAR
TANSEN (COURT MUSICIAN OF AKBAR)
A LARGE AUDIENCE
MINISTER IN AKBAR'S COURT
HARIDAS (MASTER OF TANSEN)

MOTHER, GIVE ME THE LIGHT OF KNOWLEDGE

LK 33. SCENE I

(Akbar's palace. A large audience has assembled before Akbar. His court musician, Tansen, is playing soul-stirring music. Tansen sings.)

*Kalpana go kalpana
tumiy amar bandana
dure tomai rakhbona
kalpana go kalpana
mithya mohe kandbona
kurup prane dakbona
khudra jaye hasbona
kalpana go kalpana
mrittyu dake jagbona
atma ami marbona
bhul pathe ar chalbona
kalpana go kalpana*

(Imagination, O imagination!
You are my life's adoration.
You I shall not keep afar.
Imagination, O imagination!
In false, binding lies I shall not cry.
I shall not welcome the life of impurity's ugliness.
With paltry victory I shall not smile and rejoice.
Imagination, O imagination!
To death's call I shall not respond.
The soul am I, no death have I.
No more, never, shall I walk along the wrong path.
Imagination, O Imagination!)

AKBAR   Tansen, your music carries me into the highest world, and there I enjoy such happiness, such delight. Tansen, I shall give you anything you want. You can have anything from me for the asking.

TANSEN   O Emperor, you have already given me name and fame by allowing me to play for you. What more do I need?

AKBAR   Tansen, although you get everything from me, if you have any special desire, ask me and I shall grant it. Anything that you want from me today I shall immediately give you.

TANSEN   I have everything I want. But I have one thing to tell you. You think that I am the best musician. But there is someone who is far better than I. He is the one who taught me how to play. I am no match for him.

MINISTER   O Akbar, O Emperor, your Tansen is very clever. He wants to gain more favour from you with his false modesty. Don't believe him. He thinks that by telling you that there is somebody better than he is, he will gain more favour, more love, from you. This Tansen is so clever. He is the greatest musician, but he is also the greatest trickster. Don't believe him, my Lord.

AKBAR   No, Tansen, I don't believe you. But if it is true, then you should have told me about him before this.

TANSEN   O Emperor, you will never believe me. If I had told you about him, do you think he would have come to you? He does not care for name and fame as I do. He would not want to play here at your palace.

AKBAR   He must come and play here. I shall force him. I am the Emperor Akbar. Everyone is at my behest. He has to come and play. Go and bring him here.

TANSEN   I can go and bring him here, but I tell you, if you force him to play, he will play, but he will never play his real music. He is above name and fame. He shuns society.

AKBAR   All right, then I shall go to his house.

TANSEN   Well, if you go to his house, perhaps he will play. But he always shuns great men. If he sees that the Emperor has come, he will not play at all. If I request him, even if I plead with him, it will all be useless, because you are a great man, the greatest man on earth. Perhaps if you come with me as my servant, and if I tell him that my servant would like to hear his music, then he may condescend to grant my request.

AKBAR   All right, Tansen, I will visit your teacher as your servant. I want to hear your master's music since you are praising him to the skies. But he had better be good!

LK 34. SCENE 2

(Haridas' home. Enter Tansen, and Akbar in the guise of Tansen's servant. Haridas is meditating.)

TANSEN Master, here is my servant. He has been begging me for a long time to bring him to hear your music. Today I have brought him.

AKBAR *(to Haridas)* Lord, I will be so grateful to you if you play. For some time I have been longing to hear your music. Today my master, Tansen, has brought me to you. Please play.

HARIDAS I am sorry. Today I am not in the mood to play at all. I do not know why. Otherwise I would listen to your request. You look quite nice and smart. I am happy that my Tansen has such a good servant. You look beautiful, you look powerful. I am sure you are pleasing your master in every way.

TANSEN Master, it is true that this servant is pleasing me in every way. I am most pleased with him and proud of him and, as a reward, I have brought him here. Please play for him just a little. It will be difficult for me to bring him here again.

HARIDAS Tansen, when I refuse to do something, rest assured that I will never do it. I am not in the mood today. Today my mind is all concentrated on God. You came to me to learn music. I taught you many things, and now when you play I get tremendous joy. Today I wish you to play for me. Let your servant and me hear your music. It will transport me into the highest realm. Your music will inspire me to go deep within and commune with my inner Pilot. Now, Tansen, please play.

(Tansen bows to Haridas and starts playing. Soon he starts playing wrong notes.)

HARIDAS   Tansen, what is wrong with you today? Your music is absurd. You are playing like an absolute beginner. You, my greatest student! Is anything wrong in your family? Are you upset?

TANSEN   No, no, my family is all right. But today I had the greatest hope that my servant would be able to hear your music. You did not listen to my request, and that has made me very sad. Perhaps it is my sadness that is creating this problem and making it difficult for me to play well.

HARIDAS   No matter how sad you are, Tansen, I can't imagine how you can play so badly.

TANSEN   Master, it seems to me that I am playing everything correctly. You are saying that I am playing badly, but I feel that I am playing everything as I used to play before, as you have taught me.

HARIDAS   Tansen, you liar! I have not taught you to play like this. It is all wrong.

(Haridas snatches away Tansen's vina and starts playing most soulfully and hauntingly. The music comes from another world. Akbar is in deep trance. Tansen is listening with deepest inner delight. Haridas sings.)

Ekti katha ekti sur ekyi jhankar
nam dhare ke dakchhe jena amai barebar
kothai achi kothai jabo
nai jena thikena
ghumer ghore karchhi shudhu
ami becha kena
kata bhangi katai gari
katai kari ashha
hiya khani dhekechhe mor
andhar sarbanasha
alor pakhi alor pakhi
abar eso phire
jyotir dhara banan kare
namo amar shire
dak ditechha urdhe jete
jabo keman kare
bandi je mor paran khani
ekti andhar ghare
alor pakhi alor pakhi
alor pakhi alo
prane amar rekhona ar
ektu andhar kalo

MOTHER, GIVE ME THE LIGHT OF KNOWLEDGE

(One thought, one tune, one resonance —
Who calls me ever and anon?
I know not where I am,
I know not whither I shall go.
In dark amnesia, myself I buy, myself I sell.
All I break, again all I build.
All I hope to be mine, mine alone.
Alas, my heart is eclipsed by dark and wild destruction-
    night.
O Bird of Light, O Bird of Light,
With your glowing and flowing flames, do enter
    into my heart once again.
You are calling me to climb up and fly into the blue.

But how can I?
My heart is in prison in the strangled breath of a
    tiny room.
O Bird of Light, O Bird of Light,
O Bird of Light Supreme.
In me, I pray, keep not an iota of gloom.)

TANSEN   *(at the end of the music)* Master, forgive me. I know I have played all wrong today. After hearing you I realise how badly I have played. Forgive me, forgive me.

AKBAR   *(bows)* I always thought that my master was the best musician, but he was sincere enough to say that you play far better than he does. I didn't believe him. But now that I have heard you, I know that undoubtedly you are a far better musician. I am so grateful to you and also I am so grateful to my master for bringing me to you today.

HARIDAS   May God bless you, my son. May God bless your devoted head. You are serving your master, who is my fondest son.

TANSEN   I am also fond of my servant.
AKBAR   Lord, I am also proud of my master, Tansen.

(Akbar and Tansen bow and leave.)

MOTHER, GIVE ME THE LIGHT OF KNOWLEDGE

LK 35. SCENE 3

(Akbar's palace.)

AKBAR Tansen, how it is that you cannot play so well? Your master lives in a poor cottage, whereas you have all kinds of advantages and opportunities. Even then you cannot play as well as he. I appreciate your sincerity in telling me that he plays far better than you do, but I cannot account for this. Why is it? What prevents you from playing as well as he does?

TANSEN O Emperor, I play for you, for human beings; I play for name and fame; I play for wealth. My teacher plays for God, the Lord Supreme. For him, there is only God. God is everything. I want to please human beings who live in the world of human pleasure; he wants to please the Absolute Supreme. When one plays for the world, one gets what he wants: appreciation, admiration, flattery. But when one plays for God, the Absolute, one gets God's boundless Grace, His boundless Blessing and Transcendental Delight. God, the Infinite Compassion, enters into his music and, at every moment, he plays celestial, transcendental, soul-stirring music — music that awakens the Universal Consciousness, music that feeds the Universal Consciousness, music that manifests the Universal Consciousness in aspiring souls.

AKBAR Tansen, you are a great musician, but your sincerity is greater than your music. Your inner depth is by far the greatest. Your inner wisdom is by far the best. I bow to your music with love. I bow to your sincerity with joy. I bow to your inner wisdom with my heart's gratitude.

NOT HOW MANY HOURS YOU MEDITATE,
BUT HOW YOU MEDITATE

SRI CHINMOY

LK 36. DRAMATIS PERSONÆ

KRISHNA
ARJUNA
CARTMAN

MOTHER, GIVE ME THE LIGHT OF KNOWLEDGE

LK 37. SCENE I

(Krishna and Arjuna are walking along the street. All of a sudden they see a man drawing a cart loaded with flowers.)

ARJUNA   Krishna, look! A man is drawing a cart loaded with all kinds of flowers. Are they not beautiful?
KRISHNA   Yes, they are really beautiful.
ARJUNA   *(to the cartman)* What are you doing with these flowers, my friend? Where are you going?

(The man pays no attention to Arjuna. He continues pulling the cart. Exit cartman.)

KRISHNA   Arjuna, let us follow him.
ARJUNA   That's a nice idea.

(Exeunt Krishna and Arjuna.)

SRI CHINMOY

LK 38. SCENE 2

(The cartman has reached his destination. Enter Krishna and Arjuna.)

ARJUNA   What are you going to do with all these flowers? It seems to me that you have already brought a few cartloads of flowers here. What a huge pile of flowers I see! What are you doing with so many flowers?

MAN   I have no time to speak to you. I am now employed in serious business. I can speak only to one person on earth, and that is Bhima, the second Pandava.

ARJUNA   Why?

MAN   Don't argue with me. He is the greatest spiritual seeker of all. When he meditates just for a minute or two before his meals, saying, "O Mighty Lord Shiva," he offers thousands of flowers to the Lord. His concentration is most intense; his meditation is most sincere. Look, in his family he has a brother named Arjuna, who only offers one flower at a time to Lord Shiva. He just shows off, meditating for hours. God alone knows when Arjuna will come to realise that his meditation, his power of concentration, is nowhere near his brother Bhima's.

ARJUNA   Krishna, enough humiliation! You are humiliating me in every way! Why do you humiliate me so badly?

KRISHNA   This is not humiliation, my dearest Arjuna. This is illumination. I am teaching the world through you. I wanted to teach you that it is not how many flowers you offer or how many hours you meditate that counts, but rather your power of concentration, your power of dedication. You pray to this god and that god. You want to please all the gods. You collect many flowers and offer them to Lord Shiva one by one, for two hours every day. Each time, while offering a flower, you utter the name of Lord Shiva. You think that, since you offer many flowers to Lord Shiva and the other gods for so many hours, you are the best seeker. This is your pride, O Arjuna. It was my boundless love and compassion for you that wanted to shatter your pride. O Arjuna, again and again I tell you, you are my dearest disciple, my dearest friend. You have established your eternal oneness with me.

(Arjuna sings.)

*Ami tomar phul tumi amar kul
ami tomar dhenu tumi amar benu
ami tomar gan tumi amar pran
ami tomar khama tumi amar rama*

(I am Your flower,
           You are my Golden Shore.
I am Your divine cow,
           You are my Flute, Divine Flute.
I am Your song, celestial song,
           You are my Life, Eternal Life.
I am Your forgiveness,
           You are my Beauty, Inner Beauty.)

PRAJAPATI AND HIS THREE STUDENTS

SRI CHINMOY

LK 39. DRAMATIS PERSONÆ

PRAJAPATI (THE CREATOR AND THE GREATEST OF ALL SAGES)
A COSMIC GOD, A MAN, AN ASURA (STUDENTS OF PRAJAPATI)

MOTHER, GIVE ME THE LIGHT OF KNOWLEDGE

LK 40. SCENE I

(The abode of Prajapati. Enter three students for spiritual instruction: a cosmic god, a man and an asura. Prajapati is highly pleased to see them.)

PRAJAPATI   Please sit here in front of me. *(All bow and are seated.)* What can I do for you three? Why have you come to me?

COSMIC GOD   We have come here for spiritual instruction. We have come here to learn from you that which will really make us great and fulfil our lives.

PRAJAPATI   Wonderful, wonderful! I shall teach you. But you have to stay here for some time. Then one day I shall invite you to come before me, and I shall give you spiritual instruction, my divine advice. *(All bow to Prajapati with deep gratitude.)* But first of all, I wish to know if you have any special desire, something that you feel you need most in your life. Mind you, this has nothing to do with your spiritual instruction. It is just something I want to know, you can say, out of curiosity. I want to know what each one of you has as your greatest desire.

ASURA   O greatest of all sages, O peerless sage. I want to conquer the world with my vital power. I want to lord it over the world. I want to prove to the world at large that I am the greatest and most powerful here on earth and there in Heaven.

PRAJAPATI   Ah, that is a splendid wish! *(Turning towards the man.)* Now, what about your desires?

MAN   O Creator, O Father of the entire universe, my sole desire is to become one with your whole creation. With my heart's pure, soulful love, I want to become inseparably one with your entire creation — totally one with each human being, with each creature, with each object that you have created here on earth.

PRAJAPATI That is a splendid idea! Indeed, it is a splendid wish. *(Turning towards the god.)* And what do you want most in your life?

COSMIC GOD O Absolute, O sage of the highest magnitude, O peerless one, O transcendental one, I wish to illumine the universe with my soul's Light. I wish to illumine your entire creation with my soul's divine Light.

PRAJAPATI Indeed, that is a marvellous desire! *(To all.)* I have three rooms here — one for each of you. Every day you will be served food in your rooms, and you will spend all your time in meditation. I shall call you when I feel that you are ready to receive my instruction.

(Exeunt the three students, bowing to Prajapati.)

MOTHER, GIVE ME THE LIGHT OF KNOWLEDGE

LK 41. SCENE 2

(The cosmic god, the man and the asura meet together in another hall of the house.)

ASURA   I know I can easily become the most powerful being both in Heaven and on earth. I know I have that capacity. I am not bragging, I tell you. What I say is just a mere fact.

MAN   I know that I can be the most loving person on earth. My heart has the capacity to love everyone and everything on earth. I know I shall do it. God has given me the most loving heart, and I shall utilise it; I shall offer it to serve Him in His creation.

COSMIC GOD   I know I shall be able to illumine the whole world with my soul's Light. God has given me that capacity, and He wants me to use it to illumine His creation. I will do it, and when I have done it, I will see God's Face brimming with transcendental Delight, for my success is undoubtedly His success.

LK 42. SCENE 3

(The three students come before Prajapati and bow to him.)

PRAJAPATI   Today it is time for me to give you my spiritual instruction, my divine advice. I wish to advise each of you separately. We will start with the god. *(The god bows to Prajapati.)* Now tell me, what kind of advice do you actually want from me?

COSMIC GOD   O Prajapati, you know what is best for me. I want my life to be really fruitful, meaningful and soulful.

PRAJAPATI   Da. *(On hearing this the god is struck with confusion.)* It seems that you have not understood my instruction. Go over there for a while and meditate on what I have said. Come back when you have understood my advice. We shall meditate here until you return.

(The god bows to Prajapati and moves away, out of their sight. The other three meditate together.)

COSMIC GOD   I don't understand it. I thought he would give me some special teaching, something that would illumine me all at once so that I could illumine the world. But what he has said, I do not understand at all. Let me meditate on it.... *(Meditates.)* Ah, I have found the answer.

(The god rushes back to Prajapati.)

PRAJAPATI   So, you have understood what I said?
COSMIC GOD   Yes, my Lord, I have understood.
PRAJAPATI   Then tell me.

MOTHER, GIVE ME THE LIGHT OF KNOWLEDGE

COSMIC GOD   *(with folded hands)* You want me to lead a most disciplined life; you want me to control all my senses. You want me to live a life of total discipline and perfect Perfection.

PRAJAPATI   *(overjoyed)* Yes, my child, you have understood my advice; you have understood my philosophy. *(To the man.)* Now it is your turn. *(The man comes with folded hands.)* Tell me what you actually want. What kind of advice do you need?

MAN   My Lord, I want you to tell me how I can feel that my life has special meaning on earth. I want to lead a life of happiness and fulfilment. This is all that I want.

PRAJAPATI   *Da.*

(The man is totally confused. He cannot make anything out of it.)

PRAJAPATI   Ah, I know it is difficult for you. Now you can move away from here for a little while and meditate on what I have said, and come back when you have understood it. It may take a little while, but we shall wait for you here.

(The man bows to Prajapati and goes aside. Prajapati, the god and the asura meditate together.)

MAN   *(from a distance)* I will never understand this Prajapati. Just one word — *Da.* What does he mean? What does he actually mean? What does he want me to understand? I thought he would tell me something very deep and secret, something sacred that would give me all joy, all satisfaction, all perfection, all at once. Instead of doing that, he just says *Da.* I can make neither head nor tail of it. Anyway, let me meditate on *Da* and if I get any answer, I will go back to him.... *(Meditates.)* Aah, I have found the answer!

(The man rushes back to Prajapati.)

PRAJAPATI It seems you have found the answer; you have understood my advice. Now tell me what you have learned.
MAN Ah, my Lord, at long last I have understood what you meant. You want me to give everything that I have and everything that I am. All that I have and all that I am you want me to give away freely, soulfully, devotedly and unconditionally to the world at large. Am I correct?
PRAJAPATI *(joyfully)* Right, you are absolutely correct, absolutely correct, my son; you have understood my advice; you have understood my philosophy. *(To the asura.)* Come up, please.

(The asura comes before him and bows with folded hands.)

PRAJAPATI Your two friends have understood my philosophy. I am sure you will also easily understand my philosophy. But before I teach you, I would like to ask you what you actually want. Is there anything specific that you need from me which will really help you in every way?
ASURA My Lord, I want you to decide on my behalf. I don't know what will actually make me the most powerful and the happiest being at the same time. Please, make me the happiest and the most powerful.
PRAJAPATI Indeed, that is a splendid desire. Now here is my advice — *Da*.
ASURA Confusion, all confusion! You have thrown me into a sea of confusion! I do not know what it all means.
PRAJAPATI O my son, do not be disturbed, do not be confused. Like these two, you can also move away from here and meditate on it for a while. I am sure you will understand

my advice. And when you get the answer, come back to me. In the meantime, we shall meditate here.

(The asura bows to Prajapati with folded hands and moves away.)

ASURA   *(from a distance)* What does this old man mean? This old man has no sense. I came to him for power, only power. If he had given me advice on how to acquire boundless power, I would have been the happiest person on earth. Here, there, everywhere I want to be the Lord, the Lord Supreme. I want the whole world to be at my feet, but he didn't understand me; he didn't feel my heart's desire. Now I am all confused. He has simply thrown me into a sea of confusion, this old man. I thought he would at least use some Sanskrit phrases, some mantras. They say that in Sanskrit mantras there is tremendous power. I would repeat them millions of times in order to get power. But he didn't use any. I thought that he would ask me to repeat a particular portion of the scriptures, but he didn't do that. I thought that he would disclose some secret and, with that secret, I would be able to lord it over the whole world, and make the world touch the dust of my feet. But alas, he just said *Da.* I am helpless and I am hopeless. I came to him for help, but I am helpless with what he has said to me. Anyway, what can I do? This is my fate, my deplorable fate. Let me meditate on his stupid word, *Da. (Meditates.)* Aah, I have understood, I have understood! It is so easy, so easy!

(The asura runs to Prajapati.)

PRAJAPATI   So, you have understood my philosophy, I am sure. Tell me about it.

ASURA   *(with folded hands)* I have understood the depth of your philosophy. It means that I must be compassionate, be affectionate, be full of concern all the time. Am I correct?

PRAJAPATI   *(overjoyed)* You are absolutely correct, my child. You have understood the very depth of my philosophy. Be compassionate. Let your outer being and inner being be full of compassion. In all that you say, in all that you do, show only compassion, a flood of compassion. Only then, here on earth and there in Heaven, will everybody appreciate you, admire you and adore you. Be a sea of limitless compassion. *(To all.)*

PRAJAPATI   O cosmic god, O man, O asura, I am satisfied with your understanding of my spiritual instruction. Go back to your homes and, from now on, do the things that you have learnt. O asura, use your compassion as power. O man, use your love as power. O cosmic god, use your illumination, your Light, as power. Asura, your compassion is your boundless power. Man, your love is your infinite power. God, your Light is your transcendental power. When you three work together my Dream becomes my Reality, and my Dream-Boat touches the Golden Shore of the ever-transcending Beyond. It is you three who can manifest me, fulfil me and make me feel that my creation is something of which I can be eternally proud. Only your loving concern for me, your total dedication to me, your constant oneness with me can make my creation and cosmic manifestation Divine, Immortal and Perfect. You will make my world a land of Beauty, a land of Light and Delight, a land of Love, a land of Compassion, a land of Illumination, a land of Perfection and a land of absolute Fulfilment. You can do it, and you must do it. Once it is done, I, the Creator, will dance with highest pride and deepest gratitude.

MOTHER, GIVE ME THE LIGHT OF KNOWLEDGE

(The three students bow.)

MAN   We shall do it, we shall do it. We shall please you, we shall fulfil you, we shall be your most chosen instruments. Through us you will manifest yourself on earth.
COSMIC GOD   In us and through us you will offer your Light to Heaven.
ASURA   O Prajapati, we are of you and we are for you.
PRAJAPATI   My children, you three *are* of me, you three *are* for me. From now on I will be nothing but a garland of gratitude if you fulfil my desire, my aspiration, my realisation.
ASURA   O Prajapati, we shall do it, we shall do it, we shall do it! With your boundless Light, with your boundless Love, with your boundless Compassion, we shall do it.
MAN   You are ours and we are yours. Forever we shall take part in your cosmic *Lila* and fulfil you here, there, everywhere. Today, tomorrow, eternally, we shall work together. Together we shall be in your heart to love you, to please you, to fulfil you. Together we shall play with you, sing with you, dance with you.
COSMIC GOD   Together we shall run towards the highest Goal, which is You, You the eternal Reality, the everlasting, the ever-fulfilling, the ever-illumining Reality.

(Prajapati blesses his students with tearful gratitude.)

PRAJAPATI   I offer you not only my gratitude but all my pride, because in you I have found three most worthy students.
THE THREE STUDENTS   We offer you our deepest gratitude, deepest love, deepest adoration; everything that is divine in us. In you we have found our Haven, our Goal.

I AM FALLEN

SRI CHINMOY

LK 43. DRAMATIS PERSONÆ

A GREAT MASTER
HIS DISCIPLE (ALSO A GURU)
KING (DISCIPLE OF THE GURU)
MINISTER

MOTHER, GIVE ME THE LIGHT OF KNOWLEDGE

LK 44. SCENE 1

(The home of a great Master. Enter his disciple, who is also a Guru.)

DISCIPLE   Master, Master, I need your blessing.

MASTER   Blessing? What for?

DISCIPLE   O Master, you know that the King has been bothering me for a long time. He wants me to initiate him. He says he is an old man and may die at any moment, so he needs initiation. Yesterday I finally agreed to do it. I told him that I would this evening initiate him. Now I have come here for your blessing, Master.

MASTER   You fool! How can you initiate the King? Don't you know that he has been wallowing in the pleasures of ignorance all his life? He has led an absolutely corrupt life, and you want to initiate him? Does he have one iota of purity or sincerity, not to speak of spirituality? How can you dare to initiate him? I can't bless you. Go and initiate him. It is your problem.

DISCIPLE   Master, he pleaded with me on so many occasions that this time I could not refuse. What shall I do now?

MASTER   Do whatever you like. You have to pay the penalty for your foolishness. And it is not only foolishness. There is also a subtle ego, an unconscious ego involved, which you have not noticed.

DISCIPLE   Master, I didn't know anything about that ego. How has it attacked me?

MASTER   My son, you won't like to hear this, but I know you will understand. When you initiate the King, everybody will come to learn about it and they will think, "What a great spiritual Master he is." You will become famous overnight, and there, I tell you, your spiritual progress will end.

DISCIPLE   Master, Master, save me, save me! If I don't initiate him, the King will punish me; and if I do initiate him, my spiritual life will be ruined. What am I going to do, Master? Please help me. I am at your feet.

MASTER   Go and initiate the King and then come back to me. Let me see what I can do for you.

(The disciple touches the Master's feet with deepest gratitude and leaves.)

MOTHER, GIVE ME THE LIGHT OF KNOWLEDGE

LK 45. SCENE 2

(The King is ready for initiation. He has shaved his head and cut off his beard and is sitting in front of the spiritual teacher. The King sings.)

He jogiraj dikkha amai dao go aji dikkha
rupantarer amar bani pabo aji shikkha
ghurbona ar dure dure
nachbo shudhu hriday pure
gaibo giti premer sure
dekhbo amai pran mukure
nirabatar lagi ami magi aji bhikkha

(O Yogi of the highest magnitude, initiate me.
Today offer me your initiation.
Today I shall learn the immortal message of transformation from you.
I shall not wander any more in the farthest corners of the world.
I shall only dance in the city of my heart.
Inside the city of my heart I shall sing songs of Love Divine,
And I shall see myself in the mirror of my sanctified heart.
Today I beg of you to offer me only one thing: silence, silence.
O Yogi of the highest magnitude, initiate me today.)

(The King touches his feet.)

KING You have taken all my impurity, all my imperfections. In return I give you my whole kingdom and all its wealth. Anything you want from me is yours. O Guru, I am at your command. My royal family is at your command. My subjects are at your command. And all my possessions are at your command.

GURU O King, from now on I expect you to lead a spiritual life, a divine life. From your example, your kingdom will begin a new life, a life of purity, a life of renunciation, a life of divine perfection.

KING Guru, I know, I know. I am most grateful to you for initiating me. I was not worthy of being initiated, but from now on, through my acts, I shall prove to you that I can be what you want me to be, and I shall not betray your trust.

(The King sings.)

Jagiyachhe bishwanath asundar prane
chalilam shashwater ahana sandhane

(The Lord of the Universe is awakened inside the
    heart of ugliness itself.
Now towards the Eternal Dawn I march,
I run towards the Eternal Dawn.)

(The Guru blesses the King with joy and pride, and then leaves.)

LK 46. SCENE 3

(The King's Guru comes to his own Master.)

MASTER So? You are becoming famous now. Unconsciously you wanted name and fame, and it shall soon be yours. Thousands and thousands of people will come to know about you and a great many will want to become disciples of the King's Guru. You have no idea what you have done to your spiritual life. You have taken boundless impurity, ugliness, filth, ignorance and inconscience from the King. You have fallen, you have fallen. You have fallen far beyond your imagination.

(The disciple touches the Master's feet.)

DISCIPLE Oh Master, forgive me, forgive me. Please purify me.

MASTER There is only one way you can be forgiven.

DISCIPLE Tell me, please. I will do anything.

MASTER Get a large sign and write on it: "I am fallen, I am fallen. By initiating the King, I am fallen." Write it down. *(The disciple gets a sign and writes it down.)* In bold letters.

DISCIPLE Yes, Master.

MASTER Now tie it around your neck with some string. *(The disciple does it.)* Now you must walk around the city and let everyone see what you have done.

DISCIPLE Oh Master, if the citizens see this, what will happen to me? The King's anger will know no bounds. He will punish me severely.

MASTER I know, I know. The King will arrest you, the King will punish you, the King will do everything. But if you want to be forgiven by God, then you have to do it. Only by being sincere and truthful will you be forgiven.

DISCIPLE   What you say is true. I am going. I shall walk along the street with this confession draped around my neck.

LK 47. SCENE 4

(The King in his palace. Enter a minister.)

MINISTER   Your Majesty, do you know what your Guru is doing? He is walking around the streets mocking you. He is wearing a sign around his neck which says: "I am fallen, I am fallen. By initiating the King, I am fallen."

(The King becomes furious.)

KING   What! What an insult! First he initiates me and then he laughs at me, telling the world that I am corrupt and useless! He shall see the power of my anger! Have him arrested.

(Exit Minister. In a few minutes the King's Guru is brought in.)

KING   What kind of audacity do you cherish? What kind of stupidity do you enjoy? Your insolence knows no bounds!
GURU   O King, I am helpless. I too have a Master, and because I initiated you my Master is totally disgusted with me. He says that you did not deserve initiation, that only a spiritual person, a sincere seeker can be initiated. You have done countless wrong things. You have led an undivine, unspiritual life, and I initiated you before you were actually ready for spiritual life. That is why my Master is furious with me. He said that only if I acknowledge my mistake by wearing this sign will God forgive me.
KING   So it is your Master who is causing me this disgrace! That rogue! I knew you were a sincere man, a good man. You would not have caused me such embarrassment. Your Master will be arrested and you will be freed. Your Master

will be thrown into my deepest dungeon and left there for the rest of his life. (To Minister.) Minister, have my Guru's Master arrested and brought here immediately!

(In a few minutes the Master is brought before the King.)

KING Aaah, you fool, you rogue, you rascal! What embarrassment you have caused me! How you have disgraced my royal family and my dear subjects! You know what you have done! I will not waste a moment more on you. You shall spend the rest of your life in prison.

(The disciple-Guru bursts into tears.)

GURU Oh no, oh no. It is impossible. Oh King, it is I who have initiated you, and it is I who should pay the penalty. Let me remain in prison for the rest of my life, but don't punish my Master. He has hundreds and thousands of disciples. They will be fatherless.

KING Let his disciples be fatherless! He has made me an object of ridicule. He has mocked me, as though I were some insignificant creature. This is *my* kingdom, this is *my* world. And *I* sentence him to lifelong imprisonment.

LK 48. SCENE 5

(One week later. The King's Guru has been fasting to protest his Master's imprisonment. He is visiting his Master in jail.)

MASTER Since I am eating, you should also eat.

DISCIPLE No, until I can bring about your release, I will not eat. It is I who have been the cause of your suffering. It is I who deserve punishment. If I had not initiated the King, he would have punished me. But by initiating him, I have involved you in the picture, and now I shall not rest until I have saved you.

MASTER No, I involved myself. When you came to me I could have said to you, "Yes, it is a splendid idea. You have done the right thing." But I told you that it was wrong of you to initiate the King. It is my fault that I am here. I should have kept silent.

DISCIPLE How could you have kept silent? When your spiritual son does something wrong it is your duty to correct him, to perfect him. It is through this humiliation that I can enter into the domain of perfection. How could you have ignored me, how could you have been indifferent to me? You did the right thing, you did your duty. You showed me your utmost concern and for that I am most grateful. *(The Master smiles.)* I shall not leave you here. I shall fast unto death, if need be.

LK 49. SCENE 6

(The King's palace.)

MINISTER   Your Majesty, your preceptor will soon die from his fast, and then some calamity may take place. Please forgive my saying this, your Majesty, but if your Guru dies in the palace in this way, your subjects may misunderstand.
KING   Call him. Bring him here.

(Exit Minister.)

(Minister returns with King's Guru, who has become extremely weak from fasting and can hardly walk.)

KING   O Master, O Guru, tell me what you wish.
GURU   O King, you know what I want. I want you to release my Master. I initiated you, I pleased you. Now you please *me*. Release my Master.
KING   *(to Minister)* Bring me a large piece of paper. *(Minister brings the paper. The King writes something on it, saying each word as he puts it down.)* "I am illumined. I am illumined by the initiation of my Guru." *(Puts the sign around his neck.)* Now, let us go to see your Master.

(Exeunt omnes.)

LK 50. SCENE 7

(The prison. Enter the King, Minister and Guru. The King and his Guru both have their signs on.)

KING I have come here to set you free. Now, have you anything to say? Whatever you do, I shall gladly accept.

(The Master places his right hand on the King's head and his left hand on his disciple's head.)

MASTER *(to the King)* My blessing illumines you. *(To his disciple.)* My blessing forgives you and liberates you.

PART IV

SUPREME SACRIFICE

THE SUPREME SACRIFICE OF KING SHIBI

SRI CHINMOY

SU I. DRAMATIS PERSONÆ

KING SHIBI
PRINCE
PRINCESS
FIRST MINOR GOD
SECOND MINOR GOD
THIRD MINOR GOD
BRAHMA
INDRA
QUEEN
SERVANT OF THE KING

(King Shibi was great. He had many divine qualities. He was noble and just. He was pure and kind. When the strong attacked the weak, he would invariably and immediately protect the weak. He loved men and animals equally. He gave his life to save the life of a dove. He was spiritual in the strictest sense of the term.)

(This play is adapted from a story in the Puranas.)

SUPREME SACRIFICE

SU 2. SCENE 1

(King Shibi's palace. King, Prince and Princess are enjoying a family talk.)

PRINCESS   Father, I love you. Father, I am afraid of you.
KING   Why do you love me?
PRINCESS   I love you because your heart is all love.
KING   Why are you afraid of me?
PRINCESS   I am afraid of you because you are so great, unimaginably great. Father, please give me some sound advice. I know you don't want me to be afraid of you all the time.
KING   My child, let me tell you the real reason that you love me and the reason that you are afraid of me. Your heart and soul know how to enter into my heart and soul and become one with them. Therefore, you love me deeply. You are afraid of me because your vital and mind are weak. Your vital does not want to expand along with mine. Your mind does not have the same amount of faith in God as my mind has. For these two reasons you are afraid of me, and not because I am so great. Expand your dynamic vital. Your problem will be solved. Fill your mind with the life-saving and life-fulfilling faith. Your problem will be solved.
PRINCESS   Father, I shall do it. Father, I shall do it. I shall prove to be worthy of having you as my father and I shall prove to be a worthy Princess.
KING   Moreover, my child, if I am great, then you are also great. You are my daughter. What I have as a father and as a King is all yours. My greatness will never frighten you. My greatness will only inspire you to enter into my greatness and claim it as your very own. Now that I have told you the real reason that you are afraid of me, I am sure all your

problems will be solved. My child, don't be afraid of me. Take what I have. Be what I am.

PRINCESS Father, I shall. Father, I shall be.

PRINCE Now it is my turn. Father, I do not love you, but I admire you. I am not afraid of you, but I am jealous of you.

KING I appreciate your sincerity, my son. Now, tell me, why do you admire me and what makes you jealous of me?

PRINCE I admire you because you are powerful, the most powerful in the world. Everybody is at your command. Everybody is at your mercy. I am jealous of you because everybody adores you and touches your feet. Alas, they do not adore me. They do not touch my feet. They just smile at me.

KING When I grow old, I shall retire. You will replace me. At that time, the world will adore you and touch your feet.

PRINCESS I don't think so. Father, everybody adores you and touches your feet not because you are most powerful, not because you are the greatest King, but because you are all love, all concern and all compassion. My brother does not have these divine qualities in the least, so why should the world adore him and touch his feet?

PRINCE Father, look! Look! She is really jealous of me. Father, I have all the good qualities that you have and a few more. I run. You can't run. I sing. You can't sing. I climb. You can't climb. I swim and you can't swim.

PRINCESS *(sarcastically)* You fool, you have mentioned all your great qualities. I assure you that these qualities will not draw even one person towards you. It is simply impossible for the world to adore you and touch your feet for such common qualities. Don't fool yourself. Try to become great inwardly, like our father, with all the divine qualities of the heart. Then only will you really be happy, adored and worshipped by all.

SUPREME SACRIFICE

PRINCE   Stop! Stop! Don't preach! I can take care of my life. I shall take care of Father's kingdom. Needless to say, I shall take care of your life, too, when I become King.

PRINCESS   For God's sake, you don't have to take care of my life. I have two fathers to take care of my life. As long as this father is on earth, he will take care of my life. When he *(pointing at the King)* ends his earthly pilgrimage, my eternal Father will take care of my life. So you will be given no chance to take care of my heart's aspiration, my life's dedication and my soul's surrender.

KING   *(blessing the Prince)* Son, my outer wealth shall satisfy you. *(Blessing the Princess.)* Daughter, my awakened daughter, my inner wealth shall illumine and fulfil you.

SU 3. SCENE 2

(Three minor gods in Heaven.)

FIRST GOD   That King Shibi, on earth, is disturbing my inner poise.

SECOND GOD   Mine too.

THIRD GOD   Dear friends, what is wrong with Shibi? What is wrong with you two?

FIRST GOD   That Shibi has become a very great aspirant. Soon he will become a most advanced soul.

SECOND GOD   Shibi's heart is as vast as the ocean of love and compassion. His soul is illumination itself.

THIRD GOD   So what? If Shibi really becomes great or is already great, then we should be proud of him instead of jealous. He is, after all, God's most devoted son.

FIRST GOD   Today Shibi is great. Tomorrow he will be greater. The day after tomorrow he will be the greatest. And then he will outshine us all.

SECOND GOD   *(looking at the third god)* When the matchless glory of his life badly eclipses your inner sun, perhaps you will know what a stupid god you are. Don't be philosophical, for God's sake. Be practical.

THIRD GOD   It is a real shame that even the gods are jealous of a human being. *(Looking up.)* O God, You are truly kind to me. You have made me a perfect stranger to jealousy. Whosoever is great, whosoever possesses God's Divine Greatness, will be admired and adored by me, be he a human being or even an animal.

FIRST GOD   Since you have come to that kind of realisation, to me you are worse than an animal.

SECOND GOD   You are absolutely right, my good friend. He is undoubtedly inferior even to an animal. *(Looking at the third god.)* Go back to your most undeveloped stone life, to the mineral kingdom, for that is where you belong.

THIRD GOD   You two are corrupting the purity and beauty of Heaven with your impure and wild jealousy. I pronounce my most powerful curse on you. Heaven will soon get rid of you two. You two have cast a slur on Heaven. Poor Heaven, my Heaven, Indra's Heaven, Brahma's Heaven!

FIRST AND SECOND GODS   One more word and you will be found in the stone life. We shall extinguish your life in Heaven!

(Enter Brahma and Indra.)

(The three gods, as if nothing has happened, show their utmost reverence to Brahma and Indra.)

BRAHMA   Occultly we have observed your most deplorable dispute. Even Indra and I are not sure if Shibi is that great.

INDRA   So we have decided to go to Shibi's palace on earth to test him.

BRAHMA   If he is really that great, then we should and we must admire him — his love, his concern, his compassion and his sacrifice.

INDRA   And if he is not all that we hear about him, then the jealous gods can be happy.

BRAHMA   Hard is it to conquer jealousy.

INDRA   Alas, I suffered from that disease for a long time, but now jealousy and I do not live together. We live separately, we think separately and we fulfil our ideals separately. Now I am ready to touch the feet of anybody who is superior to me in spirituality.

BRAHMA   Indra, I admire your sincerity. I adore your humility.
INDRA   *(to the minor gods, smiling)* You three wait here and see. We two are entering into the world. Brahma will assume the form of a huge hawk and I shall assume the form of a tiny dove.

SUPREME SACRIFICE

SU 4. SCENE 3

(King Shibi's palace. The King and Queen are sitting on their thrones. The Prince and Princess are also present. Suddenly a beautiful dove flies in.)

DOVE O King Shibi, save me, save me! In you I seek my haven.

> I fear to speak, I fear to speak.
> My tongue is killed, my heart is weak.
> I fear to be, I fear to be.
> Long dead my life of faith in me.

KING *(caressing the dove)* Sweet bird, cast aside all your fear. My concern is for you. My protection is for you. I am all for you.

(A huge hawk flies in and starts chasing the dove. The King stops him and places the dove in his protecting lap.)

HAWK King, this bird is my prey. This bird is mine! You are grabbing my possession. I have worked hard to get this bird. O King, I am hungry. As you have the right to deal with human beings, so have I the right to deal with birds. O King, please don't be greedy. I eat my food and you eat yours.

KING O hawk, you are powerful, but I believe I am more powerful. You say that you are hungry. I shall feed you. Tell me what meat you would like to eat. Do you care for deer's meat? Do you care for bull's meat? Do you care for boar's meat? Just tell me what kind of meat you like best. In no time I shall feed you.

HAWK   To tell the truth, I care only for *dove's* meat.
KING   Unfortunately, that is impossible. The dove is under my adamantine protection. Any other meat I can give you and I shall give you, immediately and without fail.
HAWK   Are you sure? Will you not eat your words?
KING   Never. I give my word of honour.
HAWK   Then, O King, give me immediately the flesh of your own body equal in weight to the weight of this dove!
KING   That's all? Take it gladly. I give you my flesh.

(Shibi orders a pair of scales and a big, sharp knife. A servant brings them.)

HAWK   I am sick of hearing about your compassion. Here is a golden chance to prove it. One thing more: I want the piece of flesh right from your chest, and I want you to put the flesh on the scale and weigh it. Until the weight of the flesh is equal to that of the dove, I will not be satisfied!

(Shibi smiles and stabs his own chest and cuts out a piece of flesh and puts it on the scale opposite the dove. The bird weighs more.)

QUEEN   *(bursting into tears)* No more, my Lord, no more! I can't stand it. You rascal hawk! Be satisfied with this one piece. Otherwise, I shall order my soldiers to kill you.
HAWK   O Queen, you had better speak to the King. I know it is not an easy task to keep one's promise.
KING   I shall keep my promise. I shall take more flesh out of my body.
QUEEN   Impossible! My heart shall not permit you to do so. I claim your body to be mine, absolutely mine. Therefore, I shall not allow you to cut this body of mine. *(Holding firm her husband's hands.)* Now, you animal! *(Looking at the hawk.)*

SUPREME SACRIFICE

Only an animal can ask for human flesh! Look, since my husband and I are one, this time I am going to offer *my* flesh to add to my husband's flesh. I am sure that after this it will equal the weight of the dove. You filthy creature!

HAWK   Queen, call me what you will. After all, it is your own husband's promise. If he fails, he fails. The world will laugh at him, at his so-called compassion. Anyway, I am not going to accept your flesh; I want only *his* flesh.

KING   You are right, hawk. My flesh, only my flesh.

(The Queen starts weeping and screaming, and cursing the hawk. The King cheerfully cuts another piece of flesh from his chest and puts it on the scale. To everyone's surprise, the dove still weighs more.)

HAWK   All right. King, you can cut flesh from any part of your body you want to. But it must all equal the weight of the dove.

KING   Thank you, my kind friend.

(This time the King cuts a very large piece of flesh from his right arm and places it on the scale. Still the dove weighs more. Everybody is surprised and horror-struck. The Prince and Princess are bitterly crying, shedding helpless tears.)

PRINCESS   It is Father's promise, therefore I am helpless.

PRINCE   Sister, I know what you mean about Father's promise. I too am helpless. Otherwise, by this time I would have kicked this ugly animal out.

KING   My daughter, my son, please, please allow me to fulfil my promise peacefully and cheerfully.

(This time the King cuts quite a few pieces from his body and puts them on the scale opposite the dove. Alas even then the dove weighs more. Disappointed, disheartened and utterly bewildered, he slowly steps onto the scale with his whole body. The scale now balances perfectly. The two birds immediately assume the forms of Brahma and Indra.)

BRAHMA   O peerless King Shibi, you deserve love, admiration and adoration from God's entire creation. I tested you. I was the hawk.

INDRA   I was the dove. Your heart is the infinite Compassion of the Supreme. Your life is the transcendental Pride of the Supreme.

(Shibi bows down to Brahma and Indra.)

SUPREME SACRIFICE

SU 5. SCENE 4

(In Heaven, the first two minor gods are hiding in shame and the third god is dancing with joy.)

THIRD GOD   I knew it! I knew that Shibi has no equal either on earth or in Heaven. The depth of his heart is unfathomable. The height of his soul is immeasurable. His life is the fully manifested compassion of the Supreme's supreme Perfection.

BUDDHAM SARANAM GACCHAMI

SRI CHINMOY

SU 6. DRAMATIS PERSONÆ

GATEMAN
DEVADATTA (COUSIN OF THE BUDDHA AND A CLOSE FRIEND OF
   AJATASHATRU)
AJATASHATRU (THE PRINCE, LATER KING)
DR. JAIVAKA (PHYSICIAN OF KING AJATASHATRU)
THE BUDDHA
DISCIPLES OF THE BUDDHA

SUPREME SACRIFICE

SU 7. SCENE I

(King Bimbisara's palace. Enter Devadatta.)

GATEMAN May I know whom you want, sir?
DEVADATTA Yes, please go and tell Prince Ajatashatru that his friend Devadatta is here.

(Exit Gateman. Enter Ajatashatru.)

AJATASHATRU Come in, come in. I am so happy to see you.
DEVADATTA I wish to have a private audience with you. May I?
AJATASHATRU Yes, come into my chamber, come into my room. Nobody is there.

SRI CHINMOY

SU 8. SCENE 2

(A most beautiful room. Enter Ajatashatru and Devadatta.)

DEVADATTA   Ajatashatru, my friend, tell me frankly: are you jealous of anybody?

AJATASHATRU   I don't think so.

DEVADATTA   I am. I am so jealous of Buddha. But my jealousy does not help me at all. He now has thousands of disciples, while I have only a few. And even those few disciples are leaving me and going to him. I hate him! I want to kill him!

AJATASHATRU   Oh, now it seems to me that I am also jealous of someone.

DEVADATTA   Ah, you are also jealous of someone? Please tell me who.

AJATASHATRU   I am jealous of my father, the King. Everybody touches his feet; everybody adores him. He has so much power and wealth.

DEVADATTA   You see, you have as much reason to be jealous of your father as I have to be jealous of Buddha. But we can easily solve your problem.

AJATASHATRU   If you solve my problem I will also try to solve your problem, Devadatta.

DEVADATTA   Ajatashatru, your father is old. This is the time for him to take rest and retire, but these old men never give way. Even until the last moment they want to enjoy the world, they want to lord it over the world. In every way you have surpassed your father. You have strength; you have power. Just throw the old man into prison and then you will become King. You can rule his kingdom peacefully and bravely. Who is there to stop you? I shall help you.

SUPREME SACRIFICE

AJATASHATRU It is an excellent idea, an excellent idea! I shall do it. And when I become King, I promise you, Devadatta, I shall help you kill Buddha.

DEVADATTA Be sure you don't eat your promise, Ajatashatru. Now you are the Prince, but you will soon be King. And it is on the strength of my advice that you will become King.

AJATASHATRU I am not a mean fellow. I shall remember your help. I want to become King, and with your advice I shall fulfil my desire. Then I shall help you get rid of Buddha.

(Months later. King Ajatashatru is consulting his physician, Dr. Jaivaka.)

AJATASHATRU   Why have I begun to suffer from all kinds of diseases and ailments since I have become King? When I was Prince I was always healthy and robust. But now I have lost all my health. Is it because of the pressure of my work?

DR. JAIVAKA   No, King, it is not that which is causing your suffering.

AJATASHATRU   Why, then, am I suffering?

DR. JAIVAKA   Your disease, King, is psychological. You have an inner disease.

AJATASHATRU   What kind of inner disease? What do you mean by inner disease, Dr. Jaivaka? How will you cure me?

DR. JAIVAKA   O King, I will not be able to cure you because your disease is not physical. Your disease is mental, psychological, spiritual. Only Buddha can cure you.

AJATASHATRU   Buddha? Lord Buddha? Do you know that Devadatta and I are intimate friends, most intimate friends?

DR. JAIVAKA   Yes, I know it. And I also know that Devadatta helped you become King.

AJATASHATRU   Certainly he did. And I promised him that I would help him get rid of Buddha.

DR. JAIVAKA   That also I have heard. I am fully aware of it.

AJATASHATRU   Then why do you say that Buddha can cure me? That is impossible.

DR. JAIVAKA   O King, do you want me to tell you the truth, or do you want me to flatter you? No ordinary doctor can cure you. Only Buddha the Doctor can cure you. Your heart is extremely pure. Your heart is feeling miserable for what you have done to your father and for what you have been doing to Buddha, the innocent Buddha, the Light of the world. Once you rolled a big stone towards him while he was meditating on his disciples, but it veered away before hitting him. On another occasion, you set a mad elephant to destroy him. But Buddha just looked at the elephant and it bowed down to him. Instigated by Devadatta, in various ways you have tried to kill him, but each time you have failed, and you will always fail. Buddha has realised the highest Truth. Your heart is crying for the highest Truth. This is your disease, the disease of your spiritual heart. If you really want to be cured, go to Buddha. He is the Divine Doctor, the Doctor Supreme. Nobody on earth but Buddha can cure you. He can and he will.

AJATASHATRU O human doctor, you are sending me to the Divine Doctor. I am grateful. My life of vital desire has ended. My life of soul's aspiration is beginning with your divine advice.

DR. JAIVAKA Your soul is more than ready to accept the Buddha's Light. Buddha the infinite Light will transform Ajatashatru, the King of ignorance, into Ajatashatru, the Light of immortalising Bliss.

SU 10. SCENE 4

(The Buddha with hundreds of disciples. Enter King Ajatashatru. All the disciples are excited. Ajatashatru prostrates himself before the Buddha.)

AJATASHATRU   O Lord of the world, out of our stupendous ignorance my friend Devadatta and I tried to kill you several times, but we failed, badly failed. Today I am at your august feet, to be killed immediately by your wisdom-sun.

BUDDHA   O King....

AJATASHATRU   Master, I am not your King. You are the King of my heart and soul. You are the Lord of my heart and soul. I am your undeserving slave.

BUDDHA   You are not my slave, you are my son, my chosen son. My compassion-sun forgives your ignorance-night. My wisdom-sun illumines, liberates and immortalises your heart's cry.

(Enter Devadatta. Falls at the feet of the Buddha.)

DEVADATTA   Siddhartha, while we two were quite young I fought with you over the possession of a bird. The strength of my unruly, undivine vital had to surrender to the strength of your all-loving heart. You won the bird. I told you that one day with my vital love of power I would conquer your heart's power of love. Since then I have tried in hundreds of ways to humiliate you, to ruin your mission and to kill you, but I have failed. You forgave me then, O Siddhartha. Now, O Buddha, my shameless life desperately begs your forgiveness.

BUDDHA   Devadatta, forgiveness is granted.

SUPREME SACRIFICE

DEVADATTA   O Buddha, if you have really forgiven this inhuman creature, then do me another favour out of your infinite bounty. Your heart of compassion took care of that innocent bird. Now I pray to you to take care of the crying, bleeding bird inside my heart. And also I pray to you to take care of its cage, this body.

(Devadatta sings three times.)

Buddham saranam gacchami
dhammam saranam gacchami
sangham saranam gacchami

(I go to the Buddha for refuge.
I go to the *Dharma* for refuge.
I go to the Order for refuge.)

SURYA AND SANJNA

SRI CHINMOY

SU II. DRAMATIS PERSONÆ

NARRATOR
MORTALS
FIRST COSMIC GOD
SECOND COSMIC GOD
THIRD COSMIC GOD
FOURTH COSMIC GOD
FIFTH COSMIC GOD
SURYA (THE SUN-GOD)
VAYU (ANOTHER COSMIC GOD)
SANJNA (A MOST BEAUTIFUL GIRL, LATER WIFE OF SURYA)
VISHWAKARMA (SANJNA'S FATHER, THE ARCHITECT OF THE UNI-
    VERSE)
YAMA, VAIVASWATHA (SONS OF SURYA AND SANJNA)
YAMUNA (DAUGHTER OF SURYA AND SANJNA)
CHHAYA (HANDMAID OF SANJNA)
SHANI, MANU (SONS OF SURYA AND CHHAYA)
TAPTI (DAUGHTER OF SURYA AND CHHAYA)
VISHNU
SHIVA
KUMARA

SUPREME SACRIFICE

SU 12. SCENE I

(The mortals on earth are offering their soulful prayers to Surya, the sun-god.)

MORTALS   *(chanting together)*

   Aum
   bhur bhuvah svah
   tat savitur varenyam
   bhargo devasya dhimahi
   dhiyo yo nah pracodayat

(We meditate on the transcendental glory of the Deity Supreme, who is inside the heart of the earth, inside the life of the sky and inside the soul of the Heaven. May He stimulate and illumine our minds.)

SU 13. SCENE 2

NARRATOR Every day Surya draws his golden chariot across the heavens, offering light and illumination to the heavens and to the earth.

(In Heaven a cosmic god is speaking to Surya.)

FIRST COSMIC GOD Surya, what is wrong with you today? Why are you so unhappy, O sun-god? Your unhappiness is creating tremendous problems for earth. Earth has become all darkness. There is tremendous chaos there. If you go on this way, if you have a heavy heart and do not do your job, the earth will be doomed. Heaven also will be doomed. It is your presence that illumines the heavens as well as the earth. Tell me, Surya, what is wrong with you today?

SURYA I shall confide in you. I am in love.

FIRST COSMIC GOD You are in love? With whom are you in love?

SURYA I am in love with a most beautiful girl whom I saw yesterday when I was riding across the heavens. Her beauty has conquered my heart. Her beauty has enslaved my mind. The memory of her beauty is torturing me. I cannot do anything but think of her. My heart is crying for her. What shall I do?

SUPREME SACRIFICE

SU 14. SCENE 3

(The cosmic gods are having a meeting.)

FIRST COSMIC GOD   Something has to be done. If Surya goes on in this way, if he does not do his job, then we will be in total darkness.

SECOND COSMIC GOD   The *asuras* will destroy the earth. Earth will cry to us for blessings, and we will not be able to offer any. Earth will cry in utter despair, and we will be helpless.

THIRD COSMIC GOD   And we will be destroyed ourselves very soon if Surya does not come back and offer his light to us.

VAYU   Don't worry. I am going in search of that girl. I shall find her, and then I shall make arrangements for her to marry Surya.

FOURTH COSMIC GOD   If you are successful, we shall be most grateful.

FIFTH COSMIC GOD   And if you are not, then we shall all be ruined.

VAYU   Don't worry, my friends. I know I have the capacity. I can easily find out who she is; I can easily get them together; I can easily arrange for their marriage.

COSMIC GODS   *(together)* All our joy, all our love, all our gratitude to you, dearest brother Vayu.

(Exit Vayu.)

SU 15. SCENE 4

(A most beautiful girl is sitting in a corner of the Celestial Dwellings. Enter Vayu.)

VAYU   You! Ah, I have discovered you at last. Please tell me your name. *(She gives him a sulky smile.)* Tell me. Tell me, please. Our Lord Surya is deeply in love with you. Because of you, he is not doing his work any more and we shall soon be plunged into total darkness. Tell me, tell me who you are or Heaven and earth will perish. Whose daughter are you?

SANJNA   My name is Sanjna. My father is Vishwakarma.

VAYU   Your father is Vishwakarma? You are his daughter? Come, let us go to your father's house. I shall tell him all about our Surya's love for you.

SANJNA   Are you sure he loves me?

VAYU   Loves you! Loves you! That is an understatement. His heart is crying for you. His heart is breaking for you. He can think of nothing but you. He needs you; he desperately needs you, and he wants to marry you. All the cosmic gods will celebrate your wedding. We shall all have infinite joy, infinite delight to see you two united.

SANJNA   *(smiling)* Come with me.

(Exeunt Vayu and Sanjna.)

SUPREME SACRIFICE

SU 16. SCENE 5

(Vishwakarma's home. Enter Sanjna with Vayu.)

VISHWAKARMA Sanjna, I have told you repeatedly not to speak to strangers. What do you mean by bringing home an unknown person to me?

VAYU O Vishwakarma, I may not be known to you, but you are well known to me. I have not come here to hurt you or to hurt your daughter. I have come to tell you something that will give you enormous joy. The sun god, Surya, without whom we cannot exist, is in love with your daughter. All the cosmic gods have met together, and they have sent me to you. Please listen to our prayer. Allow your daughter to marry Surya. Their marriage will have the blessings of the entire earth and all the higher worlds.

VISHWAKARMA I can't believe my ears! I can't believe my eyes! Surya likes my daughter?

SANJNA Likes! Likes! He loves me!

VAYU O Vishwakarma, you ask if Surya likes your daughter. She says that he loves her. But I wish to say that both of these are understatements. Your daughter has unconditionally conquered his heart. He is pining away for her.

VISHWAKARMA Then let us not delay. Let us arrange for the wedding to be celebrated as soon as possible. Where will it take place?

VAYU In the highest regions of Heaven. Tomorrow you bring your daughter, and all the cosmic gods will be there. We shall celebrate the wedding of Surya and Sanjna.

SRI CHINMOY

SU 17. SCENE 6

NARRATOR   All the cosmic gods are present. Surya and Sanjna's wedding takes place. Now Surya has become the happiest god. Once again he draws his chariot across the heavens with enormous delight. Earth is extremely happy with their marriage, since earth is once more getting sunshine. Heaven is happy, since Heaven is getting illumination as before. Sanjna is appreciated, admired and adored by everyone.

SUPREME SACRIFICE

SU 18. SCENE 7

NARRATOR Sanjna has long since given birth to two most beautiful sons, and one daughter: Yama, Vaivaswatha and Yamuna.

(The three children are together in the palace of their father.)

YAMA We are so proud to have such parents. Our father is so great; our mother is so beautiful.
VAIVASWATHA Indeed we are happy, proud and blessed.
YAMUNA I am the happiest woman in God's creation. My father is the most powerful of all the gods. My mother is the most beautiful woman of all. We are the children of the most powerful and illumining, and of the most beautiful and charming parents. None can be prouder than we three.

SU 19. SCENE 8

(In Sanjna's room.)

SANJNA   Chhaya! *(Enter Chhaya.)* Chhaya, I have made a decision. I have lived with my beloved Lord for many years, but slowly his fiery brightness is killing me. His light is so powerful that his very presence tortures me. When I look at him I am blinded; when I take a breath I breathe in only fire. I am burning up. His golden rays are destroying my very existence. It is impossible for me to stay with him in spite of his deep love for me. I wish you to replace me.

CHHAYA   *(with enormous joy)* I will be Surya's wife?

SANJNA   Yes, Chhaya. He will not know. Even when he comes home after offering his light to Heaven and earth, his brilliance remains always with him. His own brilliance will blind him, and he will not realise that you are not his real wife.

CHHAYA   I am so grateful to you, Mistress, for allowing me to replace you.

SANJNA   *(blessing Chhaya)* You take my place. I am going to take shelter in a cool, dense forest. There I shall live my own life, and everything will be mild, cool and soothing.

SUPREME SACRIFICE

SU 20. SCENE 9

NARRATOR   In the course of time Surya and Chhaya had three children — also two boys and a girl. Their names were Shani, Manu and Tapti. Although they were step-brothers and step-sisters, Yama, Vaivaswatha and Yamuna became very good friends with Shani, Manu and Tapti. They were all very affectionate to each other. And although Chhaya was secretly fonder of her own children than of Sanjna's children, she used to hide her favouritism for fear that Sanjna's children would betray her secret.

(Chhaya is secretly offering special sweets and gifts to her three children. Enter Yama suddenly and sees her.)

YAMA   *(furious)* You impostor! Are you like that, then? We never thought that you were so mean. You are offering sweets and gifts to your own children and not to us. You maidservant! We have kept the secret that you were our mother's handmaid because we did not want our father to be angry with our mother, yet even then you show favouritism to your own children. You did not marry our father. To think that you act as his wife! You are not fit to be called mother by us! Had our father known that you were not his real wife he would have killed you long ago! You worthless creature! I shall kick you!

CHHAYA   Stop, Yama! Don't you dare kick me! I curse you! You will suffer tremendous pain in your right leg, and soon you will not be able to walk on it. You will be crippled.

(Exit Yama, running.)

SRI CHINMOY

SU 21. SCENE 10

(Outside Surya's room. Enter Yama and knocks at the door. Surya is not inside. Yama waits outside the door. Enter Surya.)

SURYA   Yama, what do you want? Is there something wrong?
YAMA   Father, I have something to tell you.
SURYA   Why are you so frightened and sad? What is wrong, my son?
YAMA   Father, I have been cursed.
SURYA   By whom?
YAMA   By my mother.
SURYA   Oh, well, don't worry. What did she say?
YAMA   She said I will be crippled; my right leg will be paralysed.
SURYA   Don't worry. She is your mother. A mother's curse does not come true.

(Yama's leg is already swollen and painful. He cannot move it at all.)

SURYA   It is very strange, but it seems that her curse has come true. Well, don't worry, my son. Your mother was angry with you for some reason, but I shall cure you. *(Using his occult power he cures Yama's leg.)* My son, I have always heard that a mother's curse on her children will never come true, for the lives of her children are dearer to her than her own life. I can't understand why your mother's curse affected you. Even if you did something wrong, something very serious, still she is your mother. For her to curse you and for her curse to come true is very strange, very strange. There must be something wrong.
YAMA   Father, shall I tell you the secret?

SURYA   What is your secret, my son? Tell me.

YAMA   Father, you have the deepest love for our mother, Sanjna. But I must tell you that she left us long ago. She was afraid of you. Your brilliance blinded her. Your fiery looks burned her. Your very presence tortured her. She could not bear your power and your brilliance, so she asked her handmaid, Chhaya, to take her place and be our mother. Now she is living in the thick, cool forest. We did not tell you because we thought that you would bring our mother back and then she would die. But today I saw my step-mother, Chhaya, giving sweets and gifts secretly to her own children. I got angry and threatened to kick her. When I said this she cursed me, and her curse came true because she is not my real mother.

SURYA   *(stupefied)* Sanjna is gone? My beloved Sanjna has left me? I have been giving all my love and affection to an impostor? Yama, Yama, my son, what shall I do? I must have my darling Sanjna back. But I do not want to hurt her. I do not want to burn her with my fiery presence.

YAMA   Perhaps, Father, there is someone who will know how to diminish your fiery power. Then Mother can come back to you.

SURYA   You are right. Tell Vayu to search the entire universe until he finds someone who can diminish my light.

YAMA   Yes, Father. I shall tell him.

(Exit Yama.)

SU 22. SCENE II

(Surya's room. Enter Vayu and Vishwakarma.)

VAYU   Surya, I have found the person who can help you.

VISHWAKARMA   Surya, I am the architect of this universe. I can take away enough of your brilliance so that my daughter will be able to live with you again. Here is my lathe. I shall grind off an eighth part of your brightness and power. This eighth will fall to earth shining and blazing. But before it touches the ground I shall transform it, I shall shape it. It will become three particular things. From this eighth part of your brilliance will come the discus of Vishnu, which is the Sudarshan *chakra;* the trident of Shiva and the lance of Kumara.

(Vishwakarma carves off a portion of Surya's light. Vishnu, Shiva and Kumara appear momentarily, side-stage, with their weapons.)

SURYA   You have saved me, dearest Father. You have given me another chance to live happily with my beloved wife.

(He touches Vishwakarma's feet.)

SUPREME SACRIFICE

SU 23. SCENE 12

(The forest. Surya is searching for Sanjna.)

SURYA   *(seeing her at last)* Forgive me, forgive me, my beloved Sanjna. I did not know that I was hurting you. Now my brilliance has diminished, and you shall suffer no more.

SANJNA   I always loved you, I love you still. But the brilliance of your light was killing me. That was the only reason I left you. I forgive you, my dearest husband. With all my heart I forgive you.

(Enter Vayu, Vishwakarma and the six children.)

SANJNA   Father, Father, you have saved us. We really loved each other. Surya loved me, and I loved him wholeheartedly. Only I could not bear his fiery presence. But now that you have taken away a little bit of his brilliance, I can live with him again. You have all my heart's joy and gratitude. It is you, Father, who have given us this boon — to remain together, eternally one.

SURYA AND SANJNA   *(together)* Father, we are all gratitude to you.

HARISH CHANDRA

SRI CHINMOY

SU 24. DRAMATIS PERSONÆ

KING HARISH CHANDRA
QUEEN SHAIVYA (HIS WIFE)
VISHWAMITRA (A GREAT SAGE)
ROHITASHWA (THE PRINCE, SON OF HARISH CHANDRA AND SHAIVYA)
COMMANDER-IN-CHIEF
PRIME MINISTER
MINISTER OF EDUCATION
MINISTER OF FINANCE
MINISTER OF COMMERCE
MANY SUBJECTS
PRIEST
CROWD OF SLAVE DEALERS AND SLAVES
RICH MAN
VILLAGE BRAHMIN
CHANDALA [UNDERTAKER] (LATER, YAMARAJ THE KING OF DEATH)

(Harish Chandra was the most pious King in Ayodhya. He was sincerity incarnate. His continuous faith in an integral life was unparalleled.)

(This play is adapted from the original story in the Markandeya Purana.)

SUPREME SACRIFICE

SU 25. SCENE I

(King Harish Chandra and Queen Shaivya are roaming in the forest and enjoying themselves.)

HARISH CHANDRA   Shaivya, dearest to my heart and nearest to my soul, I have not heard you sing for a long, long time. Please do me a great favour: sing a song.

(Shaivya sings.)

Into the world of beauty's flame,
Into the world of offering's game,
Into the world of lustre-flood,
I came, I came, my existence came.

HARISH CHANDRA   Shaivya, your life's name is duty. Your soul's name is beauty. Your heart's name is purity. And the name of your voice is the flood of ecstasy. Shaivya, in you I am complete, and with you I am perfect.

(Suddenly, the King and the Queen hear a most pitiful cry.)

THE VOICE   Save me! Help me! Save me! Help me!

(Harish Chandra runs at top speed towards the sound. He comes to a spot where Vishwamitra is rapt in trance. The King is fully aware of the fact that Vishwamitra's anger is not only of the quickest but also of the wildest. Immediately he touches the feet of the sage. With his hands folded he speaks.)

HARISH CHANDRA   O sage of the highest magnitude, your august forgiveness my tremulous heart implores. I have tortured your sublime peace. Your forgiveness I deserve not, but my heart longs for your compassion-flood.

VISHWAMITRA   Your end is come. Today marks the end of your earthly existence. You heard the voice of the spirit crying. I want to conquer the spirit of sciences. I want to control the spirit. I want to lord it over the spirit. Tremendous success was fast approaching my fearsome attempt. But now, you fool, you rascal, you have ruined everything. Prepare yourself to brave my fatal curse. In the twinkling of an eye, my third eye shall utterly destroy your entire kingdom!

HARISH CHANDRA   O peerless sage, kill me; destroy my life, but not my kingdom. Innocent are my subjects. Pure is my kingdom. Destroy them not, I pray. Demand anything else. In no time I shall fulfil your express command, in no time!

VISHWAMITRA   All right. Remember your promise. If you fail to fulfil your promise, my all-destructive curse shall embrace your most beautiful kingdom. You have badly and shamelessly prevented me from fulfilling my desire of today. Tomorrow I shall come to your palace and bless you with my second and last, absolutely last desire. Tomorrow if you fail, your existence and the existence of your vast kingdom will be found in the land of nowhere.

SUPREME SACRIFICE

SU 26. SCENE 2

(The following day, Harish Chandra is seated on his supremely beautiful throne. Behind him are seated Shaivya and the little Prince, Rohitashwa. Right in front of the King are seated his ministers and the commander-in-chief. Vishwamitra rushes in.)

VISHWAMITRA Harish Chandra, give me your kingdom! Leave it with me now and forever. This is *my* kingdom. You must immediately leave my palace and my kingdom. Today if you break your promise of yesterday, your life and your kingdom's life will be doomed all at once. Yesterday I wanted to destroy you and your kingdom. But today I just want to have your kingdom. That's all.

HARISH CHANDRA O most venerable Sir, to you I offer my kingdom, my kingdom's heart and soul. My eyes and feet shall now proceed towards an uncharted land.

SHAIVYA *(to King)* My Lord, you can never go alone. You cannot deny the breath of my heart. You cannot deny our fondest child Rohitashwa. Your son and I shall follow you. You are our all. You are sincerity's all. You are truth's all.

(Shaivya sings the farewell song to the palace.)

O Lord, where is the Truth?
"Where your Beloved is."
Who is my Beloved, who?
"In whom your life is peace."

(The King, the Queen and the little Prince bow down to the sage Vishwamitra and are ready to leave the palace. The helpless ministers and the commander-in-chief offer their heartfelt and soulful affection, love, appreciation, admiration and adoration to their beloved King.)

PRIME MINISTER   Your Majesty, you will always be remembered with highest praise, deepest fondness and mightiest adoration.

VISHWAMITRA   Enough! Shut up!

MINISTER OF EDUCATION   Your Majesty, without any hyperbolical encomiums, you are a King in the highest degree amiable and adorable.

VISHWAMITRA   Enough! Shut up!

MINISTER OF FINANCE   Your Majesty, I have served you with transcendental joy and pride.

VISHWAMITRA   Enough! Shut up!

MINISTER OF COMMERCE   Your Majesty, your supremely devoted life may now pass in penury, but never in obscurity.

VISHWAMITRA   Enough! Shut up!

COMMANDER-IN-CHIEF   Your Majesty, we shall, before long, thunder against this heartless brute. We shall without fail bring you back to your kingdom.

VISHWAMITRA   Enough, enough, enough! Shut up! Shut up! Shut up! You feeble heart, you insignificant creature! *(Turning towards Harish Chandra.)* Harish Chandra, delay not! My indomitable will shall brook no delay. Leave my palace. Leave my kingdom.

(The King, the Queen and the Prince leave the palace. On the way, innumerable subjects pay their last homage in silence to the royal family. Pure love wells forth from the inmost recesses of their hearts.)

SUPREME SACRIFICE

SU 27. SCENE 3

(Harish Chandra, Shaivya and Rohitashwa have travelled a few miles. All of a sudden they hear a frightening voice. They turn around only to see Vishwamitra approaching them in the greatest hurry imaginable.)

VISHWAMITRA   Stop, Harish Chandra! I had not the slightest idea that you were a rogue of the deepest dye. No doubt you have made a generous gift. But what about the *dakshina*, the sacerdotal fee? I believe you are an Aryan. I believe you are an Indian. Have I to remind you of the simplest religious practice that any gift offered to someone must needs be followed by dakshina? Tell me why and how you have managed to forget such a simple thing. Shall I call you the worst possible fool, or the worst possible rogue? I think the latter you rightly deserve.

HARISH CHANDRA   O sage, at your feet I placed everything that I had. Nothing have I now. Please give me a fleeting month. At the end of the month I shall offer you my humble dakshina.

VISHWAMITRA   Harish Chandra, remember your promise. When this month comes to an end I shall approach you and demand my absolutely legitimate due.

HARISH CHANDRA   O sage, by your grace, by God's Grace, I shall be worthy of my heart's soulful promise. At the end of the month please bless me with your august presence and collect your due.

VISHWAMITRA   All right.

SU 28. SCENE 4

(The King, the Queen and the little Prince wander from place to place, land to land, with no destination whatsoever.)

HARISH CHANDRA   Alas, how can I pay my dakshina to the sage? The fateful month is nearly over. I have left no stone unturned to get a job. No, not a single soul is kind enough to employ me. They say I am weak. They feel I shall be of no use to them. Alas, stark starvation is responsible for my poor health.

ROHITASHWA   Mother, Mother, I am very hungry. I am very tired. I cannot walk, I shall *not* walk any farther. My head, my stomach and my feet are burning like a hot oven. Look at my feet, look! They are full of blisters. I think I have run a thorn into my left foot. Where are our horses? Where is my father's chariot?

SHAIVYA   *(shedding unavoidable tears)* My child, we are nearing a temple. It is the best temple in Varanasi. I am sure they will give us something to eat. And perhaps your father will get a job there. Then we shall be rich and happy again.

(The three arrive at the temple gate in the small hours of the morning.)

PRIEST   Who are you? What brings you people here at this odd hour?

HARISH CHANDRA   We have been travelling and travelling. We are hungry and exhausted, Our son is totally exhausted and extremely hungry. We shall be so grateful to you if you bless him with some *prasad* from your holy temple.

(The priest goes inside the temple and brings some prasad for the child and gives it to him. The hungry child eats with greatest joy.)

HARISH CHANDRA   Thanks, thanks a million times to you, O chosen son of God! Would you care to fulfil another desire of mine?

PRIEST   Certainly, by all means, if it is within my capacity.

HARISH CHANDRA   Could you give me some work here?

PRIEST   Work! What kind of work? Oh, no, I can't give you any work. impossible. Your face shows all the marks of a Kshatriya. I can't employ a Kshatriya to work under me. This is a temple. Here only the Brahmins are supposed to work. Kshatriya, no. Vaishya, no. Shudra, no. Only a Brahmin. I am sorry, you must look for a job elsewhere.

HARISH CHANDRA   I shall. Anyway I deeply thank you for the food. Our son's precious life is saved. Thank you again.

(Exeunt King, Queen and Rohitashwa.)

(The family is wandering along a crowded street.)

SHAIVYA The month is over today. I am sure the sage will not forget us.

HARISH CHANDRA I am sure he will not forgive us.

(Vishwamitra comes rushing in.)

VISHWAMITRA Harish Chandra, today ends the month. Where is your dakshina, where?

SHAIVYA We know it, O great sage. But the day is not yet over. It will be at least four hours before the sun goes to sleep.

HARISH CHANDRA O sage, just before the day comes to its close please bless us with your divine presence. I shall, without fail, offer you my dakshina.

VISHWAMITRA Remember, Harish Chandra, remember your promise!

(Exit Vishwamitra.)

SHAIVYA My Lord, look, there is a market. Let us go over there and see our fate.

(They enter the market. Here they see slaves being bought and sold.)

HARISH CHANDRA Ah, at long last I have found the place. I am more than willing to be anybody's slave. I shall sell myself. *(He approaches a rich man and with folded hands begs the man to buy him.)* Please, please buy me. I badly need money. I urgently need money.

SUPREME SACRIFICE

RICH MAN   Sorry, I can't buy you. I see no strength in your body. You will be a useless slave. Sorry, I won't have you. But I will buy your wife. She can help my wife in the kitchen.

(Shaivya, overjoyed, with folded hands speaks to the kind customer.)

SHAIVYA   Be pleased to feel my heart's gratitude. I want to help my husband. You are our saviour.

(Harish Chandra sinks his head into his palms.)

HARISH CHANDRA   O merciful Lord, have I to sell my own wife, my most precious treasure here on earth and there in Heaven? No, I simply can't. My wife is infinitely dearer than my life itself.

SHAIVYA   You must not swerve from the path of truth. The preservation of truth is infinitely more important than the prestige of any human being. You cannot make a cowardly escape from reality. This is the hour when the divine courage must enfold you with its celestial wings. Who else will or can uphold the truth if not you, my beloved? You *have* to keep to your divine promise.

HARISH CHANDRA   Yes, Shaivya, I remember my promise to the sage. But to sell you, my own, my very own?

SHAIVYA   Fear not, my Lord, this heart of mine shall remain eternally yours.

RICH MAN   I can't waste any more time. *(Looking at Harish Chandra.)* Either sell your wife immediately or leave me alone. Take this sum of five hundred gold coins.

(Harish Chandra accepts the money with his head hanging in utter shame.)

RICH MAN   *(turning toward Shaivya)* You follow me.

(Rohitashwa starts crying and screaming.)

ROHITASHWA   Mother, Mother, where are you going? I can't stay without you, Mother.

RICH MAN   All right. Let me give to the father two hundred and fifty gold coins for the son. Come along, you little fellow.

A VILLAGE BRAHMIN   Shame, shame! Look at this fellow. He has sold his wife and son. How can one sell one's own wife and son? O God, did You not give a heart to this low creature when You gave him a human birth? O God, You alone know what more unthinkable things I shall have to see in Your creation. O God, take me to the other world. This world is simply unbearable!

(The master, Shaivya and Rohitashwa start walking towards their destination while Harish Chandra walks along the street distressed and disheartened, with no destination at all. Vishwamitra appears.)

VISHWAMITRA   Harish Chandra, the time is up. Give me your dakshina.

HARISH CHANDRA   Be pleased to accept this humble dakshina.

(He hands seven hundred and fifty gold coins to the sage.)

VISHWAMITRA   Shame! Shame! That's not enough. Once upon a time you were a great King. Such a small dakshina is beneath your dignity. You must give me at least two hundred and fifty more gold coins. It is imperatively necessary. If not....

HARISH CHANDRA   O venerable sage! By your grace, by God's Grace, one hour is still at my disposal. Please come to me before the last fateful hour fades. In the meantime I shall get the money.
VISHWAMITRA   Remember, remember your promise!

(Exit Vishwamitra.)

HARISH CHANDRA   O Lord Supreme, my beloved wife I have lost, and my only son I have lost. All, all I have lost except this wretched Harish Chandra. Let me go to the market again and see if I can sell my most unlucky body. If I fail to sell myself, then my boat shall sink right near the shore.

(Harish Chandra enters into the market.)

HARISH CHANDRA   O! Is there no kind-hearted man to buy me? I have come to sell myself, my body and my soul.

(A chandala [an undertaker] signals Harish Chandra. In his hands there is a stick and a skull.)

CHANDALA   Come here! Follow me! How much money do you want?
HARISH CHANDRA   Only two hundred and fifty gold coins.
CHANDALA   That's all? There you are. *(He hands two hundred and fifty gold coins to Harish Chandra.)* Now follow me. Your duty is to wait on dead bodies. You have to demand from the members of the deceased's family rice, cloth and money before you cremate the corpse.
HARISH CHANDRA   Indeed, I shall do that.

SRI CHINMOY

SU 30. SCENE 6

(Rohitashwa sits down on the steps of a bathing ghat beside the river Ganga.)

ROHITASHWA

> I remember....
> My mother loved me, her world.
> My father loved me, his dream.
> My home loved me, its "supreme."
> I remember....
> I prayed with the blooming dawn,
> I played with the glowing sun.
> My life, the nectar-fun.
> I remember....
> I sang with the twinkling stars,
> I danced with the floating moon.
> All lost, alas, too soon.
> I remember, I remember, I remember.

(Rohitashwa's face has become an everchanging panorama of dark fear and endless despair. Enter Shaivya.)

SHAIVYA   My son *(caressing him)*, don't feel sad. One day we shall meet your father. I am sure he constantly thinks of us as we constantly think of him. One day the whole world will admire and adore your father for his great sense of truth and his tremendous and unprecedented sacrifice. Rohitashwa, go and play in the garden. I shall join you in the evening. Now I have to work hard in the kitchen. Today I shall make a most delicious meal for you, my son.

ROHITASHWA Please, don't forget to come and play with me in the evening.
SHAIVYA My son, without fail I shall come and play with you.

(Shaivya leaves for the house and Rohitashwa for the garden.)

SRI CHINMOY

SU 31. SCENE 7

(The King, now a chandala, works in the cremation ground. The heat and smoke have completely changed his face. While tending the burning fire, he suddenly bursts into tears.)

HARISH CHANDRA   Ah, last night I dreamt of my beloved queen and my beloved son. I dreamt of my kingdom regained. O dream, how sweet you are! O reality, how cruel you are!

SUPREME SACRIFICE

SU 32. SCENE 8

(At the end of her day's work, Shaivya comes to the garden to play with her son, but she does not find him there. She calls aloud.)

SHAIVYA Rohitashwa, Rohitashwa! Rohit, my son, my darling, where are you? *(She looks around. Suddenly she sees her son lying on the ground fast asleep. She places her two arms around his shoulders.)* How strange! Why is my son's body so cold? What are these marks? My son, my son! A poisonous snake has taken your life away!

(Eyes filled with tears and heart completely shattered, she carries her son away in her arms.)

SRI CHINMOY

SU 33. SCENE 9

(Shaivya comes to the cremation ground. At the gate of the cremation ground a long-bearded chandala, a most ugly-looking fiend, blocks her way.)

CHANDALA   Stop here! Have you brought rice? Have you brought cloth? Have you brought money?
SHAIVYA   Alas, I have no rice, I have no cloth, I have no money.
CHANDALA   What? How dare you then enter the cremation ground? Where is your husband? Where is the boy's father?
SHAIVYA   My husband *(bitterly weeping and sobbing)* was once a great man. I don't know where he is now. I work as a slave in the kitchen of a rich man. I asked the master of the family to give me some rice, cloth and money before I came here, but he refused. He said to me brutally, "I can't give you rice, cloth and money. I can't give you all that. Never. I feed you. I feed two big bellies. Is that not enough?" So I am helpless! I came here with nothing.
CHANDALA   I understand all that. I fully sympathise with you. But how can I perform my job without my fee? If I do it free, my master will be furious. I have to listen to my master. It is my bounden duty to please my master. I have to give him everything that I get from this cremation ground. I have no choice.
SHAIVYA   O Harish Chandra, where are you? Our beloved son Rohitashwa is now with God. Here I am left alone, utterly helpless, with his body. O Harish Chandra, O my beloved, where are you?

SUPREME SACRIFICE

(The chandala, hearing his name, falls down on the ground and loses consciousness. Shaivya stoops to help him. A few minutes later he regains consciousness and takes his son in his arms.)

HARISH CHANDRA   Shaivya, forgive this lower-than-lowest creature. Your Harish Chandra is here. Shaivya, my Shaivya, you are the citadel of strength. You are the lighthouse of purity.
SHAIVYA   You! You! My husband! My beloved! Our lost son brings his parents back. Our lost son reunites his parents!

(Harish Chandra's master and Vishwamitra appear.)

CHANDALA   Harish Chandra, leave your son on the ground. Listen to me. *(Harish Chandra places his son most carefully on the ground.)* Harish Chandra, your past experiences are past indeed! All your tests are over. Victory dawns on you. I am Yamaraj, the King of Death. Vishwamitra and I have tested your sincerity, your love of truth and your sacrifice. Victory, eternal Victory, transcendental Victory, dawns today on your devoted head and surrendered heart.
HARISH CHANDRA   Alas, the third member of our family is no more with us. Our dearest son Rohitashwa fails to share our joy. Our lives without him will be filled with excruciating pangs, utterly meaningless and fruitless.
VISHWAMITRA   Where is your child?
HARISH CHANDRA   There he is lying, O mighty sage.

(Vishwamitra sprinkles a few drops of sacred water over the dead body of Rohitashwa. Rohitashwa immediately jumps up and clasps his mother.)

ROHITASHWA   Mother, Mother, where were you? Where was I?

(The King embraces his son with his heart's boundless love and pride. The three bow to Vishwamitra. The parents kiss the dust of his feet. Vishwamitra garlands the King, the Queen and the Prince.)

VISHWAMITRA   Harish Chandra, I shall cherish your life of sacrifice. The entire world shall praise your Kingdom of Heaven. Forever and forever your heart the world will treasure. I am giving you back your palace and your kingdom. Your faith in yourself and Truth's faith in you will march together along the road of Immortality. You will transmit the message of truth on the inner waves of the heart.

>You are God's Love.
>You are God's Joy.
>You are God's Pride.
>You are God's All.

(Harish Chandra and Shaivya kneel down before the sage. Shaivya sings.)

> *God then was Love*
> *So nice and fine.*
> *God then was mine*
> *Below, above.*
> *God now is Light*
> *Delight, Delight.*
> *My All, my All*
> *God now is Light.*

UPAMANYU

SRI CHINMOY

SU 34. DRAMATIS PERSONÆ

AYODADHOMMYA (A SAGE)
UPAMANYU (HIS DISCIPLE)
ASHWINIKUMAR (THE CELESTIAL PHYSICIANS)

SUPREME SACRIFICE

SU 35. SCENE I

(The sage Ayodadhommya and his disciple Upamanyu.)

AYODADHOMMYA   Upamanyu, today you have completed your formal studies, and so I wish to give you a new type of study. From now on, each day early in the morning you will take all my cows to the grazing ground to feed. You will watch them there, and you will bring them back in the evening.
UPAMANYU   Master, Father, I shall fulfil your wish. I shall fulfil your command.

(Exit Upamanyu.)

SU 36. SCENE 2

(The sage is studying the Vedas, the Upanishads and the other scriptures. Evening has set in. Upamanyu comes back.)

AYODADHOMMYA   So you have brought all the cows back?
UPAMANYU   Yes, Father.
AYODADHOMMYA   What have you eaten, my son, for breakfast and lunch? Have you had a decent meal?
UPAMANYU   Oh, while the cows were grazing, I went out for some time and begged a little food from door to door. That is what I ate, Father.
AYODADHOMMYA   Unthinkable! You didn't have my permission! You didn't ask me whether you could go out to beg food from others while the cows were grazing. You must not do that. That is not right.
UPAMANYU   *(with folded hands)* Yes, Master. Forgive me, I shall not do it any more.

SUPREME SACRIFICE

SU 37. SCENE 3

(The next day Upamanyu goes to the field with the cows. In the morning for breakfast and in the afternoon for lunch the poor boy drinks milk from the udders of the cows. Happily he watches the cows grazing all day. He sings a soulful song.)

Amar bhabana
amar kamana
amar eshana
amar sadhana
tomar charane
peyechhe ajike thai
moher bandhan hiyar jatan
timir jiban shaman shasan
halo abasan nai nai ar nai

(My thoughts, my desires, my aspiration, my
    life's disciplines
Have found their haven at Your Feet today.
The bondage of tempting attachment and pangs
    of the heart,
The life of darkness and the torture of death,
No more I see, no more I feel.)

SU 38. SCENE 4

(Upamanyu comes back in the evening.)

AYODADHOMMYA   So, today you have done a fine job. I am sure that today you didn't go out for food. But strangely enough, you seem quite strong despite not having eaten today. Have you not eaten anything?
UPAMANYU   O Master, I drank some milk.
AYODADHOMMYA   Milk? From the cows? Is that milk meant for you to drink?
UPAMANYU   Oh no, Master. What actually happened is this. When the calves had finished drinking their milk, I drank the very little milk that remained in the udders of the cows.
AYODADHOMMYA   That is unfair, unfair! That milk is not meant for you, even if it is left. It is meant for the calves if they want to come back again. The very little that was left, they could have drunk. Unthinkable! I never expected you to behave that way! All right, I forgive you. But don't do it any more!

(Upamanyu touches his Master's feet and then goes away.)

SUPREME SACRIFICE

SU 39. SCENE 5

(The next day Upamanyu takes the cows to the fields. There the cows graze happily on grass and leaves. Upamanyu sings soulful songs.)

Prabhu,
tomar hasi bhalobasi
tomar aghat bhalobasi
tomar charan bhalobasi
tomar nayan bhalobasi
atma tomar bhalobasi
deha tomar bhalobasi
tomar sakal bhalobasi
pratikshane bhalobasi
prabhu tomai bhalobasi
tumi amar parichayer banshi

(Supreme,
Your Smile I love
Your Torture I love
Your Feet I love
Your Eyes I love
Your Soul I love
Your Body I love
Everything that is You I love.
Every moment I love You.
O Lord Supreme, O Lord Supreme,
I love You, I love You.
You are the Flute of my existence.)

Ore mor kheya, ore mor neye
ore ananda bani
niya jao mor trishita kshudhita
supta chitta khani
mrittyu nritya heri charidhar
dhangsa ashani hane durbar
ogo kandari tumi je amar
chira asimer kripa-parabar
tomar majhare harabo amare
jani aji ami jani

(O my Boat, O my Boatman, O message of
        Transcendental Delight,
Carry me. My heart is thirsty and hungry,
And it is fast asleep at the same time.
Carry my heart to the other shore.
The dance of death I see all around.
The thunder of destruction indomitable I hear.
O my inner Pilot, You are mine,
You are the Ocean of Compassion infinite.
In You I lose myself,
My all in You I lose.)

UPAMANYU   I do not know what I am going to eat today. Yesterday I drank so little milk that I am now tired. I drank very little milk, but even then my Master scolded me and insulted me. What am I going to eat today? *(Suddenly.)* Ah! I can drink the milk that is left on the mouths of the calves after they have drunk from their mothers.

SUPREME SACRIFICE

(So for breakfast and lunch, as soon as Upamanyu sees that the calves have finished he licks the frothy milk from their mouths, and he is satisfied.)

SU 40. SCENE 6

(Evening sets in. Upamanyu comes home.)

AYODADHOMMYA   I am sure that today at least you have listened to my command. You have not eaten, and I am sure you have not drunk milk from the cows.
UPAMANYU   No, I have not.
AYODADHOMMYA   I am very happy that you have listened to my order. But how is it that even today I see you looking quite strong and healthy? Have you not eaten *anything*?
UPAMANYU   Master, I have licked the froth from the mouths of the calves.
AYODADHOMMYA   Froth?
UPAMANYU   After they have drunk the milk from their mothers, there remains a kind of froth around their mouths. So I drank that.
AYODADHOMMYA   Unthinkable! How could you do that? When those little, innocent creatures have some milk around their mouths, gradually they lick it off. How could you drink it? Unthinkable! I have never seen a boy like you, always disobedient. Every day you drink or eat something without my knowledge or permission. You must not do that. You must not drink any more milk or froth, and you must not go from door to door to collect food. You must not do any of that.
UPAMANYU   Yes, Master. I shall not do it.

(He bows down to the Master and goes away.)

SUPREME SACRIFICE

SU 41. SCENE 7

(Early the next morning Upamanyu, as usual, goes to the grazing ground with the cows.)

UPAMANYU Today I am very hungry and very thirsty. For the last two days I have eaten almost nothing. In the evening I get food at Master's place, but that is very scanty. Previously, Master's wife used to give me a delicious meal three times a day, and I used to eat voraciously. Now I do not have breakfast or lunch at all, so the food I get in the evening is not enough. I do not know what is wrong with me or what is wrong with them that I am not allowed to eat my three meals a day. I am so hungry! What can I eat? Ah, I shall eat some leaves, just to fill my stomach.

(He goes to a tree and eats some leaves. Slowly, his eyesight begins to fail. Evening sets in and the cows begin to go home without their master. Upamanyu cannot see, but he tries to follow them anyway. On the way he falls into a dry well, and he cannot get out.)

SRI CHINMOY

SU 42. SCENE 8

(It is dark outside. The cows have returned without Upamanyu. Ayodadhommya goes out to look for his disciple.)

AYODADHOMMYA   Upamanyu, Upamanyu!
UPAMANYU   I am here, Master!
AYODADHOMMYA   Where are you?
UPAMANYU   I don't know where I am, but I am here!
AYODADHOMMYA   Ah, you are in a well! What is wrong with you? What have you eaten today?
UPAMANYU   I have not eaten anything.
AYODADHOMMYA   Nothing?
UPAMANYU   No food, Master. Only a few leaves from a tree. Now I can't see, I have no eyesight. While I was coming back home I fell into this well, and now I cannot get out.
AYODADHOMMYA   *(shocked)* Upamanyu, again? Have you disobeyed me again? You have not asked permission from me to eat leaves. You have undoubtedly eaten leaves from the arka tree, and these leaves destroy the eyesight. Now you have lost your sight. What can I do? Disobedience, always disobedience. At first you begged food from door to door. Then you drank milk from the udders of the cows. Then you licked froth from the mouths of the innocent little calves. And now you have eaten leaves. You have to pay the penalty. I cannot help you.
UPAMANYU   Well, Master, if you do not help me, I shall have to remain here. But I shall pray to you. I shall pray to you for forgiveness. I have eaten these arka leaves, and now I have become blind. It is my own fault, so let me remain blind; but I shall pray to God to give you someone who will

be able to take your cows to the pasture every day and bring them back.

(Ayodadhommya helps Upamanyu out of the well.)

AYODADHOMMYA   Just because of your disobedience you are now suffering. I did not want you to eat anything. The first time I scolded you, you should have understood me and taken me seriously. You should not have eaten anything at all. Every time you ate, I kept telling you, "Unthinkable," "Unpardonable," and you should have learnt. You should have understood that my intention was for you not to eat anything without my permission.

UPAMANYU   Master, I ate practically nothing. I drank practically nothing.

AYODADHOMMYA   But you did eat; you did drink.

UPAMANYU   Yes, Master. Forgive me, Master. I shall not do it any more.

AYODADHOMMYA   But you are of no use to me now. You have failed me. You are blind. You cannot help me in anything. And it is all because of your disobedience. Outwardly I told you that you must not eat anything, and inwardly I also told you. You did not understand my inner message and you did not obey my outer message. If you had not eaten for a few days, you would not have died. But look at your disobedience. All right, Upamanyu, I forgive you, but I cannot give you your sight back. Pray to the Ashwinikumar, the divine doctors. Invoke their presence. If they are pleased with you, they will come and cure your eyes.

(Exit Ayodadhommya.)

SU 43. SCENE 9

(With folded hands Upamanyu invokes the presence of the Ashwinikumar most sincerely and devotedly. The Ashwinikumar enter.)

ASHWINIKUMAR   Upamanyu, you are praying to us and we have come to you. Tell us, what can we do for you?
UPAMANYU   I have lost my vision by disobeying my Master. Please cure me.
ASHWINIKUMAR   That's easy. Just eat this pill.
UPAMANYU   No, no, I can't.
ASHWINIKUMAR   Why? What is wrong with this pill?
UPAMANYU   I have to get permission from my Master. Without his permission, I can't eat anything.
ASHWINIKUMAR   You fool, your Master is so unkind, so cruel! He himself did not give you anything to eat. He did not allow you to beg food from others. He did not allow you to drink the scanty milk from the udders of the cows. He did not allow you to lick the froth from the mouths of the calves. And now you have to get permission from your Master to take this pill! What kind of Master is he? Stone-hearted, cruel, brutal! You are a fool! You don't need that kind of Master.
UPAMANYU   Oh, please do not speak ill of my Master. He knows what is best for me. I am so grateful that you have come here, but I can't eat your pill right now.
ASHWINIKUMAR   Then why did you invoke us?
UPAMANYU   I invoked you to ask you to come here and cure me.
ASHWINIKUMAR   Well, that is what we have come for. We have come to cure you, but you will not let us.

UPAMANYU   But you are giving me something to eat. If you do not give me anything to eat, but just cure my eyes, I shall be most grateful.

ASHWINIKUMAR   No, you have to take the medicine. When one is a patient, he has to eat or drink the medicine prescribed by the doctor. This is our medicine. If you don't take our medicine, how are you going to be cured, you fool?

UPAMANYU   That is true, that is true. But how can I eat anything without my Master's permission? You see, I have eaten other things without his permission, and this is my fate: I have become blind because of my disobedience. Now if I disobey him again, who knows what worse things may happen?

ASHWINIKUMAR   But your Master did ask you to meditate on us, to invoke us.

UPAMANYU   Yes, he did.

ASHWINIKUMAR   That means he wanted us to cure you. Now it is up to us to cure you in our way. We are doctors; we have to give you medicine.

UPAMANYU   That is true, that is true. But I can't take your pills without his permission. I won't disobey my Master any more.

ASHWINIKUMAR   *(pleased)* Now you have shown what real obedience is. We are most proud of you. Upamanyu, we will give you back your sight.

(He gets back his sight.)

UPAMANYU   I am most grateful to you. I am most grateful to you. *(He bows to them.)*

(Exit Upamanyu, running.)

SRI CHINMOY

SU 44. SCENE 10

(The home of Ayodadhommya. Upamanyu enters running.)

AYODADHOMMYA   So they came, the Ashwinikumar came and gave you your vision back.

UPAMANYU   Yes, Master.

AYODADHOMMYA   Upamanyu, I have tested your patience, your self-control. Today you passed your examination. You have shown the world what patience is. You have shown the world what self-control is. You have shown the world how one should please one's Master. One should please one's Master the way the Master wants to be pleased. Finally, you have pleased *me* the way *I* wanted to be pleased. I wanted you to have nothing to eat without my permission. You came to that point. You didn't even take medicine from the doctors whom I had suggested. You didn't take so much as a pill from them! There you showed your unconditional obedience to me. I am most proud of you. Today marks the end of your studies. Go home. With my blessing, you will lead a prosperous life, a spiritual life. An inner life of illumination and an outer life of perfection I offer to you. Today I give you oneness with me and all my wisdom, which is Perfection.

ONE MUST FOLLOW ONE'S OWN NATURE

SRI CHINMOY

SU 45. DRAMATIS PERSONÆ

HOLY MAN
ONLOOKER (LATER, HIS DISCIPLE)

SUPREME SACRIFICE

SU 46. SCENE 1

(A holy man is swimming in the river. An onlooker is sitting idly on the bank watching him. The holy man sees a scorpion right in front of him. Feeling sorry for the poor creature, he catches hold of it and very slowly, very gently puts it on land. While he is doing this, the scorpion stings him severely. The man begins to weep with pain.)

HOLY MAN   I wanted to save you, and I did save you. Is this my reward? Anyway, I have done my duty.

(A few minutes later the scorpion again falls into the river. Again the onlooker observes.)

HOLY MAN   Ah, poor creature, you are suffering again. I feel sorry for you.

(He lifts the scorpion again and puts it on land. Once more the scorpion stings him, this time even more severely. He screams with excruciating pain.)

ONLOOKER   You are a fool! Why did you do that? The first time you made a mistake, and the second time you repeated the same mistake.
HOLY MAN   My friend, what can I do? My nature is to love, my nature is to save. The nature of the scorpion is to hate, the nature of the scorpion is to sting. I have to follow my own nature, and the scorpion has to follow its own nature. If it falls into the water again, I shall lift it up again, no matter how many times it falls. I shall be stung, I shall cry, I shall moan; but I shall not deny my nature, which is to love, to save and to protect others.

(The onlooker immediately jumps into the river to touch the feet of the holy man.)

ONLOOKER   You are my teacher, you are my Guru. I have been searching, longing for a Guru. Today I have found in you my real Guru. Since I am your disciple, from now on if the scorpion falls into the river it is I who will put it back on land.

(Disciple sings.)

*Amar bhabana
amar kamana
amar eshana
amar sadhana
tomar charane
peyechhe ajike thai
moher bandhan hiyar jatan
timir jiban shaman shasan
halo abasan nai nai ar nai*

(My thoughts, my desires, my aspiration, my
        life's disciplines
Have found their haven at Your Feet today.
The bondage of tempting attachment and pangs
        of the heart,
The life of darkness and the torture of death,
No more I see, no more I feel.)

SUPREME SACRIFICE

(He helps the holy man out of the river. The Guru now sits on the bank and watches the scene. In a few minutes the scorpion again falls into the river. The disciple catches hold of it and puts it on dry land, but the scorpion does not bite him.)

DISCIPLE   How is it, Master, that I was not stung at all? I thought that I too would be stung by the scorpion. Twice you were stung mercilessly. I don't understand.

MASTER   My child, you don't understand? Shall I tell you? Will you believe me?

DISCIPLE   Please, please tell me. I shall believe you, Master.

MASTER   The scorpion also has a soul; and its soul told the scorpion that, if it had bitten you, instead of putting it on land you would have killed it immediately. The scorpion knew that you would not accept it, that you would not tolerate its ingratitude. From you the scorpion did not get any assurance of its safety. The scorpion did not sting you because it felt this. In my case, the soul of the scorpion knew that I would never kill it, no matter how many times it might sting me; I would just catch it and put it on land for its safety. In the everyday world also people fight, quarrel and threaten others only when they see that their opponents are either weak or unwilling to fight. If they see that somebody is stronger than themselves, they will remain silent.

DISCIPLE   Master, do you have disciples?

MASTER   I have many, many disciples.

DISCIPLE   What do you do with them?

MASTER   I give and take, and take and give. I take their poison every day, and I give them nectar. I take their aspiration, and I give them realisation. I take from them what they have, ignorance; and I give them what I have, wisdom. They give me the assurance of my manifestation, and I give them the assurance of their realisation. We need each other. You need me so that you can empty yourself into me: your impurity, imperfection, obscurity and ignorance. And I need you so that I can empty my Joy, Love and Light into you. I need you so that I can fill you with my all, with everything that is within me. This is how we fulfil each other. Your nature is to give me what you have: impurity, obscurity, imperfection, limitation, bondage and death. My nature is to give you what I have: Purity, Love, Joy, Light, Bliss and Perfection. When your nature enters into my nature and my nature enters into your nature, we both are totally manifested and totally fulfilled. This is how the seeker and the teacher fulfil the Eternal Pilot, the Supreme.

WHO IS THE GREATEST?

SRI CHINMOY

SU 47. DRAMATIS PERSONÆ

PRAJAPATI (THE CREATOR)
THE EYE
THE EAR
THE ORGAN OF SPEECH
THE MIND
THE LIFE-ENERGY
THE BODY

(A terrible dispute arose among the Eye, the Ear, the Organ of Speech, the Mind and the Life-Energy. Each one was sure that he was by far the greatest. They quarrelled and quarrelled, but they could not come to any satisfactory conclusion; so they decided to go to Prajapati and settle the problem once and for all.)

SUPREME SACRIFICE

SU 48. SCENE 1

(Prajapati's abode. The Eye, the Ear, the Organ of Speech, the Mind and the Life-Energy appear, bringing the Body with them. They all bow to Prajapati.)

THE ORGAN OF SPEECH O Prajapati, save us, save us. We are having a terrible dispute. Each of us feels that he is the greatest, and now we want to know for sure who is the greatest among us.

PRAJAPATI My children, you have put me into terrible difficulty. If I tell any one of you that he is the greatest, the others will be displeased and angry with me, and they will literally hate me. Why don't you solve your problem yourselves?

THE MIND O Prajapati, we have tried our best. We have tried to solve this problem, but it is simply impossible for us. Each one of us feels that he is the greatest. It is you alone who can solve our problem. We shall, without fail, accept your judgment.

PRAJAPATI Is it true? Are you all sure that you will accept my judgment? Whatever I say, you will believe gladly, cheerfully and wholeheartedly?

THE EYE Of course, of course. Had it not been our intention to accept you as the judge supreme, we would not have come to you. Please tell us who is actually the greatest among us.

PRAJAPATI My divine children, allow me to concentrate for a few seconds. Then I shall let you know. *(Concentrates.)* Ah, I have an excellent idea. I won't have to tell you who the greatest is. You will be able to find out for yourselves.

THE EAR O Prajapati, you are avoiding the issue. We could not solve our problem ourselves; that is why we came to you.

And now you are telling us that we *can* solve the problem ourselves. We have come here; we are bowing down to you and touching your feet, O Prajapati. Please do not avoid us, do not evade the issue. Tell us frankly, we beg of you, who is the greatest among us.

PRAJAPATI   My sweet children, just listen to me. You can easily know who is the greatest, and I will tell you how. Here you all are before me: the Eye, the Ear, the Organ of Speech, the Mind and the Life-Energy. Now will you do one thing?

THE ORGAN OF SPEECH   Yes, we shall do it. We shall at least try.

PRAJAPATI   Try. You will succeed; you are bound to succeed. Now, here is my advice. One by one you will leave the Body for a year. The one whose absence makes the Body suffer most, or prevents the Body from functioning at all, is the most important.

THE MIND   Ah, that is very easy. We shall easily find out who is really the greatest.

(With folded hands they bow to Prajapati and leave. The Body follows them.)

SUPREME SACRIFICE

SU 49. SCENE 2

(The Body, the Eye, the Ear, the Organ of Speech, the Mind and the Life-Energy are together.)

THE ORGAN OF SPEECH   Let me go out of the Body first. Let me get the first chance. I know I am the greatest. If I don't speak, the world will think that the Body is dead. It is I who bring glory to the Body. I speak, and people appreciate and admire. I teach the world with my knowledge and inner wisdom. It is I who bring all joy, pride and satisfaction to the Body. Undoubtedly I am the greatest. You have not believed me so far, but now I will go out for a year; and when I come back you all will see and realise that it is I who have all along been the greatest.

(Exit Organ of Speech.)

SU 50. SCENE 3

(One year has passed. The Organ of Speech comes back and stands before the Body, the Eye, the Ear, the Mind and the Life-Energy.)

THE ORGAN OF SPEECH   *(to the Body)* How is it that you are quite all right? I thought that you would suffer greatly. Did you not suffer from my absence?

THE BODY   I am sorry, but I did not miss you badly. As a matter of fact, I did not miss you at all. On the contrary, my silence gave me much inner strength. As you know, a dumb person does not speak, yet he exists on earth. In my case, since I am spiritual, I found your absence quite helpful. I enjoyed it tremendously. At long last I was able to take a little rest. You talked *too* much for a long time.

THE ORGAN OF SPEECH   You ungrateful creature! Just wait; I shall show you! I shall teach you a lesson!

THE EYE   O Speech, I always knew that you were not the greatest, and here is the proof. In your absence we *did* exist, we *did* enjoy everything. Now it is my turn. I shall show you all. I shall prove to you all who is the greatest.

THE EAR   For God's sake, O Eye, don't brag! Until my turn is over the rest of you cannot know who the greatest is.

THE EYE   Oh, be quiet! I am leaving now. Just watch what happens to you all, you fools!

(Exit Eye.)

SUPREME SACRIFICE

SU 51. SCENE 4

(A year later the Eye comes back to the Body, the Ear, the Organ of Speech, the Mind and the Life-Energy.)

THE EYE   How strange, how strange! I can't believe my eyes! How is it that you were not affected at all by my absence? You seem to be quite happy and healthy.

THE BODY   O Eye, you are perfectly right. In your absence I enjoyed something really deep and profound.

THE EYE   What nonsense do you speak? What did you enjoy? Tell me! What kind of deep realisation did you have during my absence?

THE BODY   O Eye, in the past you showed me many uncomely things, many ugly things on earth. I saw tremendous suffering through you. But this year I have not seen any ugliness, darkness, imperfection, poverty or other undivine things, and for that I am truly happy. A man without sight can easily live on earth. There are many people who cannot see, but still manage most satisfactorily. I enjoyed your absence, and I have profited and gained tremendously from it.

THE EYE   O ungrateful Body, wait! Wait! I shall smash your pride one day! Just you wait!

THE EAR   O Eye, I told you before you left that you could never be the greatest, and now you see that my prophecy has come true. Now it is *my* turn. We shall see how well you can get along without me!

(Exit Ear.)

SRI CHINMOY

SU 52. SCENE 5

(A year has passed. The Ear comes back.)

THE EAR   O Body, I can't believe my ears! I can't! How is it that you have not suffered in the least during my absence? How could you live one full year, one long year, without me? It is unthinkable, unimaginable!

THE BODY   O Ear! I did not suffer at all in your absence. When you were here, I used to hear gossip; I used to hear about others' jealousy, about others' shortcomings, imperfections, limitations — about all kinds of deficiencies in human nature. But for one full year I did not hear anything undivine. Nobody bothered me, nobody brought me news; I did not hear any quarrels. I myself was my only thought, my only idea and my only news. I was so happy. I didn't miss you at all. On the contrary, you did me a great favour by leaving me for a year. From the human point of view, you know that a deaf person can easily live on earth and do everything except hear. Who cares for hearing, as long as one can stay on earth happily and peacefully? Your presence is not at all essential, and here is the proof.

THE EAR   O ungrateful Body, wait, wait! A day will come when I shall teach you a serious lesson. Then I shall humble you; I shall bring down your pride and smash it. There will surely be some way for me to make you feel how great I am. Wait; wait and see!

THE MIND   Now it is my turn. O Organ of Speech, O Eye, O Ear, you have all failed. Now it is my turn.

THE ORGAN OF SPEECH, THE EYE AND THE EAR   *(together)* Try, Mind, try. Like us, you too will be unsuccessful. Don't boast. We know your capacity, which is incapacity!

SUPREME SACRIFICE

THE MIND   *(angrily)* The time will soon arrive when you will see how badly you need me, you fools, you brainless sheep! I will prove to you in my absence that you are all idiots, nothing but idiots! Wait and see what happens to you when I am gone!

(Exit Mind.)

SRI CHINMOY

SU 53. SCENE 6

(A year later the Mind returns.)

THE MIND What? Are you all right? It is beyond my imagination! How, *how* can you exist without me? O Body, didn't you feel *anything* during my absence? Didn't you see that the world hated you for your stupidity and your ignorance? It is I who am all knowledge, all wisdom inside you. I am sure that, the moment I left, the world began to despise you, to ridicule you. You must have behaved like a real fool, an idiot, an imbecile. Tell me what actually happened in my absence.

THE BODY O Mind, in your absence I enjoyed something very vast, something very profound.

THE MIND What is all this nonsense? What did you enjoy during my absence that was so vast and deep? It is unthinkable, unbelievable!

THE BODY Mind, you caused tremendous suffering for me. You brought doubts into me, you brought suspicion into me and, what is much worse, you brought jealousy into me. O Mind, in your absence I had such peace, such peace! I did not think of anybody with suspicion, fear, doubt, anxiety or worry. I was all peace, all peace. If one does not have a mind one *can* exist on earth. There are many who do not have a mind at all, but they live on earth in their own way. Look at children. They do not have the mind. They need to be told everything. Yet how pure, how sweet, how loving, how divine they are! But when you come, everything is lost. They gain the mind and their whole existence becomes mean, suspicious and destructive. You are not needed, not at all! In the spiritual world we see how happy we are when we go beyond the mind. At each moment we enjoy the vast, infinite Peace, Light and Bliss. When we transcend the mind, we become one with the universal consciousness. No, Mind, you are not indispensable.

LIFE-ENERGY   My friends, all of you have tried and all of you have failed. Now I shall try. I have no idea what my fate will be but, if I succeed, we will all be able to share the glory. If I fail, then I will be one of you, and have the same deplorable fate. I shall share my success and glory with you if I succeed. And if I also am defeated, I shall share your disappointment.

THE ORGAN OF SPEECH   Stop, Life-Energy! Don't be so modest, don't be so humble! What is wrong with you today? Why are you saying such divine things? Where was your consciousness when we went to Prajapati in order to know who is the greatest? For so many years you quarrelled and fought with us, as we did with you. Now today you are saying that you will share your success with us. Why this sudden generosity? We don't care for your false modesty. You go out and see. Your pride will also have to bite the dust. You will also fail miserably, just like us.

LIFE-ENERGY   Even if I fail I shall not curse the Body. I shall accept my defeat cheerfully and gladly.

THE OTHERS   *(together)* Go ahead and leave. Stop giving us your philosophy, and leave!

(Life-Energy is about to leave the body.)

THE BODY   Oh stop, stop! Where are you going? I am practically dead. I can't exist without you. I can live perfectly without the Organ of Speech, the Eye, the Ear and the Mind; but without you, it is impossible for me to exist. O Life-Energy, don't leave me!

THE EYE   Oh, I am blind! I can't see anything! I am lost! I am in total darkness! Everything around me is dark!

THE EAR   I don't hear anything! What is wrong with me? I can't hear. I am now totally deaf. On the earth, children are playing, but I don't hear their shouts. There are rivers, but I don't hear their murmuring. There is no sound. I am dead. My existence is nullified.

THE ORGAN OF SPEECH   Oh, I am gone! I am lost! I can't say a word! I have so many things to tell the world, so much advice to offer, but I can't, I can't. I am dead! I have no strength, no power!

THE MIND   Oh, I am lost! I can't think of a thing! I am worse than a fool. I don't have even one idea. Nothing comes to my mind. What is wrong with me? I can't exist in your absence, O Life-Energy. I have to think, I *have* to! If I can't think, I am lost. O Life-Energy, don't leave me, don't leave!

(Prajapati appears before them. All bow to him with deep gratitude. Prajapati blesses them, one by one.)

PRAJAPATI   So, my children, now you know who is by far the greatest among you.

(Except for the Body and the Life-Energy, the others are sad, depressed and angry.)

PRAJAPATI   I have come to you with divine advice. Listen to me. This advice will make you happy and immortal on earth. It is time for you all to enter into a new Cosmic Game. From now on you, Organ of Speech, will only tell the Truth. Truth is all; Truth is above all. It is my Truth that holds the world. Tell the Truth. Nothing is greater than Truth. Don't utter anything false; don't mix with falsehood any more.

Use the Truth as your divine weapon to please the world and to win the world. *(To the Eye.)* O Eye, from now on try only to see the Beauty in my creation. See Beauty in human beings, Beauty in every object! Beauty, only Beauty. If you see Beauty, then you can become one with my inner and outer divinity. It is in Beauty that one can see and grow into Perfection. Beauty is the manifestation of Truth. Beauty is the only Reality of Truth. *(To the Ear.)* O Ear, from now on hear only the Truth. The message of Truth comes only from real spiritual seekers. When you have a spiritual Master, whatever you hear him say is the Ultimate Truth. Cry to hear his voice, his Truth, his Light, it is only by hearing the Truth that your inner awakening will take place. It is only by listening to him that you will be able to realise the Highest. Use your capacity to hear only divine things from divine people, and not to enjoy gossip and other undivine utterances from the world. *(To the Mind.)* O Mind, from now on remain in the Heart. There you will be safe. The aspiring Heart will always receive Light from the Soul, and this Light the Heart will offer to you at every moment. When you receive the Light from your Heart, you will be illumined. There will come a time when you will be able to transcend yourself. You will enter into the ocean of Peace, Light and Bliss. Mind, no longer allow doubt, suspicion, fear, anxiety and worry in your life. You can have boundless Peace, Light and Bliss when you remain in the breath of the Heart. You can transcend yourself. *(To the Body.)* O Body, remain always pure, pure, pure. If you do not remain pure, my Reality, my Truth and my Existence will not be able to manifest themselves divinely and supremely. It is in your Purity that the members of your family can have abiding joy. When you lack Purity, everything is deplorable, nothing is beautiful, nothing is meaningful, nothing is worth having or achieving. It is through your Purity that every divine quality can enter permanently into the human nature. O Body, you have the capacity to transform yourself with the Light of the Soul, with the messages offered by the Life-Energy, with the Truth pronounced by the Organ of Speech, with the Beauty perceived by the Eye, with the divine wisdom that the Ear brings you from seekers and spiritual Masters and with the vastness that the Mind brings. O Body, it is with your Purity and in your Purity that the members of your family can enjoy perfect freedom and at the same time manifest me totally and integrally on earth.

(The Body, the Organ of Speech, the Eye, the Ear, the Mind and the Life-Energy bow with deepest gratitude to Prajapati.)

HE EATS GRASS BUT CARRIES A NAKED SWORD

SRI CHINMOY

SU 54. DRAMATIS PERSONÆ

KRISHNA
ARJUNA
ASCETIC

SUPREME SACRIFICE

SU 55. SCENE I

(Krishna and Arjuna.)

KRISHNA   Arjuna, I am in the mood to go out for a walk. Would you like to accompany me?
ARJUNA   Certainly! It is a great joy, a great honour to walk with you.
KRISHNA   Come, let us go.

(Exeunt omnes.)

SU 56. SCENE 2

(Krishna and Arjuna are walking together along the street. All of a sudden they see an ascetic.)

ARJUNA   Look, there is an ascetic meditating.
KRISHNA Yes, let him meditate. Let us not bother him.
ARJUNA   But look, Krishna, something is very strange.
KRISHNA What is it? I don't see anything.
ARJUNA   Look, he is eating a tiny blade of dry grass. I see green grass all around, but he is eating dry grass.
KRISHNA It is certainly strange, Arjuna.
ARJUNA   But that is not the thing. It is something unthinkable, unbelievable! The man has a naked sword by his side. Krishna, it is really incredible! On the one hand he will eat only dry, lifeless grass, because he does not want to destroy life. His compassion for living things is so great that he won't even eat green grass. But at the same time, he is carrying a naked sword. Tell me, Krishna — why is he behaving like this? What is wrong with the fellow? It seems to me that his life is a life of contradiction. A blade of grass and a naked sword don't go together.
KRISHNA Yes, you are right. To eat only dry grass and carry a naked sword is certainly incongruous. Why don't you go and ask why he does this? I shall wait for you.
ARJUNA   No, please come with me.
KRISHNA All right, I am coming. I am following you.

(They go up to the ascetic.)

ARJUNA   Please tell me, venerable sir, why you act this way? I see that you are leading a simple life, an austere life, a pious life. But why are you carrying this sword? Please tell me the reason for this strange behaviour.

ASCETIC   The reason is very simple. I have four persons to kill with this sword, four unpardonable rascals.

ARJUNA   Who are they? I may be of some help to you if they are so bad.

ASCETIC   I don't need your help. Thank you anyway.

ARJUNA   May I please know their names? Such bad people must not stay on earth. They should be killed if they are really so bad. You say you don't need my help, but in case you change your mind, I am the person who can be of service to you.

ASCETIC   Thank you. I am happy to hear it. I shall tell you their names after all. The first is Narada.

ARJUNA   Narada! What has he done? What has he done to you?

ASCETIC   All the time Narada sings the glories of my Lord Krishna. He never shuts up. He does not even give my Lord time to take his rest. All the time he has to sing, and Krishna has to hear his songs. With his constant singing, singing, singing, he is always disturbing my Lord's sleep. I shall kill that wretched Narada if I see him!

ARJUNA   May I know who the second person is?

ASCETIC   The second rascal is Draupadi, the wife of the Pandavas. As soon as she got into a difficult situation she had to cry, "Lord, save me! Save me!" My Lord had to go and use his force in order to save her modesty. What kind of audacity she had! Who asked her husband to mix with bad people and play dice with the Kauravas? If her husband did something wrong, she should have to pay the penalty for it. Why did she have to call on my Lord Krishna to save her modesty? He had to waste his precious time and energy just to save her modesty. I hate her. I hate her for that, and I shall kill her as soon as I see her!

ARJUNA   What are you talking about? How do you know that story? You are an ascetic.

ASCETIC   Do you think that I do not care for the world's news? I know what is happening in the world. Listen: The story of Draupadi is very simple. Draupadi's husband, Yudhishthira, lost to Duhshasana in a dice game. And his last promise, unthinkable, was that he would give his wife, Draupadi, to the winner. Naturally Duhshasana defeated Draupadi's husband, that senseless man. She had to stay with the Kauravas, their enemies. They wanted to undress her in front of their kings and potentates. Draupadi tried to hold fast to her sari, but finally she surrendered and said, "O Krishna, save me, save me!" Immediately my Lord had to grant her an endless stretch of material. They went on and on pulling at her sari, but it was endless. That is why I hate Draupadi. As for Yudhishthira, it is beneath my dignity even to think of him. He was the real culprit. Anyway, it was Draupadi who invoked my Lord to help her. I hate her. In season and out of season, at any time, she calls on him. When the Pandava family was in the forest, do you know what happened?

ARJUNA   I do not know what happened.

ASCETIC   You don't know? That means you don't read, then.

ARJUNA   Oh, I am an illiterate person. I do not read books, but I would be very happy to hear from you what happened. I have great fondness for the Pandava family. I like the Pandavas better than I like the Kauravas.

ASCETIC   Yes, they are nice people. My Lord Krishna always takes their side. But they have no sense. They exploit my Lord Krishna. When the Pandava family was in the forest, it happened that the sage Durvasha came to visit them with all of his followers and disciples. The Kauravas, the enemies of the Pandavas, had sent Durvasha to pronounce a curse on the Pandavas. Durvasha had once gone to the Kauravas, where he was given princely honours by the eldest of the Kauravas, Duryodhana. Now, since he was very highly pleased with Duryodhana, Durvasha said he would grant him any boon. So Duryodhana asked him to go into the forest where the Pandavas were and cause them trouble. My Lord Krishna had given the Pandavas a pot out of which any number of people might be fed. But this miracle could take place only before Draupadi had taken her last meal of the day. After Draupadi had eaten her last meal, the Pandavas could not feed a single person on earth. Duryodhana asked Durvasha to go there one day after Draupadi had finished her last meal. Durvasha listened to Duryodhana's request. He came after Draupadi had finished her meal, only to torture her. When he came in he said, "I am very hungry, very hungry. I and my followers are going to bathe in the Ganges, and when we return you must feed us." Draupadi knew that she could not feed them. But she also knew that if she did not feed them he would curse her and her husbands. So she invoked my Lord Krishna for help. My Lord Krishna — do you know where he was?

ARJUNA   No.

ASCETIC   He was seated on his throne. He was nowhere near the forest, but immediately he had to use his occult power to come physically to save her. Sri Krishna said, "Please give me something to eat. I am very hungry, Draupadi." Draupadi answered, "You are hungry? O Krishna, I have invoked you to help me because I have no food, and you have come here to torture me. How am I to feed you? I have no food here." Lord Krishna said, "You have to give me food. Examine your pot." She replied, "There is nothing left, O Krishna. I am not telling you a lie. We have all eaten, and there is nothing left. I can show the pot to you." She brought the pot before Krishna. To her surprise there was a grain of rice in it. He ate it. Then he said, "I am satisfied. Now ask me anything. I am pleased with you." She said, "Then save me. The sage Durvasha is coming. He has gone now with his thousands of disciples to bathe in the Ganges, and when he comes back he will want food." With his spiritual power, Krishna immediately made food for thousands of people. But Durvasha, with his yogic vision, came to know that Sri Krishna was there. He said, "It is useless for me to go there, because now they will be able to feed us. I don't want to go there. I am satisfied." So look how Draupadi caused problems for my Krishna. My Lord Krishna had to save her again. I shall kill her! I won't let her go on like this, exploiting my Lord.

ARJUNA Who is the third person, please?

ASCETIC The third person is that Prahlada. Whenever there is any danger, immediately Prahlada says the name of my Lord Krishna, who goes to save him. Prahlada has no right to bother my Lord so often. He has to be punished.

ARJUNA Please tell me who Prahlada is.

ASCETIC Oh, you don't know Prahlada? He claims to be one of the greatest disciples of Krishna, which is absolutely untrue. Prahlada's father used to hate Krishna. The very name of Krishna used to irritate him. His son was just the opposite. Constantly he was all love, all admiration for Krishna. So what did his father do? His father took Prahlada and threw him into a tub of boiling oil. On another occasion, he knocked him onto the ground in the path of a mad elephant, all because his son was worshipping Krishna. But the boiling oil did not kill the boy, nor did the elephant crush him. Sri Krishna, my Lord, was there to save him. Sri Krishna's presence saved him every time. I hate Prahlada! I shall punish him. I shall punish him for wasting my Krishna's time. All these three that I have mentioned I shall kill.

ARJUNA   Now may I know who the fourth person is?

ASCETIC   The fourth! He is the worst of all! The wretched, wretched Arjuna! I want to kill him here and now. If I see him anywhere I will kill him, without delay.

ARJUNA   Arjuna! What has he done?

ASCETIC   That third Pandava has brought disgrace to his family and to the whole world!

ARJUNA   How? Please tell me how Arjuna has brought disgrace to his family and to the world?

ASCETIC   Look at his audacity. He asked my Lord Krishna to be his charioteer on the battlefield. Sri Krishna is not only my Lord, he is the Lord of the Universe. And Arjuna asked him to be his charioteer! Look at his audacity! I shall kill him! I shall kill him! Until I kill him I shall not leave this earth.

ARJUNA   *(smiling)* You are absolutely right. I am sure that one day you will meet these four and you will be able to kill them.

ASCETIC   I am so happy to hear these words from you. Yes, I shall certainly do it.

(Exeunt Krishna and Arjuna.)

NOT SO EASY TO CHANGE ONE'S FATE

SRI CHINMOY

SU 57. DRAMATIS PERSONÆ

SHIVA
DURGA (WIFE OF SHIVA)
KUMARA, GANAPATI (THEIR SONS)
OLD MAN (A GREAT DEVOTEE OF SHIVA)

SUPREME SACRIFICE

SU 58. ACT I

(Shiva, Durga and their sons, Kumara and Ganapati, are eating together. Suddenly Shiva stands up and begins to leave.)

DURGA   What is the matter? We have not quarrelled at all. I have not said a word to you and you have not said a word to me. What is wrong? Why are you leaving? What are you doing? The children are here. Have you no sense?

SHIVA   I am coming back. I have to do something very important.

(Shiva leaves and the children follow their father.)

CHILDREN   Father, Father, Mother has not said anything wrong. She is quite innocent. Why are you going away? Has anything gone wrong, Father?

SHIVA   Nothing is wrong with me, Kumara and Ganapati. Please go back and eat with your mother. It is something inner. You won't understand now because you are children. A few years later you will know what your father does in the inner world. I shall come back shortly.

(Exit Shiva.)

GANAPATI   Mother, Father is not angry with you. He says he has to do something inner which we won't understand right now. He will be coming back soon.

(Durga gives them a smile and they start eating. A few minutes later Shiva returns.)

DURGA Now tell me, why did you leave? What was wrong with you?

SHIVA Nothing was wrong with me. A great devotee of mine was attacked by a hooligan. He invoked me and I went to help him. But I saw that right after invoking me, he himself put up a brave fight and defeated the hooligan. I need not have worried at all. My devotee had the strength to punish the hooligan. I went there to save him, but now he has taken care of himself. I am always concerned for my devotees.

DURGA Yes, I know how much concern you have for your devotees. You have next to none! I have never seen anyone as indifferent as you.

SHIVA Indifferent?

KUMARA Mother, Mother, you are insulting our father.

GANAPATI He will not eat. He will go away.

DURGA You children have no idea how indifferent your father is to some people.

SHIVA Tell me who?

DURGA I know that you have a great devotee on earth. He is an old man. He begs from door to door. He makes next to nothing. Early every morning he begins praying to you, and he prays to you all day. Nobody meditates so devotedly and sincerely on you as he does. He prays to you twenty-four hours a day, yet he has to go begging from door to door to maintain his life on earth. He has nobody on earth to take care of him. And even you do not take care of him. You don't give him any money; you don't do anything for him so that he does not have to go out begging every day. Poor man! Even in winter, when everybody shivers with cold, he has to go out begging alms from door to door. This is your compassion for him; this is your concern for him.

SHIVA What can I do? That is his fate.

DURGA What is his fate? You can change his fate.

SHIVA   No, I cannot change his fate.

DURGA   Why not? Occultly can't you put some money right by his door? In the morning, before he goes out, you can put a pile of gold coins right in his path. When he gets it he will not have to beg any more.

KUMARA   Father, that is a wonderful idea, Why not? You can do it, you can do it!

GANAPATI   Father, please do it. Since Mother wants it and it is a nice thing to do, why let the poor man suffer? If he is your greatest devotee, he should be given some money and he should be made happy. Poor man; he needs some comfort. There is nobody to look after him.

SHIVA   All right, I shall listen to your mother and to you two.

SRI CHINMOY

SU 59. SCENE 2

(The cottage of Shiva's devotee. Shiva enters in occult form and places a pile of coins outside the door, then leaves.)

OLD MAN *(to himself)* Now I am old. A day will soon come when I will lose my eyesight. Since I have to go from door to door, let me start practising walking along the street with my eyes closed. From now on, let me beg with my eyes closed, and then when I really lose my eyesight, I will have no problem. *(The old man closes his eyes and goes to the door. He is pretending.)* Oh, I have lost my eyes, I can't see! *(Praying.)* O Shiva, you are so kind, you are so full of compassion. My vision is gone, but the strength of my legs still remains. Even now you have given me the capacity to walk, and my hands still work. I am so grateful to you. I am waiting for the hour when you will call me.

(Old man sings.)

Tumi shudbu bandhu amar
tumiy amar pran
baul haye desh bideshe
gahi jena bhalobese
jiban bhare tomar jaya gan
tumi shudbu bandhu amar
tumiy amar pran

SUPREME SACRIFICE

(You are my only Friend.
You are my life.
Like a divine mendicant,
    from one country to another,
May I sing a song of You
With all my love.
May I sing the Song of Your
    Victory all my life.)

(The old man goes out with his eyes still closed and almost steps on the money.)

SRI CHINMOY

SU 60. SCENE 3

(The old man returns home and opens his eyes. His bowl is piled high with food.)

OLD MAN Oh, I have found a trick. From now on I will definitely go out with my eyes closed. People have more compassion for me then. They have given me much more than usual.

SUPREME SACRIFICE

SU 61. SCENE 4

(Shiva's home.)

SHIVA   *(to Durga)* See? I listened to you, but he went out with his eyes closed and he didn't get the money that I left for him. If he had seen it, by this time he would have been very rich. And for the rest of his life he would have been most comfortable. But he didn't see it. Who can change his fate? His fate is like that.

DURGA   My Lord, now I understand. Many times I thought that you were unkind to people who think of you, who meditate on you. But now I realise that although you try your best to help them, their fate, their karma from the past, in some way does not allow them to receive your blessings. Today I have seen that receptivity is needed. They have to develop the capacity of receiving. If not, no matter what you give them, either they will not be able to receive it or they will not value it.

GANAPATI   But Father, you could have done something else.

SHIVA   What is that?

GANAPATI   You could have gone to his place and personally given him the money. Then he would not have missed it.

KUMARA   That is a nice idea. Why didn't you do that, Father? Tomorrow you can go and do it. Father, do it, do it, do it!

SHIVA   Kumara, Ganapati, you two sons of ours are really stupid. You do not know what will happen.

TOGETHER   What will happen, Father?

SHIVA   When I go to him he will say, "Lord, you have come!" When I give him the money he will say, "Lord, you have come here to deceive me! You are giving me money so that I will lead a comfortable life and forget you. I have no money now. That is why I depend on you. I go begging from door to door and all the time I pray to you. When I come back I also pray to you. When I am in front of other people's doors I beg, beg of you. I beg alms, and at that time I pray to you and repeat your name. The moment I become rich I will stop thinking of you. Please, please, don't be so unkind to me. I want only to think of you, pray to you, meditate on you. This is the only boon I want from you, my Lord. The little food that I need in order to live on earth you can give me in other ways. But do not take me away from your heart. I want to remain in your heart through my prayers, constant prayers." What shall I say to him when he tells me this?

DURGA   Nothing. Now I know why you say that your heart is all the time in your devotees. You are all for them. This particular devotee of yours far outshines the others. He is teaching the world that what is most needed is not money or wealth, but your heart, your feet, your compassion. This devotee of yours is teaching the world that you, you alone, are the supreme object of love and adoration. In you is the fulfilment of the world; with you is the perfection of the world.

(Shiva blesses Durga with tearful joy and pride.)

THREE MIRACLES BY A BRAHMIN'S HANDS

SRI CHINMOY

SU 62. DRAMATIS PERSONÆ

BRAHMIN
WIFE OF BRAHMIN
INDRA (LORD OF THE GODS)

SUPREME SACRIFICE

SU 63. SCENE I

(A beautiful garden. A cow enters and destroys quite a few beautiful flowers and plants. Enter the owner of the garden, a Brahmin. He becomes terribly angry when he sees what the cow has done.)

BRAHMIN   You stupid brainless creature! I shall kill you! *(He grabs an axe lying nearby and kills the cow.)*

(Enter his wife, who starts weeping at the sight of the dead cow.)

WIFE   You madman! You have killed a cow. You are a Brahmin, a member of the highest caste, and you have killed a cow! This is a terrible sin! Now what will happen to you? God alone knows.

BRAHMIN   Shut up! I know what I have done. I know what is best. In the garden I see my own creation, my own beauty, my own success, my own glory. I have worked so hard, so very hard for this garden, and now this cow has destroyed all its beauty. I have done the right thing.

WIFE   The right thing! You have taken the life of a poor animal just because he destroyed a few plants. Is not this punishment much worse than the poor creature deserved?

BRAHMIN   What do you know about justice? Unless and until I punish the culprit severely, the culprit will never know the damage that he has done to me and my garden. Anyway, you know I am not the doer. I have read the scriptures. The scriptures say that I am not the doer. It is my hands that have done it. And where is the motive force of my hands? Who has acted in and through my hands? It is Indra, Lord Indra, who is responsible. He is the lord of my hands.

(Enter Indra in the guise of an old man.)

INDRA   Ah, I have never seen such a beautiful garden! I am sure Heaven itself is not as beautiful. Even the Garden of Eden could not be as beautiful as this garden. Who has done it? Who has made it so beautiful?

BRAHMIN   *(proudly)* I have done it. I have done it all with my own two hands. Everything.

WIFE   I have also helped him a lot.

BRAHMIN   Very little, very little. Next to nothing. I have done practically all of it.

INDRA   No matter who has done it, I have never seen such a beautiful garden in my whole life. I shall tell all my friends to come here and visit your garden. It is so beautiful, so charming, so soul-stirring. Did you not appoint some servants to take care of your garden and to help you in gardening?

BRAHMIN   How many times have I to tell you that it is I who have done it, I! With my own two hands.

INDRA   You have done it with your own hands?

BRAHMIN   Yes. Only two hands. God has not given me more than two hands. Only two hands. With these two hands I have done it all.

WIFE   I have also helped you. Don't forget that I also have two hands. With these two hands I have helped you.

INDRA   And with your two hands you have helped? I never knew that four human hands could perform such a miracle. Such a beautiful garden! I am so delighted, so moved. Wherever I go, I shall surely tell people about your garden. *(Noticing the cow.)* Wait! What is this? I see a cow lying down. Is something wrong with it? Is it your cow?

BRAHMIN   Oh no. Not our cow.

INDRA   Then whose cow is it?

BRAHMIN   It is some neighbour's cow. Don't talk about that cow. It came and destroyed many of my beautiful plants, so Indra has killed it.

INDRA   Indra has killed it! How?

BRAHMIN   With these two hands. Indra is the motive force behind my hands. He is responsible for what my hands do. So Indra killed it with these two powerful hands.

INDRA   Well, make up your mind, Brahmin. Just a few minutes ago you told me that you made this garden with your own two hands. You did not give Indra any credit then. But when it comes to doing something bad, very bad, you put the entire blame on him. You must either sacrifice the praise, or accept the blame as well.

BRAHMIN   *(embarrassed)* Yes, it is I who have done it.

(Indra shows his divine form. The Brahmin starts trembling. Both husband and wife fall at Indra's feet.)

BRAHMIN   Lord, forgive me, forgive me.

(He touches Indra's feet.)

INDRA   Your hands have done three significant things. First, they created tremendous beauty on earth in the form of this garden. Your hands did the right thing. Then they did a cruel and ugly thing: they killed a helpless animal. And of all animals, a sacred cow. That was a terrible thing, unpardonable. Then these hands of yours touched my feet. My feet are compassion, my feet are forgiveness. Because your hands touched my feet, my compassion forgives you for killing one of my sacred cows. With your hands you have performed three miracles. To create beauty is a divine miracle. To take the life of an innocent gentle animal is an undivine miracle. And your last miracle, touching my divine feet of compassion, has brought you my forgiveness. Now I wish you to go to the owner and inform him that you have killed his cow.

BRAHMIN   I don't even know who the owner is. And how can I tell him? He will beat me. He will put a curse on me. He will kill me.

WIFE   That is true.

INDRA   You must go. If you don't, then God will certainly punish you. The most serious catastrophe will take place. Your son will die very soon.

WIFE   *(starting to cry)* Our only son will die! Our only son!

INDRA   Some accident or some person will kill your son as your husband has killed this cow.

WIFE   *(weeping bitterly)* O Indra, you are the Lord of the Gods. Something within tells me that you are the owner of the world. That means that you are the owner of this cow, too. We have told you what we have done. Now please forgive us.

INDRA   *(smiling)* You have spoken the Truth, realised the Truth. I forgive both of you. O Brahmin, your wife has realised the Truth before you. It is she who has saved you. Finally all your problems are over. She has offered you the knowledge, the real knowledge that I am the Lord. I am the owner of this vast creation. I have forgiven you. Your wife is your real illumination.

THE WINNER

SRI CHINMOY

SU 64. DRAMATIS PERSONÆ

SHIVA
DURGA (WIFE OF SHIVA)
KUMARA, GANESHA (THEIR SONS)

SUPREME SACRIFICE

SU 65. SCENE 1

(Mother Durga is wearing a necklace of pearls. She looks extremely beautiful. Enter Kumara with his bow and arrow and Ganesha with a sacred book.)

KUMARA   Mother, Mother, your necklace is so beautiful. I want to have it for myself, I want to have it!
GANESHA   Mother, *I* want to have it. It is so beautiful!
KUMARA   Mother, I am younger than Ganesha. *I* should get it.
GANESHA   Mother, I am nicer than Kumara; therefore *I* should get it.
KUMARA   I am stronger than he is; therefore *I* should get it.
GANESHA   Mother, I am wiser than he is; therefore *I* should get it.
DURGA   My sons, I shall give my necklace to the one who can please me most.
KUMARA   Mother, I can easily please you.
GANESHA   Mother, I can please you more.
DURGA   All right, here is the competition for both of you. Both of you have to travel around the universe, and whoever comes back to me first after travelling around the universe will be the winner. Now both of you start on your journey and come back as soon as possible.

(Kumara knows that he is the swifter and the stronger of the two. He immediately mounts his peacock and rides away, far, far into the distant worlds. Ganesha sits and meditates.)

GANESHA   *(thinking aloud)* My vehicle is the mouse and it is slower than the peacock. What am I going to do? Let me meditate and see if I can get some brilliant idea. *(He meditates.)* Mother is the goddess who pervades the universe. She is the universe. If I go around my mother, that means I will have gone around the universe. If I just go around my mother once then I will be the winner. *(He walks around his mother.)* Mother, I have gone around the universe.

DURGA Sit here now and read. Let us wait until your brother, Kumara, comes back.

(Ganesha starts reading sacred books. Enter Lord Shiva.)

SHIVA Here is the mother and only one son. Where is our other son, our little son? Where has Kumara gone? Is he playing outside?

DURGA No, he has gone to circle the universe. I wanted both the brothers to race around the universe. Kumara is still on his journey; he has not yet come back.

SHIVA And what about Ganesha? Why is he still sitting here?

GANESHA Father, I have already won.

SHIVA How? You have already won and still your brother is not within sight?

GANESHA Father, I know that my mother is the universe. So I went around my mother, and I have won the race.

(Shiva, with deepest joy and pride, blesses Ganesha.)

SHIVA You are right, you are right. You have true wisdom, Ganesha. Your mother is the Universal Mother. She pervades the universe. You have gone around her and that means you have gone around the universe. My son, I am so proud of your wisdom. Now you read.

SUPREME SACRIFICE

(Ganesha reads spiritual books. Enter Kumara hurriedly.)

KUMARA   Ganesha, have you not yet started? Have you surrendered before actually making a try? Have you surrendered to me? You knew well that I would beat you, so you did not even start, right? Can you imagine! I have never seen such a cowardly fellow as you. Mother, look, he is still sitting there. He didn't even try, and I went all the way. I went all, all, all the way around the universe, through all of God's vast creation, and I have come back to you. Mother, give me the necklace. *(Shiva smiles.)* Father, why do you smile? Have you not heard about our competition? Mother wanted us to go around the universe. She promised to give whoever returned first this beautiful necklace of pearls that she is wearing. Father, I have won, I have won! Look, he has not yet even started! *(Ganesha smiles.)* You know how to smile. That is what you know. But you don't know how to act, how to run, how to jump, how to do anything. You only know how to smile, smile, smile. And you know something more: you know how to eat. *(Durga smiles.)* Mother, why do you smile? Why are you all smiling? Can't you appreciate my sincere effort? Can't you appreciate my victory? It is mine. Please give me the necklace. It is I who deserve it. You must keep your promise, Mother.

DURGA   My son, Ganesha is the winner.

KUMARA   How? Why? What do you mean, Mother?

DURGA   He has gone around the universe, and he has come back before you.

KUMARA   Mother, don't tell a lie. How? He didn't even start, as far as I can see. Look at the sweat on my brow. My whole body is perspiring. Look at him. He is sitting there like a lazy fellow. I see nothing in him, no tiredness, no sign of effort. How tired, how exhausted I am, Mother! Look!

DURGA My son, I am the Universal Mother. I embody the universe. He went around me, and the moment he did so, he became the winner. It took him only a few seconds to go around me and now he is sitting quietly. He is the winner. And you have been gone, you know how many hours. You have taken many hours to come back.

(Kumara throws down his bow and arrows and sits on the floor, dejected.)

KUMARA Am I such a fool? Am I such a fool?

(Shiva blesses Kumara.)

SHIVA My son, I am proud of you anyway. We are proud of your speed and strength. We are all proud of you because it is you who will always destroy the hostile forces, the undivine forces that will attack the cosmic gods, the gods in Heaven. You will be the commander-in-chief of the gods fighting against demons and other hostile forces. The world has two things: darkness and ignorance. It is you who have the capacity to destroy darkness, the undivine, hostile forces. And your brother, with his inner wisdom, has the capacity to transform ignorance into knowledge. With his wisdom he will transform ignorance into knowledge-light. With your power you will destroy darkness. *(To both.)* So both of you are equally dear to me and to your mother. You two beloved sons of ours, from each of you we expect what you have to give. *(To Kumara.)* What you have is power. What he has is wisdom. With your power you are pleasing us most and with his wisdom he is pleasing us most.

SUPREME SACRIFICE

(Shiva blesses both his sons.)

DURGA   *(to Kumara)* With his wisdom your brother has won this particular race. *(Places the necklace around Ganesha's neck.)* That is why I have garlanded him. But both of you are equally dear to us.

(Kumara bows and sings.)

Hari jadi ma tor kachhe
seito amar joy
tor hate ma ja diyechhi
ta shudbu sanchai
ar baki sab mulya bihin
kebal apabyay
pira dayi pather bojha
kajer kichhui noy
atma-gyaner pare amar
tor kachhe ma har
hale jani pabo ami
shreshtha puraskar

(Mother, if I lose to You,
That is my only Victory.
Whatever I have given into Your hands,
Is only my savings.
To me the rest is of no value, a mere waste,
And it only tortures me
      and stands as a burden on my way.
I cannot put it to use.
When I lose to You,
After I have achieved
My full realisation,
I know my greatest reward I shall receive.)

WHY SHOULD I BE RESPONSIBLE?

SRI CHINMOY

SU 66. DRAMATIS PERSONÆ

NARADA (A SAGE)
RATNAKAR (A ROBBER AND MURDERER)
FATHER OF RATNAKAR
MOTHER OF RATNAKAR
WIFE OF RATNAKAR
SON OF RATNAKAR

SUPREME SACRIFICE

SU 67. SCENE I

(A forest. The sage Narada is walking through, singing the praises of Lord Vishnu. The notorious robber and murderer, Ratnakar, suddenly attacks him.)

NARADA   Ratnakar, what are you doing? Don't you see that I am singing to the Lord Vishnu? I am invoking him. I am chanting his name.

RATNAKAR   Vishnu? Who is Vishnu? There is only one person on earth and that is I, Ratnakar. I have killed hundreds of people, and I have cut off one thumb from each person. When I have one thousand thumbs, I shall make a garland of them and wear it around my neck. Nobody can save you from me.

NARADA   No? Don't you know that I have spiritual power, occult power? I can easily free myself from you. So don't threaten me.

RATNAKAR   Ha! Spiritual power, occult power! I shall kill you right now! *(He is about to stab Narada with his dagger.)*

NARADA   Wait a minute! What do you want? Do you want money?

RATNAKAR   Yes.

NARADA   How much do you want?

RATNAKAR   Whatever you have.

NARADA   I can give you whatever I have, and again, with my occult power I can give you double what I have. Look, I have a hundred-rupee coin, Can you see?

RATNAKAR   Yes.

NARADA   Now search me, Search all my garments. There is no money.

(Ratnakar searches him thoroughly.)

NARADA   Now just close your eyes.

(Ratnakar closes his eyes. From nowhere Narada takes another hundred rupees.)

NARADA   Look, Ratnakar, what I can give you.

RATNAKAR   *(amazed)* Where did this money come from? I searched you thoroughly.

NARADA   Ratnakar, Ratnakar, no matter what amount you want I will be able to give it to you, and I *will* give you. But before that I want to ask you something.

RATNAKAR   What?

NARADA   You know that what you are doing is absolutely wrong. You are acting like an animal, killing people and taking away their money. Now don't you think that you will be held responsible for all this in your life after death? Don't you know that you will be condemned to hell and punished severely? Why do you do this kind of thing? You alone, you and nobody else, will suffer for all these horrible deeds.

RATNAKAR   What do you mean, I alone? I do it because I still have a sense of responsibility. I have two old parents; I have a wife, a beautiful wife, and a beautiful son, I have to think of all of them. I am responsible for my parents, for they are invalids. I am responsible for my wife, who is helpless without me. And my son is only a little boy, so I have to think of him. It is for all of them that I do it.

NARADA   And do you think that they will also take responsibility for you when you get punishment in your after-life? When you die, you will be the one to be punished for this karma in the other world, Ratnakar.

RATNAKAR If I am punished I am sure they will share my karma with me, since I am doing all this for them. I have no other way to make money. This is the only way I can support my family.

NARADA All right, this may be the only way, but I tell you, these people will never take responsibility for you.

RATNAKAR Why not? They should! It is only fair, if I am doing it for them. Today, if anything happens to me, my parents will perish. My wife and son will probably die, too. I am sure they will all be willing to share my punishment in the after-life since it is I who am maintaining them in this life.

NARADA All right, Ratnakar. Let us see. You feel that your parents, your wife and your son will take responsibility for your undivine actions because you are feeding them, you are clothing them, you are taking care of them by doing all this. Go home and ask them. If they agree, then I shall give you any amount of money you want, and double the amount. I tell you, Ratnakar, they have a claim on your earnings but have nothing to do with your sins. This hard fact will give you a rude shock and then you will take to holy living. I want you to go home and see. I will wait here.

RATNAKAR You are a holy man. You won't break your promise?

NARADA I won't break my promise. I am doing this out of my compassion for you. I can easily leave this place with my occult force — as easily as I brought the money I showed you. Right now I can use my occult power and chase you away from here with my light.

RATNAKAR Oh yes? Show me, show me!

(Narada opens his third eye, and immediately Ratnakar starts trembling.)

RATNAKAR   Stop, stop! The volcanic fire from your third eye is burning me to ashes. I am going. I am going to see my family and I will bring you the news. They will take responsibility for me.

NARADA   Go and see.

SUPREME SACRIFICE

SU 68. SCENE 2

(Ratnakar's home.)

RATNAKAR   *(to his parents)* Mother, Father, I have been working hard for you.

FATHER   Yes, my son, you are working very hard and we are pleased with you.

RATNAKAR   They say that killing people is bad, robbing is bad. I have been killing, robbing, doing many, many things, only to support you and the rest of my family. Now, O Father, O Mother, tell me. I am your dearest son. Will you not take responsibility for my actions when I die, when I am punished by the law of karma in the other world?

BOTH PARENTS   Son, why should we accept the responsibility? When you were a young boy we brought you up, we fed you. We looked after you and we did not ask you to take responsibility for our actions. At that time it was our duty. Now you are grown up, mature, and now it is your duty to feed us, to take responsibility for us.

(Ratnakar is taken aback. He goes to his wife.)

RATNAKAR   Now, darling, will you not accept responsibility for me? You say that I am dearer to you than your life. I have done so many wrong things. Every day I harass people, I torture people, I kill people and take their money. What for? Only to feed you and to feed my family. I am sure you will take some of the responsibilities in my next life, in the other world, when I am punished. I am sure you will also share the burden.

WIFE   Me? Why should I be held responsible? I am your wife, but it is your responsibility. Did you ever hear of a wife going out to make money for her husband? It is the duty of the husband to make money and feed the wife. Are you a fool? I thought you had some sense. People will laugh at you if you ever say that I have to take the responsibility for supporting myself. It is your duty to support me. So why should I be held responsible when it is your duty?

(Sadly Ratnakar goes to his son.)

RATNAKAR   My child, will you not take responsibility for what I am doing? I am torturing people, strangling people and killing people. What for? Only to support you, your mother and my parents.

SON   Father, I am only a child. I do not know how to work. I am unable to support myself. You take care of me. For that I am grateful. But how can I be responsible for what you are doing? I am not doing a thing; I am helpless. When I grow up I will be responsible for you — to feed you and support you. I will take care of my grandparents and my mother. But now, Father, I cannot be responsible for you. It is you who have to take responsibility.

RATNAKAR   *(giving a smart slap to his son)* You ungrateful creature! *(He kicks his wife.)* You ungrateful creature! *(He strikes his parents.)* You ungrateful parents! I have nothing on earth to hold on to.

SUPREME SACRIFICE

SU 69. SCENE 3

(In the forest again. Ratnakar has returned to Narada.)

NARADA   So, you have come here to take your money? Take as much as you want. Why are you so sad? Tell me, what is the news? What is your news?

RATNAKAR   My news is that I have given up my family. I will not be responsible for them since they do not feel responsible for me. They are a bunch of ungrateful creatures: my son, my wife, my parents. I do not want them. I do not need them. Right here, tell me what I should do. I will listen to you.

NARADA   My only advice to you is this: repeat only one name — Rama, Rama, Rama. He will forgive you. He will give you salvation. And it is you who will immortalise him on earth. He will take human incarnation and you will write his biography. Long, long before he is born, before he comes into this earthly existence, you will write his biography. You will tell about his immortal life, his life of dedication, his life of glory, his life of fulfilment. All this you will write down in his biography, From now on repeat his name: Rama, Rama, Rama. Just repeat it and let me hear.

RATNAKAR   Mara, Mara, Mara.

NARADA   Can't you say his name?

RATNAKAR   I can't.

NARADA   Rama, Rama. See what you have done? You cannot repeat his sacred name because you have done thousands of terrible things. Thousands of times you have acted like an animal. You are so impure, you are so mercilessly caught by the hostile forces that you have become like a real *asura*. Now you cannot even repeat Rama's name. You can only say

Mara, which is "Rama" said the other way around. All right, then, say Mara. Repeat Mara and in a few years' time you will be able to say Rama properly. Rama is the heart. Even if you cannot properly pronounce his name, he won't mind. With a soulful heart if you pray every day, repeating the name Mara, Rama will come to your rescue. He will forgive you, he will liberate you. It is to you that he will give the glory of immortalising him here on earth. You will write his biography, you will reveal him and manifest him. You will be the harbinger of his coming. When he comes down into the world and operates on the physical plane, you will see that the biography which you have written about him will immortalise you. He has chosen you to immortalise him, Ratnakar. And the day you start writing his biography, Lord Rama will enter into you and change your name. When you start writing his biography your new name will be Valmiki the Sage. Valmiki will be your real name. "When the power of love replaces the love of power, man will have a new name: God." With your love of power you wanted to destroy the world, but with your power of love you will liberate the world. You will be a messenger of truth, a messenger of fulfilment.

(Narada blesses Ratnakar and departs.)

RAMA FAILS

SRI CHINMOY

SU 70. DRAMATIS PERSONÆ

RAMA
MINISTERS AND PRIESTS
A MAN OF VERY LOW CASTE
VASHISHTHA (PRECEPTOR OF RAMA)
MOTHER OF HANUMAN
HANUMAN (A GREAT DEVOTEE OF RAMA)

SUPREME SACRIFICE

SU 71. SCENE I

(Rama's palace. Rama has invited all his ministers and priests to discuss a serious matter. Everyone has arrived except his preceptor, Vashishtha. Vashishtha has a special seat of his own. Suddenly a man of very low caste enters and deliberately sits on Vashishtha's seat.)

EVERYONE NEARBY   Get up! Get up!
A MINISTER   How dare you sit on this seat? This is Vashishtha's seat. He is the preceptor, the Guru of King Rama.

(Enter Vashishtha.)

VASHISHTHA   Why is this man sitting on my seat? *(To the man.)* How dare you sit there? I shall kill you! Rama, if you are a true disciple of mine, you must kill this rascal.

(Rama gets his bow and arrow. The man runs for his life.)

VASHISHTHA   Rama, you have to kill this rogue, this infidel! I can give you only three chances at most. If you fail in your first attempt, you can try two more times. And if you fail in your third attempt to kill him, I will think you are a useless archer.
RAMA   You know I have killed Ravana, the King of the Demons. Is there anyone I cannot kill on the first attempt, O Vashishtha, O peerless Sage? I assure you, either I shall kill that fellow where I find him, or I shall bring him here.
VASHISHTHA   No, Rama, I don't want you to bring him here. Just kill him wherever you find him. God knows where he is by now.

RAMA   With your blessing let me leave.

(Vashishtha blesses Rama. Exit Rama.)

SUPREME SACRIFICE

SU 72. SCENE 2

(Rama is looking for the man. Finally he sees him at a distance. He gives chase, and the man runs for his life.)

RAMA   Ah, I see he is entering into my Hanuman's house. The rogue is caught! He does not know that the house belongs to Hanuman, my dearest devotee. *(Shouts)* Hanuman! Hanuman!

(Enter Hanuman's mother.)

HANUMAN'S MOTHER   O Rama, you have come. I am so grateful to you. Your presence has sanctified my home. O Rama, please wait for a few minutes. Hanuman will be coming immediately. He is getting ready to see you.

(Exit Hanuman's mother. Enter Hanuman with folded hands.)

HANUMAN   Please tell me what I can do for you, my Lord.
RAMA   Hanuman, where has he gone? Where is that rascal? Bring him out! He has insulted my Guru, Vashishtha. He sat on Vashishtha's seat. Vashishtha wants me to kill him. I have to fulfil Vashishtha's desire. Bring him out and I shall kill him.
HANUMAN   O Rama, I am sorry but I cannot bring him out.
RAMA   I can't believe my ears! Is this you, Hanuman, my dearest disciple? I was under the impression that you were ready to give your life for me at any moment.
HANUMAN   That is true. I will give my life for you. But this is not my life. It is somebody else's life.

RAMA That means you won't listen to me, to my request, my demand, my command?

HANUMAN I am sorry. Forgive me. My mother has given him shelter. *Janani janmabhumishcha swargadapi gariyasi.* "Mother and Mother Earth are superior to Heaven itself."

RAMA But I am your Lord. Am I not superior to everything in your life?

HANUMAN That is true, but how am I going to break my mother's promise?

RAMA If you want to fulfil your mother's promise, then you are no longer my dearest disciple. I must come first in your life, Hanuman.

HANUMAN Yes, you do come first in my life. I have to break my mother's promise. I am prepared. To please you is to please God. Rama, how are you going to kill this man?

RAMA I am going to kill him with my arrows. Vashishtha has allowed me three attempts. He made me promise to try three times and then give up. But it will be a real disgrace if I cannot kill a human being in three attempts.

HANUMAN Please wait here. I shall bring the culprit right to you.

(Exit Hanuman.)

RAMA *(to himself)* I knew. The moment I saw the culprit entering into Hanuman's house, I knew it was his end. He could not escape me. The human emotions created some problem for my Hanuman; that is why he took his mother's side. But the divine in him is so strong, so powerful, that it has to come forward, and it did come forward. That is why he is bringing the culprit to me.

SUPREME SACRIFICE

(Hanuman brings the culprit before Rama.)

HANUMAN   He is ready, Rama. You can satisfy yourself now.

(Rama aims at the culprit and shoots. The arrow drops without piercing his heart. Rama is wonder-struck.)

RAMA   What? How can this be? I killed Ravana, the most powerful demon on earth, and now my arrow fails. Let me try a second time. *(The same thing happens the second time.)* Only one more chance is left! Let me make my third attempt. *(The same thing happens the third time.)*

HANUMAN   Lord, you have to keep your promise now. You have three times tried to kill him, and three times you have failed. Now you can't try any more.

RAMA   No, I can't. I won't. But Hanuman, tell me: how could all this happen? I am the King of Kings, and my arrow fails today so miserably for the first time.

HANUMAN   I shall tell you the secret. I told the man to begin repeating in silence, the moment you drew back your bow, "Victory to Lord Rama." And the second time you drew it back, I asked him to repeat, "Victory to the consort of Sita." The third time, "Victory to Dasharatha's eldest son." So each time he prayed for your victory. Now if someone sincerely prays for your own victory, how can you kill that person? Your soul's divinity was pleased with him because he was praying for your victory. It was your vital and your mind that wanted to kill him. Naturally your soul's will shall always conquer the will of your vital and mind. You are the Lord of the gods. He prayed to you for your victory. Naturally your soul gave him protection, even though your mind and vital were begging for his destruction. The power of your soul is infinitely greater than the power of your vital desire.

RAMA My dearest disciple, I accept my defeat with deepest joy and blessingful pride. I accept my defeat by you, my dearest devotee. You have taught me a lesson. My soul's will shall always conquer my vital and mental craving. I have failed in my outer attempt. But my body's failure is my soul's success. The success of my soul over my body is infinitely more meaningful and fruitful than my outer success.

HANUMAN This knowledge that I have offered to you was granted to me by you. Is there anything I have that has not come from you? My knowledge, my power, everything that I have, everything that I am, has all come from you. In order to glorify me, in order to immortalise me, you are acting like my student. But I know that I am your eternal student. I know you are my eternal teacher.

(Hanuman sings.)

Janar age tomai ami henechhi
pabar age tomai ami jenechhi
debar age tomai ami peyechhi
taito tomai mor amire sanpechhi

(Before I knew You, I struck You.
Before I received You, I knew You.
Before I gave myself to You,
    I received You.
Therefore to You I have offered,
    sacrificed and surrendered
    my ego-reality's existence.)

PART V

THE SACRED FIRE

THE SACRED FIRE

SRI CHINMOY

SF I. DRAMATIS PERSONÆ

THE ABSOLUTE
THE WORLD-SOUL, SOUL OF ENGLAND, SOUL OF AMERICA, SOUL
    OF INDIA
GEORGE WASHINGTON
MARY BALL WASHINGTON (HIS MOTHER)
LAWRENCE (GEORGE'S HALF-BROTHER)
THOMAS JEFFERSON
JOHN ADAMS
JAMES MADISON
JAMES MONROE
JOHN QUINCY ADAMS
LOUISA ADAMS (HIS WIFE)
ABRAHAM LINCOLN
MARY TODD LINCOLN (HIS WIFE)
A FRIEND
THE SOUL OF BENJAMIN FRANKLIN
THE SOUL OF WILLIAM PENN
THE SOUL OF NATHAN HALE
THE SOUL OF RALPH WALDO EMERSON
THE SOUL OF HENRY DAVID THOREAU
THE SOUL OF WALT WHITMAN
THE SOUL OF EMILY DICKINSON
THE SOUL OF MARY BAKER EDDY
WOODROW WILSON
MARGARET WILSON (HIS DAUGHTER)
FRANKLIN D. ROOSEVELT
ELEANOR ROOSEVELT (HIS WIFE)
HARRY TRUMAN
AN ADVISOR
DWIGHT D. EISENHOWER
JOHN F. KENNEDY

THE SACRED FIRE

SF 2. ACT I, SCENE I

(The Abode of the ever-transcending Heights. The Absolute and the World-soul are having a conversation.)

WORLD-SOUL   Father, Lord, Beloved, my All. What is wrong with You? I have always seen You as infinite Delight. You have always been the Source and Flow of boundless Delight. Today I notice blighted sorrow and chilled depression on Your Face. I beg of You a thousand times not to torment my heart's inseparable oneness with Your Universal Heart.

ABSOLUTE   Stop, stop, you culprit!

WORLD-SOUL   Father, my Lord, Beloved, am I the culprit? May I know what I have done?

ABSOLUTE   Go deep within. You and your daughter will immediately realise what you have done.

WORLD-SOUL   My daughter, too? She is also a culprit?

ABSOLUTE   She is a worse culprit!

WORLD-SOUL   But Father, You have blessed me out of Your infinite Bounty with a number of daughters. Like me, which one has wronged You?

ABSOLUTE   I tell you, the term "wronged" is a shameless understatement. You and your England-daughter!

WORLD-SOUL   What have we done?

ABSOLUTE   What have you *not* done? And I tell you, one more person is involved. Do you want to know who she is?

WORLD-SOUL   Yes, Lord, I do want to know.

ABSOLUTE   She is your grand-daughter, America. Your daughter and your grand-daughter are constantly fighting, and most ruthlessly. Look what they have done! They have killed My Heart of Joy. They have killed all My unhorizoned inspiration. They are destroying My Vision's new creation. And you, you fool, you have done nothing!

WORLD-SOUL   Father, I am not a fool. I am just weak.

ABSOLUTE   You are not only weak but also stupid! During the day you swim in the sea of stupidity and during the night you swim in the sea of weakness. You can't even control your own daughter and your grand-daughter. What prevents you from throwing some illumining light on them?

WORLD-SOUL   Father, I have tried. I am still trying. But neither of them is ready to listen to me. They are eager to fight and kill each other. Lord, I am helpless.

ABSOLUTE   You are not helpless. You are useless, that's all. Listen, tomorrow at 5:00 a.m. sharp I want you and your daughter and her daughter here.

WORLD-SOUL   Father, You have saved me. *(Clasping His Feet.)*

ABSOLUTE   Not yet, you mountain-high fool, you sea-deep coward. Don't forget to come tomorrow!

WORLD-SOUL   Father, I assure You, tomorrow my daughter England, my grand-daughter America and I shall come without fail and place ourselves at Your all-fulfilling Feet.

ABSOLUTE   *Okay, okay.*

THE SACRED FIRE

SF 3. ACT I, SCENE 2

(The World-soul, the soul of England and the soul of America are seated at the Feet of the Absolute.)

ABSOLUTE   World-soul, My daughter, yesterday I was cross with you, but today I have forgiven you. Do you know why?

WORLD-SOUL   Father, I do not have to know why. Since You have forgiven me, my heart is all gratitude to You.

ABSOLUTE   No, no, let Me tell you why I have forgiven you. I am so moved by your daughter's exquisite beauty and I am so fascinated by your grand-daughter's indomitable strength.

WORLD-SOUL   Father, it is true; my daughter has exquisite beauty, my granddaughter has indomitable strength. Now, may I be allowed to say what I have? I have fathomless ignorance.

ABSOLUTE   Daughter, I do not want to remain bound to My yesterday's invention. From there I have moved to today's discovery. Your daughter is extremely beautiful, your granddaughter is extremely powerful and you are extremely fruitful. Now, My sweet England, why are you not allowing your daughter America to go in her own way? She feels that she is mature enough to take care of herself. Let her try.

WORLD-SOUL   Father, that is exactly what I have been telling my daughter all along. But she has turned a deaf ear to my advice.

SOUL OF AMERICA   Grandmother, I too have been telling my mother the same thing. But she simply won't listen to me. I wish to tell You, my Lord, and you, my grandmother, that there is a reason why my mother is not allowing me to be free. She is terribly jealous of me, of my capacity.

SOUL OF ENGLAND   No, I am not! America, don't brag. A war between us is imminent. Then you will see that you will be nowhere. You are bound to kiss the dust of my feet.

SOUL OF AMERICA   Mother, the joy of victory and the sorrow of defeat are in the Hands of the Absolute Lord. He will give you what you deserve and He will give me what I deserve.

(A sweet smile flashes across the Face of the Absolute.)

SOUL OF ENGLAND   America, enough, enough! You do not have to bless me with your divine philosophy. You stay with your philosophy. A philosopher is one whose mind is fertile and arms are futile. Fruitless vision is your name, whereas my name is fruitful action.

SOUL OF AMERICA   Mother, the Lord will decide your fate and mine. Why worry now?

SOUL OF ENGLAND   For God's sake, I am not worried in the least! Let me remind you of one thing. The Lord has taught His creation that only the brave deserve the fair. I am sure you have got the point.

SOUL OF AMERICA   Mother, I have.

ABSOLUTE   I am an old man. What both of you have been discussing is far beyond My comprehension. But England, My sweet England, I tell you the supreme truth: there is a beauty in the rising sun and there is a beauty in the setting sun. Both equally charming, illumining and fulfilling. You have so far enjoyed the beauty of the rising sun, but from now on you will have to enjoy the beauty of the setting sun. And you, My brave America, before long you shall start enjoying the beauty of the rising sun — the sun that illumines, the sun that liberates, the sun that immortalises the soul and the body of aspiring humanity. England and America, I tell you one thing. My Heart's desire is an amicable settlement between you both.

SOUL OF AMERICA   Lord, my dearest and bravest son George Washington also desires that very thing. But alas, as You know, it has now become a hopeless case. Mother wants to maintain her supremacy. And we do not want that; therefore, the only thing for us to do is to fight it out.

ABSOLUTE   Well, I am telling both of you something extremely important. And I want my daughter World-soul to pay all attention to what I am saying, too. England and America, mother and daughter, you two have been quarrelling and fighting and strangling each other. But there shall come a day when you will change your relationship. Instead of remaining mother and daughter, instead of remaining bitter foes you will become loving comrades and illumining and fulfilling souls.

WORLD-SOUL   Father, Father, my heart is eagerly awaiting that golden day. I am counting the hours, nay, the minutes! Lord, I wish to offer You a soulful song.

ABSOLUTE   Ah, that is what My Heart needs.

(World-soul sings.)

There is no rhyme for my Lord save Love.
There is no rhyme for my life save Power.
I know, I know, yet dare I not
Smash asunder my ignorance-Tower.

ABSOLUTE   Marvellous, marvellous, marvellous! I am so proud of you. Once upon a time, when you were a little child, I used to teach you singing. Needless to say, Daughter, you have far surpassed your Father. But I am happy to accept defeat at the hands of My own daughter.

WORLD-SOUL   Father, sometimes I forget that You are infinite. Yesterday You assumed one aspect to threaten and frighten me and today You have assumed another aspect to inundate my entire existence with Your immortalising Love.

ABSOLUTE   True, My daughter, true.

SOUL OF ENGLAND   Lord, Grandfather, I too wish to offer You a beautiful song. I envy my mother. She was divinely lucky to have You as her music Teacher. Many times I have heard her singing songs which were taught her by You. I don't deny that she has a very good singing voice. In fact, I must say that I am no match for her.

ABSOLUTE   Sweet England, I am sure that you, too, have an excellent voice. Sing! Let me hear you, please.

(Soul of England sings.)

Into the world of beauty's flame,
Into the world of offering's game,
Into the world of lustre-flood,
I came, I came, my existence came.

ABSOLUTE   Beautiful, marvellous, wonderful! You liar, why did you underestimate your singing ability? You are an excellent singer.

SOUL OF AMERICA   Lord, my mother and my grandmother are really good singers. Unfortunately, I can't sing at all.

WORLD-SOUL   Don't display your false modesty.

SOUL OF ENGLAND   We don't appreciate your false modesty.

SOUL OF AMERICA   Lord, do believe me, I am not a singer. But may I dance instead of singing for You?

ABSOLUTE   Of course, of course. That is a good idea. My bravest child, dance for Me. Nothing will please Me more.

(Soul of America dances.)

ABSOLUTE Incredible, incredible! I have never seen in all My existence such a beautiful dance. America, My bravest child, and by far the best dancer, if I were young I would have definitely joined you. With greatest difficulty I am resisting temptation.

(The Absolute, World-soul and the soul of England give a thunderous applause.)

SRI CHINMOY

SF 4. ACT II, SCENE I

(George Washington and his mother, Mary Ball Washington, at home.)

GEORGE WASHINGTON   Mother, Mother, my heart is all gratitude to you. It was you who did not allow me to join His Majesty's Navy when I was quite young — hardly fourteen. I need not tell you, Mother, that your son and loyalty are inseparable. And who gave me this most precious sense of loyalty? You, Mother, only you. As a result, I am able to dedicate myself completely to the cause of American independence.

MARY WASHINGTON   My son, you think and feel that you and loyalty are inseparable. But another name for my son George is modesty. You are your country's top-ranking general. You and you alone are America's supreme need and divine choice to lead your country to victory! You will seat your country on the throne of victory and place the victory-crown upon its head.

GEORGE WASHINGTON   Mother, your son loves only one thing on earth.

MARY WASHINGTON   What is that, my son?

GEORGE WASHINGTON   Peace. Peace in our country, peace in Great Britain, peace throughout the world.

MARY WASHINGTON   My son, although you are only twenty-seven, your country has chosen you as its supreme hero to command all the military forces of the colonies. George, you have two other names: loyalty and modesty. But did you know that I also have another name?

GEORGE WASHINGTON   What is it, Mother?

MARY WASHINGTON   Pride, my son, pride in you. You are at once my pride and your country's pride unparalleled.

GEORGE WASHINGTON My countrymen think that I am a patriot to the core. Alas, I do not dare to tell them that although I like patriotism, I love peace. My heart is being ruthlessly tormented by the mere thought of breaking with our mother country so violently. True, I definitely want freedom, but I want this freedom in a peaceful way.

MARY WASHINGTON Son, that is not to be. No, you will have to fight against Great Britain, for that is the only way. I believe this is a God-ordained war. It is you who have to offer your country the smile of victory, freedom-dawn. Hunger, you and your soldiers will brave. Cold, you and your soldiers will brave. Countless dear ones you and your soldiers will lose. Frequent defeats you are fated to suffer. But there will come a time when victory's sun will shine on the life and soul of America. And that sun will bless you, embrace you and treasure you.

GEORGE WASHINGTON Mother, you think too highly of me.

MARY WASHINGTON Son, it is not a matter of thinking. I see the truth; I tell the truth. You know that your mother has always been a perfect stranger to falsehood.

GEORGE WASHINGTON I don't deny that you and sincerity are bosom friends, But your prophetic words frighten me far beyond your imagination.

MARY WASHINGTON I do not care for imagination. You must not think that what I am saying is a mere figment of my imagination. This is not imagination, but my glowing realisation. Yours is the inevitable victory. You will be the father of this country. As your mother, I wish to bless you, my son. As your future daughter, I would like to be blessed by you.

(Mary comes over to him.)

GEORGE WASHINGTON Mother, *(dropping down on his knees)*, I need your blessing to win this war. You are still my mother. Let victory dawn; then, future daughter, I shall dare to bless you. *(Mary blesses him.)* Mother, you are very kind.

MARY WASHINGTON Son, you are very great, and good, too.

GEORGE WASHINGTON Mother, who is my source, whose vision is in me? Who is the confidence-power in me? You and you alone! And whose blessing light shall carry me to victory's golden shore? Yours and yours alone!

THE SACRED FIRE

SF 5. ACT II, SCENE 2

(Several years later. Night. George Washington's elder half-brother, Lawrence, who died many years before, appears before his younger brother in a dream.)

LAWRENCE   George, I am sorry to ruin your sleep. I am sure you went to bed at nine o'clock as usual. You have hardly slept two hours. George, I am so proud of you. I am so proud of you. I am so proud of you. I salute the indomitable spirit of the General in you. I bow to the peerless wisdom of the President in you. I take endless pride in the Father of the Nation in you. George, I have come to you to cheer you up. Don't be sad. While I was on earth, you and I were extremely fond of each other. On the strength of our mutual fondness, I have come to tell you something special. I have known you from your very birth, George. You have always been a true lover of peace. You have always valued peace infinitely more than anything else. Our country needed you to fight for her. Our country needed you to liberate her from bondage-night. You surrendered your own will to our country's will; therefore, my pride in you knows no bounds. Under your supreme leadership our country has won the war. For many long years you have struggled far beyond any human imagination; therefore, I know how richly you deserve some rest. But our country needs you again. This time it needs you desperately to build an undivided nation. Our country needs your guidance inimitable. I assure you, George, that you will be the first and last president to be everybody's choice. Many will succeed you, but you, with your lofty ideals, will be their pole star. You will be their guiding hand. George, your dear brother Lawrence urges you to accept the presidency. Heed not your will, brother, but our country's will.

GEORGE WASHINGTON   O brother of my heart and soul, it is true that I commanded the whole American army, but today I gladly take your wish as a supreme command. Brother Lawrence, to please you is to please the real in me. I am definitely willing to become the President of America.

LAWRENCE   I am most grateful to you. The entire nation will be grateful to you. I am truly proud of you, as the entire nation will be proud of you, George. Let me tell you something really sweet. Your young friend and greatest admirer, Henry Lee, will say something to the whole nation after you have left the body. His loftiest message will be echoed and re-echoed from the Atlantic to the Pacific. Nay, the whole world will admire his supreme discovery. Don't get excited, George. Of course, it is very easy to give advice; my own excitement is running riot. But this young friend of yours will declare, five days after paying his last respects to your deceased body, that you were first in war, first in peace and first in the hearts of your countrymen.

GEORGE WASHINGTON   How do you know that?

LAWRENCE   Brother George, I live in Heaven. One can see and know everything from here. I am like someone who is at the top of the tree, who clearly sees and knows what is happening or what is going to happen all around the foot of the tree. Brother, Heaven is all vision, and I am enjoying this divine vision. Earth, where you are, is all mission. You are struggling, sometimes consciously and sometimes unconsciously, and you will be struggling surprisingly hard to fulfil your God-ordained supreme mission. George, you know perfectly well that I have never been a singer. But, to my genuine surprise, and no doubt yours, I have set a tune to Henry Lee's transcendental utterance.

(Lawrence sings.)

First in war, first in peace, first in the hearts of his countrymen.

GEORGE WASHINGTON   Excellent, excellent, Lawrence! You are an excellent singer.
LAWRENCE   Thanks a lot, George. But it is getting rather late. I must go back to Heaven now.
GEORGE WASHINGTON   Oh no, please stay with me a little longer.
LAWRENCE   George, I always get the greatest joy by pleasing you.
GEORGE WASHINGTON   And I, by pleasing you. Tell me, when are you going to come back again to encourage me, inspire me and elevate me?
LAWRENCE   I shall definitely come as soon as I can. I shall definitely come as often as I can. But I tell you one thing, a top secret. Don't disclose it to anyone. I shall come to you for the last time on December 14, 1799. At that time I shall come to you to bring you to my home, where I am living now.
GEORGE WASHINGTON   Really? Lawrence, don't forget that significant day. I shall be eagerly expecting you. I tell you, Lawrence, I don't have the slightest desire to be thought of as the Father of the Nation. My grateful life and my soulful heart desire only to remain your eternal brother.
LAWRENCE   I, too, want that. I, too, want to remain your eternal brother. I am sure the Almighty will grant our prayer.

SF 6. ACT II, SCENE 3

(George Washington is admiring the beauty of one of his farms.)

GEORGE WASHINGTON   Indeed, England was right. The English said that we are not in a position to rule our country. Look how my countrymen are angrily and endlessly fighting over absolutely unimportant things. Each one treasures his own ideas as flawless and perfect jewels. To me, all of their ideas are nothing but ridiculous idiosyncrasies. England is mocking us. Although we have won the war for independence, the British are making fun of us. We must immediately put an end to it. And also, we must shatter England's idea of the supreme necessity for a king. We don't need a king. Of late, out of their tremendous love and respect for me, my countrymen have started calling me King. But no, I reject this honour! Have I not fought against the injustice of the King of England? Why enter into the same ridiculous position? No, it is beneath our country's dignity to follow in the footsteps of England. In England people become scared to death at the very mention of the King's name. They think that to defy the King's authority is the worst possible crime. They are not afraid of bullets and death. They are afraid only of His Majesty's supreme authority, nay, autocracy. Look at the height of their stupendous stupidity! They sincerely believe that their King was chosen by God Himself. As if God has nothing else to do either in Heaven or on earth! And even after touching the highest height of stupidity, still they are not satisfied. They think that to disobey the King is to disobey God. O Almighty One, if You have time, forgive their stupidity. If You have more time, illumine their minds so that they do not fall helplessly into the sea of stupidity any more. The King is a man, a mortal like me. He can never be infallible. Why worship a king who is as prone to committing mistakes as any other ordinary human being?

(Enter Thomas Jefferson.)

THOMAS JEFFERSON Sir, I have brought your song. I do hope that you will be satisfied with my tune.
GEORGE WASHINGTON I am sure you have done a good job. Jefferson, I have two more names for you: excellence and perfection.
THOMAS JEFFERSON I shall eternally remain grateful to you for offering me these two most precious names. But it is you alone who are entitled to these names: excellence and perfection.
GEORGE WASHINGTON All right, let us share our excellence and perfection.
THOMAS JEFFERSON That is a splendid idea. Let us do that. Now, here is your song.

(Thomas Jefferson sings, accompanying himself on the violin. Then, he and George Washington sing together.)

GEORGE WASHINGTON Dear Jefferson!
THOMAS JEFFERSON Sir Washington!
GEORGE WASHINGTON All-where your wings of capacity fly.
THOMAS JEFFERSON You are the sun-vast pride of your banner high.
GEORGE WASHINGTON You are our America's peerless brain.
THOMAS JEFFERSON You freed us from bondage-chain.
GEORGE WASHINGTON In your mind is our country's vision-light.

THOMAS JEFFERSON   Your shoulders, our country's mission-height.

GEORGE WASHINGTON   You have told us no more dark night.

THOMAS JEFFERSON   You have given us nectar-delight.

GEORGE WASHINGTON   Marvellous!

THOMAS JEFFERSON   Now, let me teach it to you.

GEORGE WASHINGTON   You know that God has not granted me a singing voice.

THOMAS JEFFERSON   Sir, I do not subscribe to your conviction. Unless you have tried, how can you know? Please sing with me. I am sure you will also excel in music, as you excel in everything else.

GEORGE WASHINGTON   Helpless, I am surrendering to your clever and inescapable encouragement. Let me try. Teach me how to sing.

THOMAS JEFFERSON   I am teaching you with great pleasure and honour.

(Thomas Jefferson and George Washington sing together. Washington carries the tune perfectly.)

THOMAS JEFFERSON   You see, sir, I was right.

GEORGE WASHINGTON   You were an inventor. Today, you have become a discoverer — the discoverer of a singer in me.

THOMAS JEFFERSON   Let us each sing our respective lines.

GEORGE WASHINGTON   That is a nice idea. Let us do that. *(They sing.)* All glory to you, Jefferson! I was a soldier, but you have turned me into a singer. Look at your capacity-height and my gratitude-light.

THOMAS JEFFERSON   Sir, you are our country's constant pride, in everything that you do and say.

GEORGE WASHINGTON   I thank you, Jefferson, from the depths of my heart. Now, if you don't mind, may I change the subject?

THOMAS JEFFERSON   Of course. To please you is to please myself.

GEORGE WASHINGTON   If that is so, then right from today I want you and Alexander Hamilton to work together peacefully. I have chosen both of you to be my two strong shoulders. Alas, my shoulders are causing me endless worries.

THOMAS JEFFERSON   Forgive me, sir. I know Hamilton and I are two real culprits. We create constant troubles for you. Sometimes, even when we see and know that the other party is perfectly right, we find it difficult to admit it outwardly. Such is our unpardonable weakness. But, on my part, I shall try my utmost to work with Hamilton peacefully from now on. It was kind of you to bless us by calling us your two shoulders.

GEORGE WASHINGTON   Not mere shoulders, but my giant shoulders. Jefferson, it is you who have written our Declaration of Independence. There you have said something truly precious to my heart and soul. You said that we derive our just powers from the consent of the governed and not otherwise. A gift of immortal glory you have offered to our country. Your matchless mind is all illumination. If you do not come forward and put an end to the constant sad dispute between yourself and Hamilton, who will and who can? It was with great joy and pride that I made you Secretary of State and Hamilton Secretary of the Treasury. Both of you are more than qualified in your respective fields. But alas, I do not know what prevents you two from working together peacefully.

THOMAS JEFFERSON   I am sure you know what prevents us from working together. It is our unlit jealousy. It is our disproportionate sense of supremacy.

GEORGE WASHINGTON   Your diamond sincerity, Jefferson, deserves all my heart's unalloyed admiration. Now, please tell me if I have understood your point of view and Hamilton's point of view. At your journey's start both of you had the same notion: that some people have more wisdom and more honesty than others. Am I correct?

THOMAS JEFFERSON   Yes, you are perfectly correct.

GEORGE WASHINGTON   But you feel that these wise and honest people are as likely to be found in one class as another, whereas Hamilton thinks these people are more likely to be found among well-educated, well-established and successful men, rather than among the other classes.

THOMAS JEFFERSON   True, sir.

GEORGE WASHINGTON   To me the difference is very small, almost negligible. Both of you are making a mountain out of a molehill. You two can easily reconcile your points of view in the twinkling of an eye, if you want to.

THOMAS JEFFERSON   We know that. But our ego-ignorance still lords it over us.

GEORGE WASHINGTON   Ignorance-life does not become you, especially in your position of responsibility and leadership. So, my dear brother, please try for an immediate reconciliation.

THOMAS JEFFERSON   I shall. I give you my word of honour, sir.

THE SACRED FIRE

SF 7. ACT II, SCENE 4

(John Adams is conversing inwardly with the Absolute.)

JOHN ADAMS   O Almighty Being, I feel from within that in a few hours' time my earth-pilgrimage will come to an end. Before I breathe my last, do bless me with the necessary capacity to offer You my constant gratitude-heart. I am grateful to You for having brought me into a religious family. I am grateful to You for having kept me active from birth to death, physically, vitally, mentally, psychically — in every possible way. I am grateful to you for having granted me the unparalleled opportunity to be one of the pioneer freedom-fighters. I am grateful to You for giving me the divine inspiration to urge the country to make George Washington Commander-in-Chief in our just battle for freedom-light. I am grateful to You for having given me the capacity to defend Captain Preston. Nobody was bold or kind enough to defend his case. But every man is entitled to a fair and just trial. I told my countrymen that the British officer only did his duty. As we were fighting for our country, he was under obligation to defend his country. I am grateful to You for the golden opportunity You gave me to serve You as head of the country. I am grateful to You for allowing my son, like me, to be head of the country. Finally, I am extremely grateful to You that I was able to listen to Your wishes. You did not want our country to be involved in a war against France when France attacked a few of our ships. You wanted to maintain peace as long as possible. I became my country's enemy. My countrymen called me a traitor. But I heard You inside my heart calling me a lover of peace and wisdom. Almighty Being, You gave me all this capacity; therefore, I am sincerely grateful to You.

ABSOLUTE   John, My son, I am well pleased with you and your life's multifarious activities. You know, My son, today is the fourth of July.

JOHN ADAMS   *(his face immediately brightening)* The most significant day in our country's life. The fourth of July, the fourth of July! My soul shall fly, my soul shall fly!

ABSOLUTE   John, My boundless Pride is carrying you to Heaven for a rest which you so richly deserve. Your great friend and great rival Thomas Jefferson also will arrive in Heaven in a few hours' time. I shall carry his soul, too. I have chosen this day for you, My son, and for My other son, for both of you unquestionably deserve the beauty and glory of this day.

JOHN ADAMS   Lord, Lord, it was Jefferson who wrote in the Declaration of Independence, "All men are created equal." I have always carried this peerless message of his in my heart.

ABSOLUTE   Jefferson wrote the Declaration of Independence, but behind it was your constant, divine encouraging insistence. My Vision-Light was illumining not only your country but also the whole world through the Declaration of Independence. Both of you have proved to be My real divine instruments. John, I am so glad that you gave real importance to the fourth of July. You urged the nation to celebrate the fourth of July with amusing games, enchanting balls and inspiring bonfires. John, many people misunderstood you in many things. They even went to the length of calling you a stubborn mule. But I have always called you a truth-fighter with a volcano-will.

JOHN ADAMS   O Supreme Being, I implore Your last Blessing before You take me to the other shore.

THE SACRED FIRE

ABSOLUTE   Before I bless you and take you to My other Home, I shall sing a song for you.

(The Absolute sings.)

O green-blue Sacred Fire,
O sun Freedom-Light,
O Heaven's Goal Delight, America,
O my child of speed,
My supreme Promise-Seed.

JOHN ADAMS   *(overwhelmed with joy)* Lord, Your Blessing is Your Name. My gratitude is my name.

SF 8. ACT II, SCENE 5

(In Heaven. The Absolute, George Washington, John Adams, Thomas Jefferson.)

ABSOLUTE George, John and Thomas, you three have worked very hard for your country's independence. Now your country is a free nation. Are you not happy?

JOHN ADAMS Of course we are.

THOMAS JEFFERSON But it was all Your Grace, Your unconditional Grace.

GEORGE WASHINGTON Of late I have been feeling that if America could make more inner progress, then her outer success would be more illumining, more fulfilling.

ABSOLUTE You are completely right, My son. Now, tell Me something. Who said this while he was on earth: "Liberty, when it begins to take root, is a plant of rapid growth."?

GEORGE WASHINGTON Me! it was I who said that!

ABSOLUTE You are right in remembering what you once said. And I am right in telling you that your words are correct, O Father of America — Father, indeed, in body, vital, mind and heart; Father in action; Father in realisation. John, do you know who said this: "If it be the pleasure of Heaven that my country shall require the poor offering of my life, the victim shall be ready, at the appointed hour of sacrifice, come when that hour may. But while I do live, let me have a country, and that a free country...."?

JOHN ADAMS Of course I know, Father. It was I who said it while I was on earth. And this was not a mere emotional outburst. It was an inner experience of mine. I am really and truly grateful to You, Father, for having given me that heart-nourishing and soul-illumining experience.

ABSOLUTE   John, everything that I have is for you and for your brothers and sisters, for humanity, for my entire creation. Your enemies called you a stubborn mule, John, but I call you a determined truth-fighter.

JOHN ADAMS   I thank You from the very depths of my gratitude-heart.

ABSOLUTE   Thomas, you wrote the Declaration of Independence. To Me, it was not a mere declaration. It was something infinitely more. It was the freedom-cry of humanity's aspiration-day from the frustration-night of ignorance.

THOMAS JEFFERSON   Father, out of Your infinite Compassion You made me Your humble instrument.

ABSOLUTE   And with your most striking receptivity you received Me, my world-illumining Light. For your extraordinary service to your country, you would have been known as a great man. But for the offering of your independence-declaration you are known as a good man, a God-messenger, a Vision-son of God.

THOMAS JEFFERSON   Father, I also said something on earth.

ABSOLUTE   Let Me know what it is.

THOMAS JEFFERSON   "The God who gave us life gave us liberty at the same time."

ABSOLUTE   True, absolutely true, My son. George, John, Thomas, I hear that you have been practising three splendid songs. Can I hear them?

THOMAS JEFFERSON   Certainly You can, Father.

JOHN ADAMS   Father, our teacher is Thomas.

GEORGE WASHINGTON   But, You have not given us the capacity to sing, Father. So if we do not sing well, then it is our fault and not Thomas'.

THOMAS JEFFERSON   I shall take the full blame if they don't sing well.

ABSOLUTE All right, all right. Let us not remain in the world of blame. Let us remain in the world of practicality and reality. Teacher, you sing first.

(Thomas Jefferson sings.)

O star spangled banner of the Hour Supreme,
You are God's Sound-Delight.
In you is God's Silence-Might.
For you is the World-Pilot's Transcendence-Dream.

(The Absolute, George Washington and John Adams offer thunderous applause.)

ABSOLUTE Now, John, you sing your song.

(John Adams sings.)

O high I flew to see God's Home
And far I ran to see God's Eye
And deep I dived to feel God's Love.
Behold the wings of my victory-sky!

The Absolute, George Washington and Thomas Jefferson offer thunderous applause.)

ABSOLUTE Now, Father of the Nation, you sing.
GEORGE WASHINGTON Father, I am also the father of the non-musical family. And now I am going to prove it.

(George Washington sings.)

My life began with duty's pride,
My life shall live with beauty's light.
My life shall sport with reality's soul,
My life shall end with Divinity's Height.

(The Absolute, John Adams and Thomas Jefferson offer thunderous applause.)

ABSOLUTE   Thomas, you and your students have sung most beautifully and most soulfully. You have done a very good job in teaching them how to sing. I am offering you My special blessingful Gratitude on behalf of these two brothers. I wish you three always to be together here in Heaven and there on earth.

SF 9. ACT III, SCENE I

(James Madison goes to the graveyard and reads aloud the message on the stone over Thomas Jefferson's grave.)

JAMES MADISON "Here lies Thomas Jefferson, author of the Declaration of Independence, of the Statute of Virginia for Religious Freedom, and Father of the University of Virginia." *(Shedding tears of joy, pride and gratitude.)* Oh, tall and great you were. Tall, very tall. I am short, very short. As a tall tree in both the inner world and the outer world, do accept the soulful homage of a tiny helpless plant.

THOMAS JEFFERSON *(appearing in spirit)* James, who says that you are helpless? Who says that you are a tiny plant? Don't underestimate yourself. Nobody should blame you for the deplorable experience that the British have given our country by capturing Washington and setting fire to the White House. It was an absolutely unwarranted war. To me it is quite clear that England is doomed to swim always in the sea of ignorance. Just ask the eyeless British why they have to lord it over others. Have they nothing else to do? Anyway, let us forget that sad disaster as soon as possible. On my part, I am praying to the Almighty to grant the ignorant British some wisdom-light.

JAMES MADISON Jefferson, you are divinely great, supremely magnanimous.

THOMAS JEFFERSON James, I am really proud of you for forming our national government. Now our states will not indulge in fruitless quarrels. You were so right when you said, after the Revolutionary War, that if we are to survive and excel, then there can be no other way than to form a national government. I am proud to call you the Father of the Constitution. I am extremely grateful to you for introducing the Bill of Rights. Freedom of speech, freedom of the press, freedom of religion, the right to have a trial by jury if you are accused of a crime and the right to meet and complain about an unfair law — these are the things that a free country needs. James, once more I tell you, I am proud of you beyond your imagination.

JAMES MADISON   May I always be worthy of your pride in me! May I be worthy of your unconditional encouragement. I admired you most while you were in the body, and now that you are in the spirit I worship and adore you.

SRI CHINMOY

SF 10. ACT III, SCENE 2

(James Monroe alone in his room.)

JAMES MONROE   Lord, I love my country dearly, yet I am not happy. I have two beautiful homes, yet I am not happy. George Washington, the Father of the Nation, showed me much affection, yet I am not happy. The great Jefferson said to me, "Monroe is so honest that if you turned his soul inside out, there would be no spot upon it", yet I am not happy. When I ran for a second term as president, it can almost be said that nobody ran against me, yet I am not happy. People called my time as president "the era of good feeling", yet I am not happy. While I was in office the boundary line was established between our country and Canada. This is indeed the world's most inspiring, encouraging and illumining example of disarmament: an unbelievably unfortified border. To a great extent I am responsible for that, yet I am not happy. The hero in me spoke when I asked Spain and other European nations to keep their hands off North and South America, yet I am not happy. When our Latin American neighbours wanted to free themselves from the Spaniards, I encouraged, even assisted them, yet I am not happy. Nothing on earth is giving me any satisfaction. I must needs leave this shore for the other shore where my most esteemed colleagues Washington, Jefferson and Madison are enjoying their well-deserved rest. Needless to say, I too need some rest. *(With folded hands.)* It is the fourth of July, the most significant day in our country's history. May I be blessed with the boon from You that, like Adams and Jefferson, I too may leave my body today. *(A bright light from Above descends on Monroe.)* Lord, You have heard my prayer. Not only do I offer You this earth's body, but also my Heaven's soul I surrender to Your divine care.

SRI CHINMOY

SF II. ACT III, SCENE 3

(John Quincy Adams has collapsed in the House of Representatives and his wife, Louisa, is at his side.)

JOHN QUINCY ADAMS   Louisa, soon I shall pass behind the curtain of Eternity. My sorrow knows no bounds that my fellow citizens do not want to put an end to slavery. Everybody should be free. Everybody deserves that right. It is man's birthright. Like my father, I have been misunderstood by many.

LOUISA ADAMS   John, God alone knows how kind and good you are. Your heart cries to elevate the weak, to help the needy. Your service to the country is the colossal pride of Heaven. Name and fame you spurned. You dared to serve your country as a congressman after having served as President. What does this prove? It proves that what always comes first and foremost with you is not personal recognition but the service of your country in any capacity. John, I am proud to be your wife. I shall pray to the Almighty that He allow me to follow you to the other world, for without you my life will be fruitless and useless. John, you are a supreme fighter to the end. Our Lord in Heaven will bless you with tremendous joy and pride. You are sailing your life-boat to Him. Mine, too, I shall sail to Him before long.

JOHN QUINCY ADAMS   Louisa, you have always been my mind's loving illumination. Today you have blessed my heart with divine consolation. I shall remain eternally grateful to you.

LOUISA ADAMS   I, too, shall remain eternally grateful to you; in addition, I shall remain unconditionally devoted to you, to your ideal, to your soul, to your Goal. In you I have seen my life's perfection.

JOHN QUINCY ADAMS The same holds true in my case. Both of us have loved each other, perfected each other and fulfilled each other in the Heart of our Heavenly Father.

SRI CHINMOY

SF 12. ACT IV, SCENE I

(Abraham Lincoln and a friend at the White House.)

FRIEND   Lincoln, you are really great, you are really good. God gave you a unique heart. What our great thinker Emerson said of you is so true. Your "heart is as great as the world. But there is no room in it to hold a wrong."

ABRAHAM LINCOLN   Friend, I have done nothing to make any human being remember that I have lived.

FRIEND   That is your modesty speaking. Outwardly you are very tall. Inwardly, also, you are very tall.

ABRAHAM LINCOLN   I am nothing, and I am prepared to remain nothing all my life. But I want our country to be something great, really great, so that the world will appreciate and admire it. Alas, how can the world appreciate our country while there is still slavery? As long as there is slavery in the nation, there can be no oneness-discovery. When I was young, I once saw a beautiful Negro girl for sale at a slave auction. I took an oath on that very day to put an end to slavery. Since then I have been praying to God every day to grant me the opportunity and capacity to put an end to this most deplorable state of affairs.

FRIEND   I tell you, Abraham, God will definitely listen to your prayer. Just wait and see. If God does not fulfil such a good and pure desire as yours, then what kind of prayers will He fulfil?

ABRAHAM LINCOLN   Friend, you are kind. Pray for me; pray for the fulfilment of my heart's desire.

FRIEND   I shall. And I am sure God will grant your prayer.

ABRAHAM LINCOLN   Do you know that there is someone here who failed in business in 1831, who was defeated for the

Legislature in 1832, who failed in business again in 1833, who suffered a nervous breakdown in 1836, who was defeated for speaker in 1838, who was defeated for Elector in 1840, who was defeated for Congress in 1843, who was defeated for Congress in 1848, who was defeated for Senate in 1855, who was defeated for Vice-President in 1856, who was defeated for Senate in 1858?

FRIEND   And who was elected President of the United States in 1860! My dear friend, what you have *been* is of no consequence. What you have *become* is of *paramount* importance.

ABRAHAM LINCOLN   I suppose you are right. Thank you for sharing with me your encouraging and inspiring discovery.

SF 13. ACT IV, SCENE 2

(Abraham Lincoln and his wife, Mary, at home.)

MARY LINCOLN   Abe, why are you so sad? Is anything special bothering you? It is time for us to go to the theatre. People are waiting for us.

ABRAHAM LINCOLN   I know, I know.

MARY LINCOLN   Then what is tormenting your soul at this unexpected hour?

ABRAHAM LINCOLN   I feel that I have so much to do for our country, yet I have done nothing.

MARY LINCOLN   Don't be a fool! What other President can equal you? From a log cabin to the White House. Unbelievable! A very short time after you became President the Civil War began. Sadness and determination became your immediate friends. It is you and you alone who led the fight to protect the Union and to end slavery. And you succeeded. What can compare with your Gettysburg address: ".... government of the people, by the people, and for the people!"

ABRAHAM LINCOLN   It was not your husband who spoke those divine words, but God Himself who spoke those words in and through me. I was just an instrument of His.

MARY LINCOLN   I do believe it. But He didn't choose me or anybody else to be His instrument. God found in you His supremely chosen instrument. But come, Abe, let us go to the theatre. People are waiting for us.

ABRAHAM LINCOLN   Alas, I am also waiting for my country to know and feel that I have done the right thing by ending slavery. Let us go.

THE SACRED FIRE

SF 14. ACT IV, SCENE 3

(The souls of Benjamin Franklin, William Penn, Nathan Hale, Ralph Waldo Emerson, Henry David Thoreau, Walt Whitman, Emily Dickinson and Mary Baker Eddy with the soul of America.)

SOUL OF AMERICA   Children, from the soul's world you have come to visit me. Therefore I am extremely grateful to you all. Benjamin, you were a supreme statesman. You were a supreme scientist, you were a supreme lover and builder of your country. Your sublime contribution to me can only be felt and not described. Benjamin, the oldest and the wisest of all, do you still care for America?

SOUL OF BENJAMIN FRANKLIN   I do, I do. While I was on earth I said: "Where liberty dwells, there is my country." Even now I treasure this life-illumining feeling.

SOUL OF AMERICA   Marvellous, marvellous! William was founder of Philadelphia and you, Benjamin, are Philadelphia's first citizen. Yesterday I composed a song on Philadelphia. It is only you and William who deserve it. Therefore I want to present it to you both.

(The Soul of America sings.)

Philadelphia, Philadelphia, Philadelphia, Philadelphia.
O sweet city of brotherly love,
O God-perfection below, above.
Philadelphia, Philadelphia, Philadelphia, Philadelphia.
Your world-attention Liberty Bell
Proclaimed the death of our bondage-hell.
O freedom-lovers' utopia!
Philadelphia, Philadelphia, Philadelphia, Philadelphia.

(Everybody applauds with tremendous joy.)

SOUL OF AMERICA   Now I wish all of you to quote something from your own lofty messages which you offered to the soul of the earth while you were in the physical. *(Looking at William Penn.)* William, O English Quaker, preacher and writer, you followed the inner light, which is a *must* for everybody. Because of your religion and religious feeling, repeatedly you were imprisoned. Such is human stupidity. Now it is your turn.

SOUL OF WILLIAM PENN   "In all debates, let Truth be the aim, not victory."

SOUL OF AMERICA   Marvellous, marvellous!

Nathan, who told you that you were a spy? No, you definitely were not. You were a supreme lover of your country. You were at once earth's colossal sacrifice and Heaven's hallowed satisfaction. Yours was the heart of sublime promise-light. Yours was the life of glorious sacrifice-might. Many martyrs are buried in oblivion-night and many more shall be. But you will always be remembered not only by your own countrymen but by all freedom-lovers in all freedom-loving countries. Nathan, suppose you are given another chance; this time what would you do?

SOUL OF NATHAN HALE   Mother, this time I would give my life for my country's spiritual liberty. This is the liberty from desire-life and temptation-life. This liberty is a giant stride towards world-transformation and perfection. The outer liberty is of very little value if the inner liberty is wanting. In the inner world, we prepare ourselves for God the One. In the outer world, we offer ourselves to God the Many. A hero I was in the outer world. A hero my heart longs to be in the inner world. Here I shall have to conquer the bondage-day and ignorance-night for myself and for all human beings on earth.

SOUL OF AMERICA   Son, I am so pleased to hear that. Yours is not a human promise. Yours is a divine promise. The Lord Himself is speaking in and through you. By the way, Nathan, how I wish to hear from your lips now the soul-stirring message you gave before you breathed your last, before you embraced the gallows.

SOUL OF NATHAN HALE   Mother, I have set a beautiful tune to my message. May I sing it for you?

SOUL OF AMERICA   That is a great idea. Sing it for me, my son.

(Nathan Hale sings.)

I only regret that I have but one life to give for my country.

(Everybody applauds.)

SOUL OF AMERICA   Marvellous, marvellous.

Ralph, you were the peerless sage of America. You were the vision-light of America. You brought to the fore the mental illumination-beauty of America. Great was your love of America and America's freedom-consciousness. I am reciting your poem.

(The soul of America recites:)

By the rude bridge that arched the flood,
Their flag to April's breeze unfurled,
Here once the embattled farmers stood,
And fired the shot heard round the world....

(Everybody applauds.)

SOUL OF RALPH WALDO EMERSON   "There can be no excess to love, none to knowledge, none to beauty, when these attributes are considered in the purest sense."
SOUL OF AMERICA   Marvellous, marvellous!
   Henry, nature's beauty captured your heart and soul. As a naturalist you were divinely great. You were a life-elevating writer. Now, Henry, it is your turn.
SOUL OF HENRY DAVID THOREAU   "Things do not change, we change."
SOUL OF AMERICA   Marvellous, marvellous!
   Walt, you were a hero-seeker of Truth. You were a hero-lover of mankind. Your *Leaves of Grass* is treasured by both Heaven and earth. You not only saw the soul in the body, but also saw the body as the soul-reality. A transformed and illumined body-consciousness for God-satisfaction was your goal. By the way, while you were on earth, you were extremely fond of taking long-distance walking tours to other countries. Now that you are in Heaven you do not walk. You fly and fly. Do you miss your walking days?
SOUL OF WALT WHITMAN   I do, Mother, I do.
SOUL OF AMERICA   Walt, now it is your turn.
SOUL OF WALT WHITMAN   "O America! Because you build for mankind, I build for you."
SOUL OF AMERICA   Marvellous! marvellous!
   Now, Emily, your heart's inner aspiration-beauty pleased me far beyond your imagination. Your heart's inner music blessed America's children with glowing simplicity, purity and luminosity. You gave to the American consciousness a new dimension, a new type of soul-search — soft, delicate and lucid. Now Emily, your turn.

SOUL OF EMILY DICKINSON

> If I can stop one heart from breaking,
> I shall not live in vain;
> If I can ease one life the aching,
> Or cool one pain,
> Or help one fainting robin
> Unto his nest again,
> I shall not live in vain.

SOUL OF AMERICA   Marvellous, marvellous!
  Mary, you were the founder-leader of Christian Science. In mental healing you supremely excelled. Your divine, self-giving service gave birth to the First Church of Christ, Mother Church in Boston. Infinity and Eternity sing their Immortality's soul-song in your church, God-Abode. Now it is your turn.
SOUL OF MARY BAKER EDDY   "Divine Love always has met and always will meet every human need."
SOUL OF AMERICA   Marvellous, marvellous!
  I am so proud of each of you. It is you who have made me really great. It is your consciousness-light that has made me shine in the vanguard of world-aspiration and world-achievement. How I wish you all could live with me once more and stay indefinitely. Alas, it seems that it can't be. It is getting late. The doors of Heaven may close. You all have to go back to Heaven. But do come back soon. Each time I see you, my children, I swim in the boundless sea of light and delight. I have something for you to carry back with you: my entire satisfaction-life's gratitude-sky.

Because of you, world-greatness I claim.
Because of you, world-goodness I claim.
Because of you, world-success and world-progress
    I claim.
I am what you divinely and supremely have made
    me to be.

THE SACRED FIRE

SF 15. ACT V, SCENE I

(Woodrow Wilson in his White House Office.)

WOODROW WILSON   Alas, a world war has begun with all its atrocities. I want my country to stay out of the war. To me, war is undivine and inhuman; therefore, it is beneath my dignity to fight. I have urged my nation not to enter into the vortex of war. We have had enough of war. What we need and what we shall always need is peace. *(He glances at the morning news and is horrified.)* I can't believe my eyes! German submarines have sunk our ships! I wanted to remain out of the war. Now I see that this can never be. Fight we must to defend our country. But I shall tell my country and the world that, for America, this will be a war to end all war.

SF 16. ACT V, SCENE 2

(Woodrow Wilson and his daughter Margaret, at home.)

MARGARET WILSON   Father, God gave you a very big heart. Your heart cried for world peace. You did not want America to enter into the war, but Germany and circumstances compelled America to become involved. You told the world that, on our part, this was a war to end all war, and you fulfilled your promise. Now, again, you want to manifest your lifelong resolve. You want to avert all future wars. You want peace all over the world; therefore, you are sacrificing your very life-blood to form the League of Nations. You are facing tremendous opposition. To my utter sorrow, you are encountering the worst opposition from your own countrymen. But I feel from deep within that soon you will definitely be able to form the League of Nations. Your divine vision will see the face of supreme reality.

WOODROW WILSON   Margaret, my daughter, you have always been my confidante. Today your heart of illumination has consoled me tremendously.

MARGARET WILSON   Father, it is a great pleasure, a great joy and a great honour to be of help to you.

WOODROW WILSON   Daughter, ideas live; men die.

MARGARET WILSON   Men like you, with lofty ideas, never die. Because of their divine ideas, they remain immortal on earth. They are treasured equally by both Heaven and earth. Father, the League of Nations must see the light of day before you leave this body.

WOODROW WILSON   How I wish it could be possible! Margaret, right from your childhood you were God-oriented. Now you have decided to go to India and practise spirituality. It is only in the spiritual life, you realise, that God-realisation is possible. I admire your genuine longing for God and bless your devoted heart. But I have one request to make of you. Please tell me that you will fulfil my request, my heart's desire. You will go to India only after I have gone to the other world, not before.

MARGARET WILSON   Father, I promise that I shall stay beside you like your most faithful shadow until you join the other world. Only then shall I go to India, the land of my heart's dream, the land of my soul's real reality-existence.

SRI CHINMOY

SF 17. ACT V, SCENE 3

(Franklin D. Roosevelt is sitting at his desk.)

FRANKLIN D. ROOSEVELT   Lord, I am grateful to You for granting me the capacity to serve my country as its President. True, I am paralysed by polio, but You have blessed me with ceaseless activity. You have spoken through me these celestial words: "This great nation will revive.... The only thing we have to fear is fear itself." And the most important of all the blessings that You have showered upon me is my dear wife, Eleanor. Without her I could have done nothing. Without her I could have become nothing.

(Eleanor Roosevelt enters.)

ELEANOR ROOSEVELT   Franklin, I overheard you. Now it is my turn to speak. Because of you, I am the wife of our President. Because of you, I am the First Lady of the country.

FRANKLIN D. ROOSEVELT   And because of you, one day when I am physically gone, I will be known as the husband of the First Lady of the world.

ELEANOR ROOSEVELT   Why? Why such extravagant absurdities?

FRANKLIN D. ROOSEVELT   No extravagant absurdities. Because of your devoted, selfless service to the nation and the world community, you deserve that greatest honour. I clearly see it. When the world claims you as its First Lady, an unprecedented honour, I shall swim in the sea of light and delight in Heaven.

ELEANOR ROOSEVELT   You have always been a great patriot. Now you are a matchless President. But since when have you become a prophet?

FRANKLIN D. ROOSEVELT   Right from today. My vision can never fail.

ELEANOR ROOSEVELT   I also have a vision. Your dream of the United Nations will, without fail, blossom. Wilson's dream — the League of Nations — will be blossoming powerfully and significantly with a wider, brighter and more fulfilling capacity in your dream of the United Nations. Wilson entered into a war to end war. You, too, did the same after America was attacked. Both you and Wilson are God's sons of all-loving and all-fulfilling peace. Your dream will one day be fulfilled, I assure you.

FRANKLIN D. ROOSEVELT   Let us thank God that He has blessed both of us with prophetic vision.

ELEANOR ROOSEVELT   Indeed, you are a great prophet, Franklin.

FRANKLIN D. ROOSEVELT   And you are a prophetess, Eleanor.

SRI CHINMOY

SF 18. ACT V, SCENE 4

(The White House. Harry Truman is working in his office.)

HARRY TRUMAN   Japan, I warned you. You paid no heed to my warning. You are planning to bother us more and more. We simply can't tolerate you any more. Your cruelties and atrocities will remain unparalleled in world-history. But tomorrow — not even one day more shall pass — I shall end this war. Your Hiroshima and Nagasaki will be totally destroyed by our world-shattering and world-destroying atom bomb, and you will then be compelled to surrender. We want peace. Once victory is won, we shall again work for peace. Be with us and work for world peace if you want to save your face from the infamy of a world war caused and declared by you.

SF 19. ACT V, SCENE 5

(The White House. Truman and one of his advisors.)

ADVISOR So, Mr. President, you have won the election. We all are extremely proud that you have become our President for a second term. We were afraid that you would not win the second election, but you did. All glory to you, Mr. President.

HARRY TRUMAN Not in vain did I travel thirty thousand miles. Not in vain did I give three hundred fifty speeches. I have won. That means my Fair Deal has won. Our country, which basically wants and needs the Fair Deal, has won.

ADVISOR Mr. President, Theodore Roosevelt is immortal for offering his "Square Deal" gift to the nation. Franklin Roosevelt is immortal for offering his "New Deal" gift to the nation and you will be immortal for offering your "Fair Deal" gift to the nation.

HARRY TRUMAN Whether or not I am going to be immortal I leave in the Hands of God. That is His business. My business is to become honest. My business is to see that my countrymen lead an honest life. Many businessmen stood against me when I proclaimed the Fair Deal. They were afraid that they were going to lose their businesses. What could I do? I was helpless. My sole purpose is to see the truth and serve the truth. Talking about businesses and businessmen, once upon a time I, too, was a businessman. I ran a clothing store, and I sadly failed. But this time, not in the capacity of a businessman but in the capacity of a truth-lover, and for the purpose of promoting the supreme necessity of truth in the minds and hearts of my countrymen, I am sure I shall succeed.

ADVISOR Mr. President, you must and you shall.

SRI CHINMOY

SF 20. ACT VI, SCENE I

(New Delhi, India. Dwight D. Eisenhower is on a goodwill tour all around Asia. At night he has a dream in which the soul of India appears.)

SOUL OF INDIA   President Eisenhower, you are great. You were a five-star general. You are great. You have won the world war. You are great, you are greater and you are greatest because you want peace. I am the soul of India. I want peace too, peace all over the world. India has many faults, but India's true love for peace nullifies all her shortcomings. My son Krishna wanted peace between the Pandavas and the Kauravas. But when he saw that peace was not going to take birth in a divine way, he agreed to settle the issue through war. He advised the Pandavas to fight for the right cause. On being attacked, your country had to fight in World War I and World War II to defend herself and thus establish and maintain the Kingdom of Truth and World Peace. Your country's vision and my country's vision run parallel. Although at times your America and my India are at odds, they basically love each other, for both have the self-same goal: a peaceful life. My son Gandhi cried and cried for peace. Almost all of your predecessors also cried for peace. The whole world is so proud of Washington, the Father of your nation. He wanted nothing but peace. From him, all of you have imbibed the message of peace. Eisenhower, you and your country want peace. My children and I want peace. Therefore, we are one. In your first inaugural address, your prayer to God was pure and sublime. You said, "Give us, we pray, the power to discern clearly right from wrong, and allow all our words and actions to be governed thereby, and by the laws of this land. Especially we pray that our concern shall be for all the people regardless of station, race, or calling." In your second inaugural address, you said something divine and supreme. You said, "This is our home, yet this is not the whole of our world. For our world is where our full destiny lies — with men, of all peoples and all nations, who are or would be free. And so the prayer of our people carries far beyond our own frontiers, to the wide world of our duty and our destiny. May the light of freedom, coming to all darkened lands, flame brightly — until at last the darkness is no more."

DWIGHT D. EISENHOWER   O Soul of Mother India, you have an astonishing memory. I fully agree with you about India and America. I feel that India has the God-ordained vision and America has the God-ordained mission. Both vision and mission must be united to give birth to humanity's perfection in life. You are so right. You are so right.

(Eisenhower sings "O Sweet Liberty".)

SRI CHINMOY

SF 21. ACT VI, SCENE 2

(John F. Kennedy's Inauguration.)

JOHN F. KENNEDY   We observe today not a victory of party but a celebration of freedom .... Let every nation know, whether it wishes us well or ill, that we shall pay any price, bear any burden, meet any hardship, support any friend, oppose any foe to assure the survival and the success of liberty. My fellow Americans: ask not what your country can do for you; ask what you can do for your country. My fellow citizens of the world: ask not what America will do for you, but what together we can do for the freedom of man.

THE SACRED FIRE

SF 22. ACT VI, SCENE 3

(John F. Kennedy is making a speech on television.)

JOHN F. KENNEDY O world-leaders, I wish to tell you all something. I need your one-pointed attention. Together we shall save our planet, or together we shall perish in its flames. Many countrymen have joined me in a ban on atmospheric nuclear tests. And some have not. I offer my most sincere loving gratitude to those countries who have joined me in this world-protecting and world-fulfilling mission. And I place the countries that have not joined us at the Feet of God for their immediate illumination. What more can I say?

SF 23. ACT VII, SCENE I

(The World-soul, the soul of England and the soul of America in the Abode of the ever-transcending Heights.)

WORLD-SOUL   My sweet daughter, England-soul, are you not happy now? Possession is not happiness. Renunciation is happiness. And if renunciation is God-ordained, then it is perfect happiness. It was God who wanted you to renounce your possession-authority. Look, now your daughter America is happy and you are happy. Needless to say, I am happy too.

SOUL OF ENGLAND   Mother, once I was temptation-possession, but now I am illumination-oneness. And I unmistakably and gratefully know that it was all your doing.

WORLD-SOUL   My daughter, what we need to know is not so much whose doing it was, but whether the thing is done. I am glad beyond measure that the thing is done, the *right* thing is done.

SOUL OF AMERICA   Grandmother, Mother has taught me many nice things, and two things I treasure most: her mind's lofty nobility and her life's non-sentimental, or non-emotional but measured and confident progress along the road of Eternity's perfection.

WORLD-SOUL   You are absolutely right, my granddaughter. Now I would like both you and your mother to do me a big favour. Please sing me the song that says, "My Captain says go on."

(The souls of England and America sing.)

THE SACRED FIRE

There was a time when I stumbled and stumbled.
But now I only climb and climb beyond
And far beyond my Goal's endless Beyond.
And yet my Captain commands: "Go on, go on!"

(And then they sing:)

America, America, America!
Great you are, good you are,
Brave you are, kind you are.
O my America, America.
Your Heaven-freedom
Is earth's aspiration-choice.
With you, in you
Is God-Hour's Victory-voice.

PART VI

DESHABANDHU:
BENGAL'S BELOVED FRIEND

DESHABANDHU: BENGAL'S BELOVED FRIEND

DF 1. *Dramatis personæ (in order of appearance)*

THREE CHILDREN OF THE COSMIC GODS
NETAJI (SUBHAS CHANDRA BOSE, THE PROTÉGÉ OF C.R. DAS)
DESHAPRIYA (JATIN RAMMOHUN SEN)
DESHABANDHU (CHITTA RANJAN DAS)
RAJA [KING] MANILAL SINGH
DEBENDRA (AN ATTENDANT)
PANDIT MOTILAL NEHRU (FATHER OF JAWAHARLAL NEHRU)
VAISHNAVA (A DEVOTEE OF VISHNU)

DESHABANDHU: BENGAL'S BELOVED FRIEND

DF 2. SCENE I

(Place: The Garden of Eden. Time: Full moon night. The children of the cosmic gods are singing in Heaven, Bishwabasir jai.... *[Victory to the citizens of the world!....] Enter Netaji Subhas Chandra Bose. "Netaji" means "great leader".)*

NETAJI Since I left India, I have never heard such a soul-stirring song! The sentiment, the thought, the language, the rhythm, the melody, the tone — each and every petal of this song-flower is unique, and the flower itself is intoxicating me with its beauty and fragrance. Since I left my Mother Bengal, I have never heard such a beautiful song. But alas, I thought that it was the children of Bengal who were singing the song. Now I see that it is the children of the cosmic gods who are singing. Where am I? Where is my Motherland? O my Mother India, I do not mind in the least if I am not favoured with a place among those who sacrificed their all to liberate you from the cruel shackles of British domination. My only sorrow is that you are still in stark bondage, ruthlessly insulted and painfully humiliated at every moment.

(From the opposite side, enter Deshapriya, another martyr. Deshapriya is from Chittagong; "Deshapriya" means "one who is dear to Mother Bengal".)

DESHAPRIYA Ah, Netaji! You are here! I am so fortunate today to meet with Mother India's greatest and most beloved son. Your name and your supreme glories are echoing and re-echoing throughout the length and breadth of India. I have just come from our Motherland, where I paid a short visit.

NETAJI   You are coming from India? Tell me, tell me, how is our eternal sufferer, Mother Bengal? Mahatma, Jawaharlal and others — how are they? What are they doing?

DESHAPRIYA   Our Mother India is free! The English have left our Motherland on their own.

NETAJI   Tell me, tell me more! Why do you stop? Am I in a fantasy-world? Our Motherland is liberated? Our one and only dream has been fulfilled? Then how is it that you are not happy in the least? On the contrary, your eyes are flooded with tears.

DESHAPRIYA   Alas, our Mother India is now divided. She can no longer pride herself on the oneness of her sweet children. The whole of India is drenched with the blood of Hindus and Muslims. Poverty, untold misery and catastrophe have become India's daily companions. My Mother Chittagong has fallen under the inexorable curse of division. The poisonous air of division-night is about to devour and destroy me completely. There is no food, no clothing — only birthless and deathless fear. Premature death, accidental death and unnatural death — this is what India's fate has become. Soon, Netaji, I shall visit Bengal again. My sole aim, like yours, is to unite India. We must uproot the separation-poison-tree!

NETAJI   What are you saying, Deshapriya? I am unable to understand you. On my way to Japan from Singapore, I fell asleep in the plane, and then I do not know what happened to me. One thing I do remember, though, is that my dearest and fondest *Azad Hind Fauj*, our Indian National Army, failed to bring about India's independence.

DESHAPRIYA   No mighty endeavour can forever remain unfulfilled, Netaji. At God's choice Hour, God Himself lovingly breathes life into our glorious dreams. True, your *Azad Hind Fauj* could not give India her freedom, but you and your indomitable army of liberation-fire will forever and forever remain immortal in the heart-history of India. Even Mahatma has bowed to you and your army with tremendous admiration.

NETAJI   Enough, enough, my dear friend! No more embarrassment! What I have done for my Mother Bengal is next to nothing; what I have done for my Mother India is next to nothing. Now tell me, are they honouring our beloved Deshabandhu (Chitta Ranjan Das), our political Guru, whose lofty inspiration I imbibed at my journey's start? Today I want to prostrate myself at his mighty feet. He was my blue-vast inspiration-ocean. If my cherished countrymen have even an iota of appreciation for me, then I am offering it all to him, for it is he alone who rightly deserves it. His boundless affection-smiles and unparalleled wisdom-teachings have made me what I am now. My earth-bound life and my Heaven-free soul are profusely and eternally grateful to him.

DESHAPRIYA   Indeed, dear Netaji, it is his unconditional blessings that have also made *me* what I am now. Let us go and pay our prayerful homage to our beloved Deshabandhu. I am sure he will be overwhelmed with joy to see you!

(Exeunt omnes. Netaji song is heard from offstage.)

DF 3. SCENE 2

(Time: Dawn. The children of the cosmic gods are playing in Heaven at the command of Lord Indra. For a whole year, they will be observing great festivities for India's independence.)

FIRST CHILD   Delight, delight everywhere! The moment we desire anything, we get it! We get everything for the asking. We do not have to pray and meditate in order to achieve anything. Yet, a burning desire I cherish to accept human life. Do you know, my friends, why I entertain this kind of desire?

SECOND CHILD   I *do* know why.

THIRD CHILD   And I also know! Our Lord Indra accepted the human body. The Guru of the cosmic gods, Brihaspati; the great sage Narada; Lord Brahma; Lord Vishnu and Lord Shiva from time to time also accept human life. Leaving Heaven, they play their respective roles for Mother Earth by taking human form.

FIRST CHILD   But why? Here there is no dearth of anything. Again, perhaps there is no true joy in enjoyment if no austerity is needed to achieve something. Therefore, perhaps there is no joy here in Heaven after all. Yes, this is the very reason for Heaven-dwellers to descend to earth. How strange! Although human beings are desperately longing for a divine life, their desire is not fulfilled. At the same time, we divine beings have everything, yet there is somehow a sense of sorrowful unfulfilment.

THIRD CHILD   In order to inseparably and eternally remain with the Lord Supreme, one has to take a human body. One must aspire to be His close companion on earth.

FIRST CHILD   Let us go and take a human body on earth! We know how weak all human beings are, how helpless they are, how insufficient and incomplete they are. Nevertheless, God has very special Blessings, very special Compassion and very special Concern for them. Therefore, He Himself descends to earth in human form, in a human body.

SECOND CHILD   I, too, have a strong desire to enter into the world. Let us all go together!

THIRD CHILD   Are you insane? Do you know that there is an animal in the desert that eats cactus? Its mouth bleeds, yet it continues to eat the cactus! *(All of the children burst into laughter.)*

FIRST CHILD   I have heard that the Mother of Illusion takes away all the knowledge and power of the cosmic gods when they enter into human life. Therefore, fear is torturing me!

THIRD CHILD   Then why are you pining for human birth? You can see from here what they are doing on earth. Today, here in Heaven, a play is being staged about the life of Bengal's beloved son Deshabandhu. Let us go and watch!

SECOND CHILD   I am also eager to watch. Since we do not know earth-life well, let us first become fully acquainted with it here, in the safety of Heaven. Let us go and watch the play about the life of Deshabandhu Chitta Ranjan.

FIRST CHILD   Look, look! A new scene!

(They retire to one side of the stage and watch. Deshabandhu song is heard. The curtain rises to show an earthly scene.)

(Place: Darjeeling. Deshabandhu [Friend of the Nation] is bedridden. His days are numbered; death is fast approaching. Beside him are Raja Manilal Singh and Debendra, two of his attendants.)

RAJA Gurudev, you are the peerless wealth of our country. God will not allow you to leave your Motherland. But I do hope you are observing a proper diet!

DESHABANDHU I am regularly irregular in my diet.

RAJA When you are well, you must go to England for a change of scenery, to recuperate completely.

DESHABANDHU Where will I get the money? Do you not know that I am utterly poverty-stricken?

RAJA But there is so much money in your party fund.

DESHABANDHU That fund is sacred. I cannot touch it!

RAJA All right, we shall raise funds. Your health is of first and foremost importance.

DESHABANDHU No, no. I have given up all my lofty dreams. Mother India's bondage-life has stabbed my heart with excruciating pangs. I must not flee to England for comfort. Again, who would give me the money? I am a veritable beggar.

DEBENDRA Gurudev, I beg to be excused! Do not allow the pitiful word "beggar" to cloud your self-offering-sun. You have renounced all your vast riches to liberate our Motherland. The other day Mahatma Gandhi said, "Deshabandhu has sacrificed everything. He is, indeed, an all-sacrificing sannyasi. He has even offered his own house to the poor and needy." I told Mahatma that my boss has offered millions and millions of rupees to the undeserving people, and the result is that now he is penniless; he has absolutely no money of his own.

DESHABANDHU Shut up! How dare you say "undeserving"? Who is deserving and who is undeserving? We must needs give our all to see the living Presence of God inside each and every human being if we dare to dream of fulfilling God's Will here on earth.

(*At that moment from behind the curtain several voices:* Bande Mataram! Deshabandhu ki jai! *"Victory to Deshabandhu!"*)

FIRST CHILD   (*deeply inspired*) Blessed, Deshabandhu, are you. Blessed is your life on earth.

THIRD CHILD   I do not know why here in Heaven they are creating such a fuss over an ordinary human being!

SECOND CHILD   An ordinary human being? Deshabandhu is not an ordinary human being! He should be our ideal. I am going to take incarnation in his Motherland, Bengal. I shall take Mother Bengal as my own, very own. I wish to be blessed by her, just as Deshabandhu has been richly and gloriously blessed.

FIRST CHILD   I shall accompany you.

THIRD CHILD   I am not going! From here in Heaven I shall enjoy watching you. Whenever you are in need of anything, I shall send it from here. When the great Mother of Illusion makes you forget that you were once upon a time the children of the cosmic gods, in secret I shall arrive and remind you of what you were, and I shall save you.

(*From behind the curtain:* Bande Mataram! Deshabandhu ki jai! *"Victory to Deshabandhu!" Then the song to Tagore's words* Ennechile sathe.... *[You came into the world with an immortal heart, and you left it here on your way back] is heard.*)

DF 4. SCENE 3

(Place: Deshabandhu's palace in Heaven. Time: Twelve noon. Deshabandhu and Pandit Motilal Nehru, Jawaharlal Nehru's father and Deshabandhu's great admirer, are conversing.)

MOTILAL   At long last our beloved Mother India has gained her independence! All her stupendous efforts have finally been crowned with success!

DESHABANDHU   Yes, I have heard that breathtaking news, my dear friend, and also I have heard that your son, Jawaharlal, has become our Prime Minister. I am so happy that he has emerged as a star of unparalleled brilliance in the firmament of India.

MOTILAL   This is due to your blessings, Deshabandhu, and the blessings of all those who truly love our Mother India.

DESHABANDHU   But alas, dear Motilal, Bengal's fate is excruciating! Our green-gold Bengal has now become a black cremation-ground. Not a single leader has sprung forth from her sacred heart to bear the responsibility of our Motherland. But, my friend, you can be truly proud of your most illustrious Jawaharlal.

MOTILAL   Deshabandhu, what about your mind-begotten son, Subhas? Subhas has conquered the heartbeat and life-breath of each and every Indian soul. Without a shadow of doubt, Subhas' place in the chronicle of our Mother India's ageless life is infinitely higher than my son's!

DESHABANDHU   Alas, I had so much hope in my Subhas and in the others. One by one, untimely, they left Mother Bengal; they deserted her. They, too, have now come to Heaven without liberating Bengal, and our Mother is helplessly drowning in a sea of tears and blood.

DESHABANDHU: BENGAL'S BELOVED FRIEND

(Enter a certain Vaishnava, like Deshabandhu a devotee of Vishnu.)

DESHABANDHU   I am so happy that you have come to bless my abode.

VAISHNAVA   I have come to you for a ticket.

DESHABANDHU   What kind of ticket?

VAISHNAVA   I need a ticket to roam freely in Heaven, on earth, in the infernal region and throughout all planes of consciousness. This is all I need for the time being; afterwards I will need a different ticket from you.

MOTILAL   May I know your name?

VAISHNAVA   Certainly! But first tell me, will you give me the ticket? If not, why should I take the trouble of telling you my name? Would you not like to show me that your life's generosity and your heart's magnanimity far surpass Deshabandhu's?

MOTILAL   What! How dare you compare my insignificant existence with his all-illumining life? Do you not know that I love him and adore him unreservedly? He kindly and compassionately showers his blessingful affection upon me and tells the world that I am his friend. Therefore, I had in mind to make a special request of Deshabandhu on your behalf to grant you the ticket that you need.

VAISHNAVA   You have to make a request of Deshabandhu? Am I at the right place? Am I standing before the right person? Is this not the abode of Deshabandhu? Perhaps it is not! In that case, I am leaving!

MOTILAL   Stop, Venerable Vaishnava — stop! This is Deshabandhu himself *(pointing to Deshabandhu.)* Stop! Do not go away! Please, do not go away!

VAISHNAVA   All right, now I can tell you my name, but in abbreviated form. I am shortening it considerably: One Thousand

Eight Sri Tribuban Das Ghana Shyama Sri Krishna Charan Bharasha Prasadananda Das.

DESHABANDHU   This is your *abridged* name? Is it your hard-earned name, or have you inherited such a splendid name?

(Deshabandhu and Motilal burst into wild laughter.)

VAISHNAVA   This is my hard-earned name! I earned it! My parents gave me the name Shibu. Now tell me, what about my ticket?

(Enter Netaji Subhas Chandra Bose and Deshapriya.)

VAISHNAVA   What is this nonsense? What is this absurdity? Why are they coming here? Please, please fulfil my desire first, before you speak to them! *(To Subhas and Deshapriya.)* Please, please wait a little! Let Deshabandhu fulfil my desire first by granting me my ticket. I am sure you, too, have come here to ask for something.

DESHAPRIYA   *(to Deshabandhu)* I have brought Subhas here to offer his devoted obeisance to you, Deshabandhu. Ah, I see Nehru here! *Pranam, pranam!* I bow to you, I salute you!

MOTILAL   Subhas is here? Our leader is here?

(He stands up and embraces Subhas.)

VAISHNAVA   Alas, these friends of yours are ruining my request! I shall be here again tomorrow.

(Exit Vaishnava.)

DESHABANDHU   Subhas, you too have come back? What will our Mother Bengal do now? Like us, you, too, have deserted Mother Bengal?

NETAJI   It is *you,* Deshabandhu, who can save our Bengal from untold and unspeakable atrocities. Once more Bengal needs your immediate pinnacle-leadership! We implore your express arrival! Once more we shall be your unwavering soldiers. At every moment we shall obey your infallible command lovingly, faithfully and self-givingly.

DESHABANDHU   Come, let us go! We shall go first to East Bengal, which they now call East Pakistan. We shall save our Mother Bengal from the ruthless torture of division-night. Come, my Subhas! Come, Jatin! You two remain always with me. If you two are with me, then there is nothing that I will not be able to accomplish for our Mother Bengal.

(The song Janani Chatrala *is heard. With adamantine will, all three hero-souls descend from Heaven to their beloved Bengal. Exeunt omnes.)*

(The song Bharat Amar *concludes the play.)*

DF 5. GLOSSARY

AZAD HIND FAUJ   another name for the Indian National Army that Netaji formed to overthrow the British.

BANDE MATARAM   "Mother, I bow to Thee!" — the mantric slogan of the Indian freedom-fighters.

BRAHMA, VISHNU, SHIVA   the Indian trinity. Brahma is the Creator, Vishnu the Preserver and Shiva the Transformer.

DESHABANDHU KI JA   (*ja* is pronounced "joy") — "Victory to Deshabandhu!"

INDRA   the chief of the cosmic gods.

JAWAHARLAL   Pandit Jawaharlal Nehru, the first Prime Minister of India.

MAHATMA   Mahatma Gandhi. It was Netaji who first called Gandhi-ji the Father of the Nation.

SANNYASI   one who has renounced the world.

Author's note

"While I was translating, so many times there were tears in my eyes. We Bengalis, both Hindu and Muslim, are all for Netaji. For him there was no Hindu, no Muslim, no Christian. All joined his Indian National Army, irrespective of religion, because they loved him so dearly."

ADDITIONAL WRITINGS ON DESHABANDHU

DF 6. DESHABANDHU (1945)

Bhalobesechhile bharat matare
    Banga desher bir
Nishwa haile bharatbasir
    Muchite nayan nir
Pratipade badha daliya charane
    Vijayir beshe ese
Pranam karecho bir prasabini
    Janani bangla deshe
Britisher kara tomar sparshe
    Hayeche tirthabhumi
Swadesh mantre dikkshita haye
    Tomar charane chumi
Sardul sama tomare manito
    British shasak dal
Tumi ene dite arter buke
    Nitya nutan bal
Himaloy jabe haran karilo
    Deshabandhur pran
Nakkshatra je nimne namilo
    Kare kabi anuman
Eman shoker banya kakhano
    Nameni moder deshe
Shatru mitra kendechilo sabe
    Tomarei bhalobese

DESHABANDHU: BENGAL'S BELOVED FRIEND

DF 7. CHITTA RANJAN DAS (1957)

How to hail Chitta Ranjan? To honour him as a Vaishnava to the marrow, a highly literary figure, a politician of the front rank, a man endowed with oratorical gifts, an unrivalled Bar-at-Law, a potential leader, a hero who knew what fighting means, is in no way adequate. The most befitting epithet for this unique personage would be "Deshabandhu" [the friend of the country] for his unstinted sacrifice for his country and countrymen.

Rare is the man whose life far exceeds his great achievements. Also rare is the man whose message to the world is his life itself. But in the life of Deshabandhu we find a rare combination of both these high qualities.

Chitta Ranjan had been to England to sit for the Indian Civil Service. Unfortunately, nay, fortunately, he headed the list of the unsuccessful. Had he won the "Heaven-Born Service", he would certainly have become a civil servant. And who could guarantee that he would not have exerted his unusual power to climb to the highest rung of the ladder? And if he had done so, how could opportunity have knocked at his door and asked him to mix with and work for his countrymen whom he so sincerely loved? What Providence wished from Chitta Ranjan was a great service to his Motherland. The devoted son was ever confident of his Motherland's brightest future. His deep patriotism gave a significant meaning and purpose to the exalted glory of India all over the world. It happened that during his stay in that foreign land a meeting was once held at Oldham under the Presidentship of Gladstone. In a speech on "Indian Agitation", Chitta Ranjan's tone and expression left no doubt that he was a citadel of strength:

> Gentlemen, I was sorry to find it given expression to in Parliamentary speeches on more than

one occasion that England conquered India by the sword and by the sword she must keep it! *(Shame.)* England, gentlemen, did no such thing. It was not her sword and bayonet that won this vast and glorious empire; it was not her military valour that achieved this triumph. *(Cheers.)* England might well be proud of it. But to attribute all this to the sword and then to argue that the policy of the sword is the only policy that ought to be pursued is to my mind absolutely base and quite unworthy of an Englishman. *(Hear, hear.)*

The years 1907 and 1908 shall shine perpetually in the history of Bengal. The current of true patriotism simply inundated the four frontiers of the province. On the fourth of May, 1908, in the small hours of the morning, Sri Aurobindo was arrested, and soon he was considered to be the supreme leader of the firebrand revolutionaries. The two significant features of the Alipore Bomb Case were the unexpected acquittal of Sri Aurobindo and C.R. Das's swift flare-up into fame. Das was then a junior counsel. Bhupal Bose, the father-in-law of Sri Aurobindo, appointed Byomkesh Chakravarti to defend his son-in-law. The old man dismissed Das as a child, saying, "I should not commit the charge of the case of my son-in-law to a younger counsel."

But somehow Chitta Ranjan Das felt an inner urge to participate in the defence of Sri Aurobindo, his dear friend, whom he had first met in England. In those days, he used to communicate with the spirit-world with the help of a planchette. One day a particular message was received by him repeatedly.

"You must defend Arabinda." To the query who he was, the reply came, *Upadhyaya*. Requested to be more explicit, the "spirit" replied: *Brahma bandhava upadhyaya* [a fire-soul of patriotism].

From that day on, it became quite clear to Chitta Ranjan that he would have to conduct the Alipore Bomb Case.

Meanwhile, for some reason or other, the counsel Byomkesh Chakravarti was dispensed with and C.R. Das was called in.

On this occasion Sri Aurobindo's sister, Sarojini Ghosh, played a significant role in saving her brother. She raised subscriptions and even begged from door to door, appealing to the very rickshaw drivers and the coolies who, on their part, never failed to respond to her throbbing appeal. At last, on the 18th of August, 1908, in *Bande Mataram,* she issued the following appeal:

> I am sincerely grateful to my countrymen and countrywomen of different provinces, creeds and grades of society for their kind response to my appeal for funds for the defence of my brother, Srijut Aurobindo Ghosh. The time has now come to engage a counsel to defend him in the Court of Sessions. Perhaps the public have not hitherto had any accurate idea of the probable expenses of my brother's defence. My legal and other advisers tell me that the amount required would not fall short of sixty thousand rupees. But only twenty-three thousand rupees have been received up to date.
> May I not hope that the balance will be received shortly?....

Deshabandhu's love and affection for Sri Aurobindo will be evident from the following incident. When some of the friends of Sri Aurobindo made a fervent request to him to conduct the case to the best of his ability, he was deeply pained:

> Am I less anxious than any of you to get Aurobindo released?

On another occasion he said that while defending Aurobindo he felt that he himself was the accused and he was arguing his own case. What a sense of identification he developed with his intimate friend!

While closing the Alipore Bomb Case, he made a short and eloquent speech. His prophetic voice will ring in the ears of posterity for all time:

> ....My appeal to you is this — that long after this turmoil, this agitation will have ceased, long after he is dead and gone, he will be looked upon as the poet of patriotism, as the prophet of nationalism and the lover of humanity. Long after he is dead and gone, his words will be echoed and re-echoed not only in India but across distant seas and lands.....

Let us here leave Sri Aurobindo to speak about the loving sacrifice of C.R. Das and the divine mystery involved in the matter.

> He came unexpectedly — a friend of mine, but I did not know he was coming. You have all heard the name of the man who put away from him all other thoughts and abandoned all his practice, who sat up half the night day after day for months and broke his health to save me — Srijut Chitta Ranjan Das. When I saw him, I was satisfied, but I still thought it necessary to write instructions. Then all that was put away from me and I had the message from within, 'This is the man who will save you from the snares put around your feet. Put aside those papers. It is not you who will instruct him.

I will instruct him.' From that time I did not of myself speak a word to my counsel about the case or give a single instruction, and if ever I was asked a question, I always found that my answer did not help the case. I had left it to him and he took it entirely into his hands, with what result you know.

Sister Nivedita was one among those who highly appreciated the rare sacrifice made by Chitta Ranjan in the interests of Aurobindo. She said, "I knew you to be great, but did not know that you are so great." She then pinned a dark red rose into the buttonhole of Chitta Ranjan's coat.

"A politician thinks of the next election, a statesman of the next generation." (James Freeman Clarke) This pleasant-sounding statement cannot be applied to patriot-politicians like C.R. Das. "With me," says he, "work for my country is no imitation of European politics. It is a part of my religion. It is a part and parcel of all the idealism of my life."

When his only son Chira Ranjan was eagerly prepared to go to jail for the country, his relatives and friends advised Chitta Ranjan to dissuade him from doing so. At this Chitta Ranjan was more than angry with them. "When will you understand this simple truth, that I must send my own son to jail first and then only am I entitled to invite the Bengali youths to launch into the service of the Motherland?" More surprise awaits us. A deep and tranquil smile played upon his eyes the moment he heard that his wife Basanti Devi and his sister Urmila Devi were asked to step into the police station, for he realised that the hour of victory was fast approaching.

His sense of duty: his father, Bhuvan Mohan Das, had declared insolvency. Nobody could lay any claim on his debt, and according to the British Law the son was exempt from being charged. But the deepest sense of duty in the devoted son Chitta enjoined him to free his father. When a sum of Rs. 75,000 was made over to clear off the father's debt, Justice Fletcher, with a heart full of admiration for Chitta Ranjan's unprecedented deed, declared, "An act of this kind is not to be seen even in Europe." Soon after this momentous event took place, his aged father died.

Chitta Ranjan had a helping hand even in social reform. The deplorable condition of Indian widows cut him to the quick. He made bold to say that it is mere stupidity on our part either to force the widows to marry once again, or make them practise celibacy the rest of their lives. According to him, it is to the widows that the chance should be given to choose their future state and not to the so-called social reformers.

Untouchability was altogether foreign to his nature. He failed to put up with the haughtiness of the higher-class people. He utterly disdained their merciless conduct towards the low. His sympathetic heart voiced forth: "Next time, how I wish to take birth among the untouchables and devote myself to their service!"

I am now tempted to relate an interesting as well as arresting incident which will display Chitta Ranjan's love and reverence for Sri Aurobindo. Deshabandhu was then the Editor of a popular periodical, *Narayan*. Nolini Gupta had sent a contribution entitled *Arter Adhyatmikata* (Spirituality in Art) from Pondicherry for publication in 1917. Chitta Ranjan was enamoured of the article and was certain that the actual writer could be nobody else save Sri Aurobindo, covering himself with a pseudonym, for the word "Nolini" also means "lotus", just as "Aurobindo" means "lotus". "Gupta" means "hidden" and was taken to be the indication of Sri Aurobindo's living incognito. Considering that it was no longer necessary for Sri Aurobindo to remain hidden from public view, he published the said article under the name of Aurobindo Ghosh instead of Nolini Gupta. Soon after, Sri

DESHABANDHU: BENGAL'S BELOVED FRIEND

Aurobindo wrote to his dear friend Chitta that he was not the writer of that article, but that there was actually one among his associates in flesh and blood bearing the name Nolini Gupta. Of course, at present Nolini Gupta needs no introduction.

1925 — Deshabandhu left the earth. The Master-Seer of the Age, from his silence-hushed Ashram, telegraphed a message to a daily journal that had wired for a comment. "Chitta Ranjan's death is a supreme loss. Consummately endowed with political intelligence, constructive imagination, magnetism, a driving force combining a strong will and uncommon plasticity of mind for vision and tact of the hour, he was the one man after Tilak who could have led India to *Swaraj*."

Tagore's glorious tribute to the mighty departed soul runs:

> With thee came down the immortal breath.
> This thou booned us with thy body's death.

"Time," says Gandhi, "cannot efface the memory of a man so great and good as Deshabandhu. At this time of trial for the nation, there is no Indian who does not feel the void created by his death."

Bengal suffered a tremendous blow. Deshabandhu was a man of fifty-five when Death snatched him away. His life was a short, but a very full and busy one. Even those who did not know him at close range felt his death as a personal loss.

THREE DRAMATIC SCENES FROM
"THE DESCENT OF THE BLUE"

DF 8. ACT VII, SCENE 10

(Alipore Court. Beachcroft, Additional Sessions Judge and the jury. Norton, C.R. Das and other lawyers. The day of Aurobindo's release. C.R. Das, after summing up his whole case, concludes his historic address.)

C.R. DAS "....My appeal to you is this — that long after this turmoil, this agitation will have ceased, long after he is dead and gone, he will be looked upon as the poet of patriotism, as the prophet of nationalism and the lover of humanity. Long after he is dead and gone, his words will be echoed and re-echoed not only in India but across distant seas and lands....."

(Beachcroft looks on, eyes indrawn. The prosecution counsel, Mr. Norton, who was listening spellbound to the peroration, now looks at C.R. Das, relaxed and relieved of his year-long tension. Beachcroft starts addressing the jury. After his address to the jury the foreman takes leave of the court to retire for consultation with his colleagues. The jurors retire. The Court rises for lunch.)

DF 9. ACT VII, SCENE II

(After lunch.)

FOREMAN   *(turning to the judge)* Your Honour, our fully considered verdict is unanimous so far as Aurobindo is concerned. We all are of the opinion that he is Not Guilty. As regards the others....

BEACHCROFT   I accept your verdict and acquit Aurobindo of the charges brought against him. *(Turning towards C.R. Das)* Mr. Das, I congratulate you on your laborious study, patience, endurance and your able conduct of the case concerning your client Aurobindo.

C.R. DAS   I thank Your Honour for your kind appreciation of my personal efforts. I thank also the members of the jury for their unflagging patience and energy in following the case in detail from day to day and for giving their well-considered verdict.

NORTON   *(coming forward and shaking C.R. Das by the hand)* You have the reward of your labour. I congratulate you.

C.R. DAS   Thank you very much, my learned friend.

DF 10. ACT XI, SCENE 2

(5 June 1923. Sri Aurobindo and C.R. Das. Sri Aurobindo's residence, Pondicherry.)

C.R. DAS   A serious problem, Aurobindo.
SRI AUROBINDO   What is it?
C.R. DAS   I wish to take to spirituality.
SRI AUROBINDO   *(smiling)* How can it be a problem at all?
C.R. DAS   It is, Aurobindo.
SRI AUROBINDO   How?
C.R. DAS   Politics dogs me night and day.
SRI AUROBINDO   But you know the two cannot normally go together. The aims and ideals of the usual political activity are almost always opposed to those of spirituality, to say nothing of the forces at work in politics....
C.R. DAS   Ah, you have understood my problem. Aurobindo, help me into the spiritual life.
SRI AUROBINDO   I wish I could.
C.R. DAS   What prevents you, dear friend? Aurobindo, you are to me something far more than even a dear friend. And you know that.
SRI AUROBINDO   Chitta, you must be aware that you cannot make satisfactory progress in your inner life if you do not move away altogether from absorption in politics. It influences the consciousness in a very undesirable way.
C.R. DAS   You are perfectly right. But....
SRI AUROBINDO   I understand your difficulty. All right, then; you go on with your political activities, but at the same time do your best to live your inner life. Gradually you may find that your interest in politics is giving way to your interest in a higher life.

C.R. DAS   What a burden you have taken off my shoulders! I see a ray of light and breathe in a little fresh air. But one thing more — I need your help also in another matter. Our "Swarajya Party" needs your unstinted support.

SRI AUROBINDO   I feel strongly for it. I give its stand my full inner support. You will always feel my presence in it.

C.R. DAS   I feel doubly relieved. With your presence in me, all will go well with me. Do you remember my prophecy about you at the Trial? — "His words will be echoed and re-echoed...."

SRI AUROBINDO   But what would Norton think of you if he were to overhear you?

C.R. DAS   Oh, he is now a different man. He works hand in hand with me. He now appears against the Government in political cases.

SRI AUROBINDO   Good that he is now on the side of the weak and the striving. His chivalry will pay.

SIX STORIES ABOUT CHITTA RANJAN DAS

DF 11. A LARGER THAN THE LARGEST HEART

There was once a great leader whose heart was larger than the largest. In law he was extremely successful and as a national leader he was also quite successful. His real name was kindness, affection and compassion. He was always for the poor and the miserable, and he used to help people far beyond their need. The tips he gave to the police, for example, were ten times the amount that they usually got from others.

"These policemen work so hard," he said. "Just because they wear Indian garments, we do not value them. But if the same work were done by Englishmen with trousers on, we would have to give them much more."

One day a man in the Congress who worked for the great leader came up to him crying. The great man said, "Why are you crying?"

He said, "I stay at your house, but just because I come from the lowest class, everyone goes away from me. I am given my food at the place where the dogs and the chickens stay. It is so dirty and filthy there. One of your servants brings my food and I eat there as if I were another dog or another chicken. Please do something for me."

Because of his low class, society did not permit him to sit with the members of the family. But still the great man felt very sad. He said to his wife, "Granted, he cannot sit and eat with us, but can you not at least give him a nice place to eat? Why does he have to eat with the dogs and chickens? Can he not be given a better place?"

His wife said, "Yes, he should be given a better place. I shall see to it."

Although the wife told the servant to take his food to a nice place, a few days later the servant was careless and took the food to the same place. So once more the Congress worker came to the great man, crying and crying: "They have given me the food there again, just because I come of a low class. I am staying with you because of your affection and love for me. Otherwise, I would not stay. This kind of treatment I hate. Whenever your Brahmin cooks see me, they run away. They show tremendous contempt for me and literally hate me. Am I not a human being?"

The great leader felt miserable, and he burst into tears. He called his wife and said, "From now on this young man will eat not only inside the house, but actually in the room where I eat. He has to eat in my room whenever I am eating. If I happen to be elsewhere and it is time for him to eat, he has to eat in my room. I make it a law."

This great man was Chitta Ranjan Das. He was known as the most beloved friend of Mother Bengal. It was he who saved Sri Aurobindo from jail. When he died, Tagore said, "You came into the world with an immortal heart and you left it here on your way back."

DF 12. THE KIND-HEARTED BARRISTER

One day a middle-aged woman was found in the street most miserably and most pitifully weeping. A young barrister came out of a nearby house. He was on his way to court. When he saw the woman shedding bitter tears, he came up to her and asked why she was crying.

"I have walked here from a far-off place," the woman replied. "I have come only to see you. In my village I have heard so much about you. People say that you are extremely kind-hearted, extremely generous and extremely self-giving. Tomorrow is my only daughter's wedding. Alas, I do not have enough money to give her a proper marriage ceremony. I am so miserable. I know that tomorrow, if the wedding does not go well, some people will sympathise with me without helping me in any way. Others will laugh at me. Still others will just hate me. I have decided if tomorrow I cannot give my daughter a decent wedding, a proper wedding, I shall commit suicide. Now that you have heard my story, is there any way you can help me out of this sad plight?"

The young barrister said, "Right now I do not have any money with me. Please tell me how much money you actually need."

The woman mentioned a certain sum and the young barrister continued, "This evening try to be here at this same place. I shall without fail give you money and make you happy. Do not feel sad any more."

In the evening the young barrister returned home and as he neared his house he saw the woman waiting for him in exactly the same place. He presented her with ten times more money than she needed. The woman was speechless. She could only gaze at him with eyes full of gratitude. He smiled and said to her, "I am really happy that I could be of some help to you at this moment of your life."

This young barrister's name was Chitta Ranjan Das.

DF 13. CHITTA RANJAN INCOGNITO

On another occasion an elderly man was waiting for the young barrister. He had heard all about Chitta Ranjan Das. He knew that in addition to being extremely kind-hearted and generous, Chitta Ranjan always tried to be of service to the poor and the needy. This elderly man had walked from a distant village. He had never seen Chitta Ranjan personally and he did not know what he looked like. By making enquiries along the way, he had discovered where the young barrister lived, and so he decided to wait in the street with the hope of meeting Chitta Ranjan.

As the elderly man sat on the footpath, recovering from his long journey, a young man came up to him and kindly asked if he could be of any assistance to him. The elderly man immediately began to give a full account of his woes. He explained that he was in terrible financial difficulty. He could not afford to send his children to school; he could not even continue to feed his family. They were depending entirely on him to save them, but all his efforts to find employment had come to nothing. He desperately needed 2,000 rupees. The elderly man concluded by saying, "I am waiting here with the hope of speaking to him as he passes by. Is there any way that you can give him my message?"

The young man was puzzled. "Who is it that you are waiting to see?" he asked.

"I want to see Chitta Ranjan Das, who is always so kind and compassionate to the poor."

"I happen to know him well," the young man said. "He is now in court. If you come with me I shall take you to him."

Then he took the elderly man by car to the high court and showed him to a small room. "Please be seated. I shall go and speak with Chitta Ranjan Das and I assure you that you will be given the necessary amount."

In ten minutes' time a junior clerk entered the room and gave the elderly man an envelope containing the necessary amount. The elderly man was so grateful. He begged the junior clerk, "Is there any way I can meet the man who has been so kind to me? He has saved my family from utter ruin. I wish to express my gratitude to him and to receive his blessings. Do you think he could spare a few moments?"

The junior clerk replied, "He has already spent a full hour with you! Now he is so busy with his other responsibilities."

"What!" exclaimed the elderly man. "How is it possible?"

"Do you not recall that he brought you here in his own car?" said the junior clerk.

DF 14. TO CLEAR HIS FATHER'S NAME

The father of Chitta Ranjan Das, Bhuvan Mohan Das, was forced to declare insolvency. I do not know about America, but in India it brings great shame on the family to be reduced to this situation. His son was so sad and embarrassed that he took it upon himself to repay the entire sum of Rs. 75,000. He was not financially responsible for his father's debts under the British Law, but his high sense of duty and honour compelled him to clear his father's name. The British Justice who was presiding over the case said, "An act of this kind is not to be seen even in Europe." From that time, Chitta Ranjan Das started giving away money to help the needy.

*

Author's note: When I was twenty-five years old I wrote about this incident in an essay devoted to Chitta Ranjan Das. It is published in my book *Mother India's Lighthouse*. In life sometimes we create something and we get the results after 40 or 50 years! I wrote the essay in 1957 and now in 1993 — so many years later — I will be meeting with his grandson Siddhartha Shankar Ray, who has become the Indian Ambassador to the United States.

DF 15. A REAL KING AND QUEEN

Once a very large meeting took place at Bhabananda Park in Calcutta. C.R. Das was presiding over the meeting and his wife, Basanti Devi, was beside him.

The eminent scientist, P.C. Ray, said to them, "Here I see a real king and a real queen. Although they are without crowns, we are all ready to listen to their commands most willingly and most gratefully."

DF 16. GOD ALONE KNOWS WHO IS DESERVING

One day a very poor Brahmin came to C.R. Das and begged him for a large sum of money so that he could take care of his children and also his children's studies and pay back his debts. C.R. Das's heart melted at the pitiful condition of the poor Brahmin and he gave him a cheque for 10,000 rupees. The Brahmin was overjoyed and extremely, extremely grateful to C.R. Das.

At the time, a friend of C.R. Das happened to be standing nearby. When the poor Brahmin left, the friend said to C.R. Das, "What have you done? It is good to give money to the poor, but such a large amount? How do you know he deserves such a large amount of money? Are you not giving money indiscriminately?"

C.R. Das said, "I do not know whether I am giving money away indiscriminately or discriminately, but I do feel that it is up to God to judge as to whether I am doing the right thing or not."

Just at that moment, one of his assistants came up to C.R. Das with a telegram. C.R. Das opened the telegram and saw that an offer of 20,000 rupees had come from a certain king if he would accept a forthcoming legal case. Twenty thousand rupees the king was prepared to give him just to accept the case! C.R. Das said to his friend, "You see, I gave ten. Now I get twenty. So, God knows what is best for you, best for him, best for me, best for everyone. God alone knows who is deserving or undeserving. My business is to be of service to mankind, especially to those who are very, very poor."

CHITTA RANJAN AND SUBHAS CHANDRA: THE LIGHT-BESTOWER VERSUS THE STRENGTH-PRODUCER

SRI CHINMOY

DF 17. EXTRACT FROM BIRTH CENTENARY OFFERING

Deshabandhu was the only one
Whose soul was Subhas Chandra's
Dream-harbinger
And whose heart was Subhas Chandra's
Hope-multiplication.

*

For eight months
Subhas was with Deshabandhu
In the same jail.
The closer he became,
The deeper grew his love and admiration
For his mentor.
The saying "Familiarity breeds contempt"
Was, for him and also for others
Who subscribed to his view,
Nothing short of absurdity.

January 1997

DESHABANDHU: BENGAL'S BELOVED FRIEND

DF 18. DESHABANDHU CHITTA RANJAN (SONG)

Deshabandhu Deshabandhu
    Chitta Ranjan
Banger hiyar ashesh gaurob
    Amulya dhan
Bharat matar mukti swapan
Tumi tomar ashrunayan
Chitta Ranjan Chitta Ranjan
Data samrat tomar jiban
Chitta Ranjan Chitta Ranjan
    Paramer das
Bhitar bahir sudha nirjhar
    Banger ullas

27 April 1993

BENGAL'S BELOVED FRIEND

Bengal's beloved friend, Chitta Ranjan,
You are the endless glory
And invaluable wealth of Bengal's heart.
To fulfil Mother India's Liberation-Dream
You became the ceaseless flow
    Of your tearful eyes.
Chitta Ranjan, Chitta Ranjan,
Self-giving emperor your life became.
Chitta Ranjan, Chitta Ranjan,
The choice instrument
    Of the Absolute Lord Supreme.
Within, without a nectar-fountain;
Ecstasy immeasurable of Bengalis
    In the heart of Bengal.

DESHABANDHU: BENGAL'S BELOVED FRIEND

NOTES TO DESHABANDHU: BENGAL'S BELOVED FRIEND

DF 6. *(p.582) Deshabandhu.* In 1945, when Sri Chinmoy was thirteen years old, he wrote a poem in Bengali about Chitta Ranjan Das. It was entitled "Deshabandhu." In Sri Chinmoy's handwritten notebook, which still survives, the singer of the highest magnitude and extremely close disciple of Sri Aurobindo, Dilip Kumar Roy, has made two minor corrections to this particular poem. He also read about two hundred of the then Chinmoy's Bengali poems, made necessary corrections and highly appreciated the talents of the budding poet.

DF 7. *(p.583) Chitta Ranjan Das.* In 1957 Chinmoy wrote this article on C.R. Das which was printed in *Mother India,* the Sri Aurobindo Ashram periodical. It was later published in Sri Chinmoy's book *Mother India's Lighthouse* (Rudolf Steiner, 1973).

DF 7,26. *(p.588) Spirituality in Art* was published in the *Mother India* of April 1959. Translation by Chinmoy.

DF 7,29. *(p.589) With thee came down the immortal breath....* Translated by Romen from the original Bengali.

DF 8-10. *(p.592) Three dramatic scenes from The Descent of the Blue.* When Sri Chinmoy was between twenty-six and twenty-eight years old, he wrote a full-length drama about the life of Sri Aurobindo entitled "The Descent of the Blue." Three scenes in that play focus on C.R. Das and his historic defence of Sri Aurobindo, as well as his later urge to follow the spiritual life. The play was published serially between 1958 and 1962 in "Mother India".

DF 11. *(p.598) A larger than the largest heart.* 15 January 1979.

DF 12. *(p.600) The kind-hearted barrister.* 26 April 1993.

DF 13. *(p.601) Chitta Ranjan incognito.* 26 April 1993.

DF 14. *(p.603) To clear his father's name.* 26 April 1993.

DF 15. *(p.604) A real king and queen.* 28 April 1993.

DF 16. *(p. 605) God alone knows who is deserving.* 28 April 1993.
DF 17. *(p. 608) Extract from Birth Centenary offering.* As a prayerful offering on the occasion of the Birth Centenary of Netaji Subhas Chandra Bose on 23rd January 1997, and the forthcoming 50th Anniversary of India's Independence that same year, Sri Chinmoy wrote a book entitled *Mother, Your 50th Independence-Anniversary! I Am Come. Ever in Your Eternity's Cries and Your Infinity's Smiles, Subhas.* Chapter four of that book is devoted to the relationship between Subhas Chandra and Chitta Ranjan. Subhas accepted Deshabandhu as his political Guru.
DF 18,2. *(p. 612) Bengal's beloved friend.* Author's translation of *Deshabandhu Chitta Ranjan* song.

PART VII

CHANDA AND TANDRA

CHANDA AND TANDRA

SRI CHINMOY

CT 1. DRAMATIS PERSONAE

[The first edition edition of the play *Chanda and Tandra* presented no *dramatis personæ* and no stage directions. Also, character lines were not preceded by character names.]

CHANDA AND TANDRA

CT 2. SCENE 1

"Mother, brother Chanchal is not allowing me to sleep."

"Sleep, day and night! Sleep, only sleep! If you complain once more, I shall pull you by the ear, Tandra."

"Just try!"

"What will you do if I do it?" Chanchal asked.

"I shall make Mother punish you."

"If you tell Mother, your life is in danger."

"Yes, you make me feel that it will be as easy for you to strike me as it is for you to steal sweetmeats."

"Shut up! When did you see me stealing?"

"I have seen it with my own eyes. I shall tell Mother. Just the other day I saw you eating sweetmeats from Uncle Narayan's room without his knowledge."

Is it called stealing if one takes sweetmeats from one's own uncle? I do it quite often. Besides, he himself has told me to take them at my sweet will."

"Another lie! When did he tell you?"

"I am a thief! I am a liar! You are a baby, but you have insulted me deeply."

Saying this, Chanchal delivered a smart slap to his younger sister. Tandra immediately started screaming as if someone had attempted to stab her. Their mother, Bharati Devi, and their elder brothers and sisters rushed into the room. Their father, Brahmamoy, was meditating, but his trance came to an abrupt end.

Seeing danger, Chanchal took to his heels. Tandra's screaming and crying would not come to an end, however. In many ways Bharati Devi tried to console her youngest child. She promised to punish Chanchal severely. But even then Tandra did not stop crying. Finally the mother lifted Tandra into her lap and put some sweetmeats into her mouth.

The eldest daughter, Sarala, was deeply concerned. She said, "Tandra, have you heard the latest news? Have you heard that Neta-ji (Subash Chandra Bose) is still alive? He is coming to Calcutta today by plane. Listen, I hear the sound of the airplane. It seems Neta-ji has arrived. We are leaving for the airport. Are you coming?"

Hearing Neta-ji's name, Tandra immediately stopped crying. Had it been any other day she would have run to the airport herself, but today she just stretched out her arms towards her eldest sister. She knew perfectly well that her mother's lap was more comfortable than her sister's, but if she stayed with her mother she would not be able to go to see Neta-ji. Even a child of six has that much intelligence.

Tandra was about to leave for the airport with Sarala when, quite unexpectedly, her brother Bharat said, "Look, Mother. Tandra's cheek is all red. Her face is swollen. Chanchal is so cruel. Day and night he strikes me, too."

Hearing that her face was red and swollen, Tandra started crying and screaming again.

Sister Sarala became furious. "Bharat, you fool! You idiot!" she cried. "We found it so difficult to console her! God alone knows when you will be blessed with some intelligence!"

"Shut up! I am not a fool."

"How dare you tell me to shut up? I am your eldest sister!" Saying this, Sarala boxed Bharat's nose and said, "Do you think only boys can box?"

Bharat did not cry. Instead, he angrily pulled his sister's hair so hard that some of it came out in his hand. Bharat realised his mistake and was about to run away, but his sister would not let him go. Holding him with one hand, she slapped him many times with the other.

Seeing that the situation was becoming grave, Tandra once more began screaming. Their mother was beside herself. Meanwhile, Sarala left for the airport. Brahmamoy took Tandra in his lap, something which he had never done before. Immediately she became silent, proud and happy that she was sitting in her father's lap.

"Unbearable, unbearable!" Bharati Devi said to her husband. "All our children have gone to the dogs. Day and night they are quarrelling and fighting, screaming and shouting. How long can it go on? And you are determined not to pay any attention to their needs!"

"Don't worry. These things are quite natural and normal. Everything will be all right in the course of time. In our childhood I am sure we behaved the same."

"Never! In our time no one ever saw such unruly boys and girls."

"Anyway, what is to be done now?"

"They must be sent to a good school."

"I shall see about it."

"Before you make any decision, I tell you, our children will kill one another."

"No, no. Soon they will become calm, quiet, polite and obedient. We will have a most harmonious family."

"I don't think so."

"Well, in that case I must say that whatever you teach them is what they learn."

"Yes, I am teaching them how to strike and kill one another, how to live like hooligans!"

"I didn't mean all that, but ...."

"I understand you perfectly well in everything else, but I never understand your 'but ....'"

"My only cause of sorrow is that you women have never learned how to think."

"Enough! For God's sake, you don't have to worry about us. The Supreme Goddess always thinks about us. We don't need your concern."

"It is not enough if the Supreme Goddess alone thinks of you people. What can she do all by herself? You must also use your brains."

"You always ridicule me. I can't stand it anymore."

At this point Tandra intervened. "Father, how is it that you have such a long beard?"

"Tandra, it is quite natural for a grown-up to have a long beard," Brahmamoy replied.

"You mean Mother is not grown up?"

"True, your mother is grown up, but women don't have beards."

"Why?"

"God has not blessed them with beards."

"Why? That is not fair. Everyone should get the same thing."

"But what can poor God do? Women would not be pleased to have beards."

"I tell you, Father, I clearly see that God is partial to men. Even my own mother is partial to my brothers. She loves them much more than she loves me and my sisters."

"But I love my daughters more than I love my sons," Brahmamoy said.

"That is true. Tell me another thing, Father. Why are your hair and beard all red? Other men do not have hair that colour."

"That is a long story."

"Never mind. I am falling asleep. I don't want to hear the whole story. But tell me, Father, what was your father's name?"

"My father's name was Ananta."

"What was your mother's name?"

"My mother's name was Sima."

"I like your father's name, but not your mother's name. Now Father, what is your name?"

"Brahmamoy."

"Father, please shorten your name. I find it too hard to say."

"Why? Just say Brahma."

"Baimo."

"Don't worry. My grandmother also used to pronounce my name that way."

"Father, to tell you the truth, I am not interested in your father and mother and grandmother. But tell me one thing. Why does brother Chanchal tell me that it is a great sin to sleep during the day? He also says that if one sleeps during the day, then he will definitely be bitten by a snake!"

"That is nonsense! But you must know that it is not good to sleep much during the day."

"Mother always says, 'Go and sleep,' whenever she sees me during the day. However, Brother says I must not sleep during the day at all. It seems that you are taking Brother's side. Now I do not know whom to listen to."

"You should always listen to your mother."

After a while, Tandra fell asleep beside her father. Bharat had also fallen asleep, weeping, after having been beaten by his sister and struck by his mother for causing more problems. Nobody there had showed him any affection. Sarala had gone out after her argument with Bharat, and Chanchal had not yet returned home. It was getting dark.

Bharati Devi, who had not eaten anything all day, kept looking around to see if Chanchal had come back. She felt miserable about the whole situation. Her anger had now shifted to Tandra. Why had she called Chanchal a thief? Tandra deserved the punishment she had got from her brother, she thought.

"What is Tandra doing? It seems that she has decided to sleep the whole day. Unbearable! Unbearable! Is there anybody else on earth who is as unhappy as I am?"

Brahmamoy gave her a smile. "What is wrong with you?" he asked.

"You stay with your family. I cannot bear it any longer. The children are not at home. The whole day they have eaten nothing. Calamity after calamity has taken place. I am fed up with this kind of life."

"Why are you cowed so easily? Don't you know that in this world nobody is as happy as you are?"

"Certainly not! My younger sister is really happy. She has no children."

"Go and ask her. She will tell you that you are really lucky because you are blessed not only with one, but with six children."

Tandra awoke then and Brahmamoy said to her, "Chanchal has not eaten anything today. Will you go and look for him?"

"Certainly, Father. Mother, please give me some sweetmeats. I shall eat some, and the rest I shall give to brother Chanchal. I know where he is. He is at his student club. If he does not want to come back I shall tempt him with the sweets. You know that he is a greedy boy."

"Again you are insulting your brother. This time he will literally kill you."

"Mother, I am sure that by this time he has become calm and quiet. All his anger has gone away. He will carry me back on his shoulders. I shall not call him greedy, but I will tell him that he is far better than our eldest brother. Every time I tell him this, he places me right on his head and starts dancing."

"Look at the intelligence of this little girl!" said Brahmamoy.

All of a sudden Vidyut ran in screaming, "Our eldest brother has broken his arm. Chanchal-da and a few other boys have taken him to the hospital!"

At this Bharati Devi became completely hysterical. "My Prashanta has brokeh his arm! When am I going to die?" she moaned.

When he had calmed his wife a little, Brahmamoy immediately left for the hospital, taking her and Tandra with him. Bharati did not forget to bring some food for Chanchal.

Meanwhile, Vidyut went out to play again.

CT 3. SCENE 2

"Chanda!"

"Coming, Mother."

"Come quickly. Let me do your hair."

"No, Mother. I don't want it to be done today."

"Chanda, I have to comb your hair. It looks like a jungle."

"In that case you have to tell me a story."

"I am not in the mood to tell a story today."

"Why not, Mother? You know thousands of stories. Just tell me one."

"I find it difficult today to get in a cheerful enough frame of mind."

"What is wrong with your mind?"

"Ten years ago ...."

"What happened ten years ago that you cannot forget even now?"

"I shall not be able to forget it ever in this life."

"Then you have to tell me that story."

"No, I won't ever be able to tell you."

"All right. I don't really want to hear it. Just tell me any excellent story."

"No, I really can't do it today. Chanda, do you know that today is the Kali Puja?"

"Mother, let us go to the Kali Ghat."

"Not today. Some other day."

"Mother, are you really mentally upset today?"

"Not exactly."

"Well, since you cannot tell me a story, I shall tell you about a funny incident that took place at our school."

"Tell me."

"An old teacher came to teach us. I do not know his name. His hair and beard are all as white as milk, even his eyebrows.

He is a staunch follower of Gandhi. He was wearing a Gandhi cap and homespun clothes."

"What did he teach you?"

"He didn't teach us. He asked us a question right at the very beginning."

"What was the question?"

"Guess, Mother."

"I can't guess. I am not feeling well."

"Mother, if I knew a mantra, I would cure your mental disease right away."

"Tell me, for Heaven's sake, what did the teacher ask you?"

"Oh, it is a common question. He asked us what we would like to be when we grow up. Gayatri said that she would need some time to answer this question. Snigda was sitting beside her, and she immediately said that she would like to be a doctor. Do you know what Tapati said? She said that she would like to participate in the next Olympics. This year no Indian girls went to Europe to compete, and the European girls joked that poor India is not blessed with any women."

"What did Badal say?"

"Mother, this is a serious injustice on your part. You always prefer boys to girls. You didn't even ask me what I said."

"I like that boy very much."

"I shall tell you his answer last. Now I will tell you a funny answer. Bhola pinched Gita and Gita was about to give him a good slap. But Gita's movement caught the teacher's attention and he got furious. He said, 'Stand up on the bench.' Poor Gita had to stand up on the bench and give her answer. She was beside herself with anger, and she said she would like to be the goddess Kali and stand on Bholanath's chest. The teacher was satisfied with her answer and he let her sit down. Durga was sitting beside me. I asked her if she would like to be the goddess Durga and fight against the undivine forces while riding on a lion. Durga said, 'I laugh at that kind of fighting. I would like to be involved in modern warfare — flying planes and dropping atom bombs.' Gopal said that he would like be a pure devotee of Mahatma Gandhi. He is ready to give his life in offering good wishes to the Muslims."

"Was there no admirer of Lenin in your class?"

"You mean a communist? We are all communists. Do you know, Mother, why I am angry with your Badal? He stole my grand ideas. I do not know how he did it. All that I wanted to say he told the teacher before I got my chance, so I was compelled to say something quite insignificant."

"What did you say?"

"Well, I was going to say that I would like to be a poet, an artist, an ideal member of society. But Badal said all that before me. What could I do? I just prayed to God inwardly and told the teacher that I would be searching for a special power by which I could put an end to untold suffering and death. I said I wanted to be the dearest daughter of the divine Mother. The teacher just gave me a smile, but made no remark. But the boys and girls in the class were about to kill me, as if I had committed a serious crime. Right to my face, one of them said, 'You have learned all this nonsense from your aunt.' I didn't understand what he meant. Mother, is it true that you are actually my aunt?"

"What is wrong if an aunt becomes a mother?"

"There is nothing wrong, but why do you have to be my aunt and not my real mother? I always took you for my real mother."

"Ten years ago I became your mother."

"But Mother, I am eleven years old."

"True. Your mother left you with me ten years ago."

"That means I have another mother."

"You did have. Your mother and I used to study together. We were most intimate friends."

"Is it true that my father was a great doctor?"

"Yes, he was. But at the time of your mother's passing, your father, who is my dearest brother, took to sannyasa. To my wide surprise, your father left the country telling me exactly what you said to your teacher today. Now you see, Badal stole your ideas, and you have stolen your father's ideas."

"Mother, I am so delighted that I have inherited my father's sublime ideals. In that case, I don't blame Badal at all. I see that two persons can easily think alike."

"Certainly. It is quite possible."

"Mother, please tell me where Father is."

"I do not know where he is. He has accepted the life of a religious mendicant. Only once a year he writes to me. His letter begins and ends with this pithy message: 'On this Kali Puja day.'"

"Why does he write only that?"

"Because on this Kali Puja day ten years ago your mother left the body."

"Why did my mother die on that particular day?"

"Who can answer this question, my child?"

"Mother, quite a few times I have dreamt of a world in which I see no suffering, no poverty, no death, but only joy, pure joy, endless joy. Very often I visit that place in my dreams."

"Do you think of me when you are in that world?"

"I do think of you, but I do not see you there."

"Is there any way that one can transform this ordinary world into your dream world?"

"I am sure one can, but I do not know how, Mother. You were telling me about my mother. Please tell me her name."

"Your mother, who was my sister-in-law, had the name Uma. From now on I am your Aunt Mukti."

"No, that can't be. You will always remain my mother. If Uma was my mother, why did she leave me?"

"She did not leave you of her own accord. She was compelled to go."

"Who compelled her?"

"Death!"

"I shall put up a brave fight against death. The other day you told me the story of Satyavan and Savitri. You told me how Savitri brought back her husband from death. I shall not allow death to enter into this world any more."

"Nobody has been able to do that so far."

"That doesn't mean that nobody will ever be able to do it. I shall do it. In my dreamland there is no death. There is only Peace, Light and Delight."

"If your father knew about your dreams he would be exceedingly glad. This time when I receive a letter from him I shall show it to you. It is my most earnest desire that someday you will see your father."

"I am sure that Father will not be able to recognise me. But I shall be able to recognise him, because you will let me know beforehand. Will it not be real fun, Mother?"

"On the eve of his departure, your father told me that he might come to see you in twelve years if such was the Will of God."

"Why should it be God's Will in twelve years? Why can't it be now? How long have I to wait?"

"Only two years."

"Mother, let us go and see him before he comes here."

"I do not know where he is, Chanda. Yesterday I received a letter from my eldest sister's husband. He has invited us to come and visit the family. He says that Tandra always speaks about you with great admiration. Do you want to go?"

"Certainly, Mother. I love Tandra very much. Tandra calls me Phuli, which means flower. Nobody shows me any respect except Tandra. I am really fond of her."

"It seems that you like to be respected and admired as happens when you become the elder sister."

"It is not exactly that. But when somebody admires me and loves me, I want to give everything away to that person. Besides, I don't have any younger brothers or sisters. I am the only child in my family."

"Who told you so? You have a number of younger brothers and sisters. The young children in the neighbourhood are all your sisters and brothers. I have no younger sister or brother. I am the youngest in my family, but look how many children call me Didi [elder sister] with such love and admiration."

"Mother, just because you teach at the college your students call you Didi. What do you teach?"

"I teach history."

"I have already completed the history book. How is it that those big boys and girls have not yet completed their history? Are they all fools? Have they no brains?"

"My child, your history book and their history book are not the same."

"Mother, I shall teach history in college when I grow up. Everybody will love me and respect me as they do you. Will it not be fun, Mother?"

"By the way, did you know that Prashanta has broken his arm? He is getting better, though."

"Prashanta-da has broken his arm! He loves me so dearly. He loves me even more than he loves his youngest sister, Tandra. Also, he tells me that I have more intelligence than Vidyut."

"Don't call her Vidyut. You must call her Vidyut-di. She is much older than you. If you don't show her respect, how do you expect the young ones to respect you?"

"Mother, when shall we go to Tandra's?"

"During the Christmas vacation."

"I must take some beautiful gifts for Tandra."

"By the way, do you want to see a picture of your mother and father?"

"Oh, yes!"

Mukti went to get the picture.

"Look how beautiful they are. Bow down to them."

"Mother, what is the use of bowing down to a picture?"

"Who told you that it is just a picture? With what care and love I have preserved it. Today is the Kali Puja. Therefore I have placed flowers before the picture to offer them my love and respect."

"Mother, today I shall not go out to play. Like you, I shall worship Mother Kali today."

"What boon will you ask her to grant you?"

"Why, a very simple boon. I shall pray to her to return my parents."

"When your mother comes back, will you not forget me totally? I am sure you will not call me Mother then. Shall I not feel miserable?"

"No, never! I shall call you my mother and I shall call her my mother. Everyone else has one mother, but I shall have two mothers. I shall really and truly be happy then."

"Then don't forget to tell Mother Kali all this, and also don't forget to tell her about your dream."

CHANDA AND TANDRA

CT 4. SCENE 3

Chanda and her mother came to Tandra's house to spend the Christmas vacation. A new life had entered into Brahmamoy's family. Everyone was happy and busy. Tandra was extremely delighted to see Chanda. She alone was making noise enough for five people.

Tandra was most pleased with the doll that Chanda had brought her. Tandra's doll was able to speak. Sometimes it said that it wanted to eat; sometimes it said that it wanted to go out for a walk. Tandra had no rest. By listening to her doll's commands she became extremely tired. If anyone said that he could not understand the language of the doll, then he put his life at stake. But Tandra was perplexed about one thing.

"Mother, do you know what my doll likes to eat?"

"Certainly I know. Whatever you like to eat, your doll also likes to eat."

"I am so happy that you understand my doll's language. How is it that you understand dolls so well? Do you have any dolls?"

"I used to have dolls when I was your age." But then Vidyut said, "Look at this stupid girl. How can a doll talk?"

Bharati Devi did not want a fight to start between the two sisters, so she said, "Tandra, Vidyut knows nothing. Don't pay any attention to her. You play with your doll. Let me go and talk to your Aunt Mukti. Where has Chanda gone? She is so shy. She just bowed to me, and now she has disappeared."

"She is shy? Do you know that she knows how to ride on a bicycle? She has promised that she will teach me how," Tandra said.

"No, Tandra. I don't want you to learn how to ride a bicycle. You will break your arm or leg, like your eldest brother, and everybody will suffer."

"Mother, do you mean that everybody who rides a bicycle breaks his arms or legs?"

"It is not that. But I want you to wait for a few years. You are too young."

"Mother, don't you see how big I am?"

Meanwhile, Brahmamoy and Mukti were engaged in serious conversation. Mukti had always been afraid of Brahmamoy, for he seemed continually moody. He paid no attention to social customs and etiquette. In a sense, he was not sociable at all. He did not know how to converse easily, so he spoke very little. Yet from his heart there flowed a river of compassion towards all human beings.

Naturally he had great love and compassion for Mukti, since she was his wife's sister. He had tried his utmost to start this conversation on a most suitable subject. The moment Mukti bowed to him he said, "I am really fortunate to have before my eyes the vision of a goddess. Although your house is not very far from ours, you don't come here very often."

"When did I ever decline your invitation?"

"You are right. I have not invited you, but I am sure your sister has invited you many times."

"Who is she to invite me? This is your house. I will come only when I am invited by you."

"Who told you that this is my house? Since the day your sister stepped into this house it has been totally hers."

"That means you pay her the rent regularly?"

"No, she is kind enough to let me live here free of charge. But I must say, if I do anything wrong, make even the slightest mistake, it is simply impossible for me to stay here."

"Why do you speak ill of my sister? Don't you know that I shall report it to her?"

"For twenty years I have lived with your sister, but I have not been able to understand and believe her. How can I dare to believe and understand you? For God's sake, don't tell her."

"Why? What will happen if I tell her?"

"A great calamity will take place."

"That means you are extremely afraid of my sister."

"Absolutely!"

"I have come to you to hear some sound advice about the spiritual life, and instead I am hearing only about family life."

"In your sister's domain, spirituality is forbidden."

"I don't approve of that. It is really an injustice on her part. Everybody should be free to act according to his will. Right from her childhood my sister has had a fiery temper."

Just then Bharati Devi entered the room, overhearing Mukti's final remark.

"So I have a fiery temper, Mukti? What more are you going to say about me? What more appreciation are you going to thrust upon me?"

Mukti became frightened and bowed to her sister, saying, "Forgive me, forgive me."

"I know, Mukti, it is not your mistake. It is your brother-in-law who has instigated you to say this. But I don't deny that my temper is of the quickest. How hard I try to control my anger, but in vain."

Saying this, Bharati left them. She had wanted to tell them something, but she had totally forgotten.

"Mukti, just because of you, this time I am saved. At times I want to accept *sannyasa* and become a sannyasi like your brother. There is nothing in this world except suffering, frustration and misery."

"You too want to become a sannyasi? You want to renounce everything? You want to be a real renouncer?"

"Don't call me a renouncer. What have I that I can renounce? My children don't listen to me, not to speak of your sister. I have no one to claim as my own. Everyone in the family thinks that he would be better off without me. Everyone wants freedom from all restraint, and nothing else."

"Tell me then, Brahmamoy, what makes you stay with your family?"

"Nothing special. I stay with my family as others do, for no particular reason. I know perfectly well that the achievements of this world are absolutely meaningless and useless, yet I am unable to give up this earthly life. Attachment within and without is all I see. Never can I escape from 'I'-ness. I really want to withdraw from this world."

"If everybody wants to withdraw from the world, then why was the world created?"

"I am sure God has a special purpose for it. But I certainly don't know what it is."

"The Indians call the world an illusion; therefore India is lagging far behind on the material plane."

"Illusion is illusion. How can you call it otherwise? Here on earth I cannot claim anything as my own. Name, fame, knowledge, even my own body, leave me without my approval. I really do not know what I am going to do with my life."

"Everything you say is true, but you have some duty to perform on earth. If you do not perform this duty, you will remain like inert matter."

"I know all that. Let me continue with my philosophy. In the process of evolution, from the mineral life there came into existence the plant life; from the plant life, the animal life came into existence; from the animal life, the human life has come into existence. Now we notice that there is a yawning gulf between the animal life and the human life. Man is far superior to the animals; nevertheless man is not fully satisfied with his present situation. On the one hand, we human beings are so helpless; on the other hand, we have the promise of becoming divine men. A tiny plant grows into a banyan tree. This tree lives for hundreds of years, but it remains a tree. It does not change into something else. But man has the possibility of change. When man is transformed, divinised, he becomes like Krishna, Buddha and Christ. Krishna, Buddha and Christ have far transcended humanity's ordinary level."

"If we can become like Krishna and Buddha, how is it that we don't become so?"

"We are too lazy, too attached, too ignorant. To become transformed and divinised we have to work very hard. We have to practise Yoga. We have to concentrate and meditate."

"I wish that you would try."

"No, Mukti, you try. The pressure of the family is simply too much for me. Your brother is a sannyasi. He has renounced the world. You have remained unmarried. I shall be very glad if you take to the spiritual life and inject some spirituality into your sister."

"What would you do if my sister renounced the world, leaving all the children with you?"

"She simply could not do it."

"In that case, you also can't do it."

"Let us not think of renunciation right now. I am not yet ready for it."

Suddenly Bharati entered again.

"Stop your philosophy now. You have talked long enough. Come and eat."

Mukti was startled. In a low voice she said to her brother-in-law, "Come with me. As long as you are with me there is no fear."

But Bharati overheard.

"Oh, I see. My husband has been telling you that I am a monster. He is scared to death whenever he sees me."

"No, Sister, he didn't say a word against you."

"What were you talking about, then?"

"We were just discussing ...."

"I understand. Both of you were speaking ill of me. I am sure you are looking for a medicine to cure my anger."

"Sister, have I ever told you a lie?"

"Then why can't you tell me what you were discussing?"

"You won't understand it, Sister."

"Am I a fool? All right, never mind. I don't care."

"No, Sister, you are not a fool. But you have no time to hear all about our philosophy. You are always busy with your children. You have great responsibilities. To bring up six children is not a task to be undertaken lightly. I am sure there are not many women who would be happy to undertake such a task. But on the other hand, when these children grow up and bring you name, fame and glory, you will be very happy and proud."

"Mukti, who will sympathise with my suffering? I have no one to confide in. I thought when you came here you would give me some comfort and peace of mind. Please stay with me for a few days."

All were eating except Prashanta and Chanchal.

"Where are Prashanta and Chanchal? Where have they disappeared to?" Mukti asked.

Bharati replied, "Don't speak of them. They have made me mad. They are nothing but my enemies, yet I cannot take my mind off them."

"Why do you have to take your mind off them? You are really lucky to have six children."

"Yes, it is easy for you to say this kind of thing. You have no idea how difficult it is to bring up children."

CHANDA AND TANDRA

"How can you say I don't know about it? Who is bringing up Chanda?"

"Chanda is an exception. She is most obedient. All my children are unruly, disobedient and worse than useless."

"Will you give me the responsibility for your children? I shall be happy to look after them."

"With deepest joy and gratitude I am ready to give you all my children."

"Then from now on you don't have to worry about them at all. I shall worry about them."

"Let them go to the dogs. I shall never think of them again. I shall have nothing more to do with them."

All this time Brahmamoy had been silent. With a smile, Mukti resumed her conversation on a different subject.

"Sister, your fish curry has turned out very well."

"Has it? I am now an old lady. I have forgotten all about cooking."

"Do you remember that our grandmother used to call you Anna Purna, the Goddess of Food?"

"She also used to call me something else. Do you remember it?"

"Yes, she used to call you Lakshmi as well. You know, Sister, I am still jealous of you. How I wish to be able to cook like you."

"Cooking is the work of a maidservant. How I wish to be learned like you."

Suddenly Prashanta came in with a letter.

"Aunt, here is a letter for you."

Mukti took the letter eagerly and started reading.

Brahmamoy asked, "Whose letter is it?"

"It is from my brother. Here is a piece of news which gives me tremendous joy. My brother wants Chanda and me to come to his ashram."

"Your brother has written to you? It is very strange that a world-renouncer has such attachment for the family."

Bharati said angrily, "Yes, everyone should be like you! Don't dare to compare yourself with my brother! My brother is a real jewel, not only to his family, but to all mankind! Mukti, tell him that I am coming with you."

Tandra said, "Aunt, I shall also go with you."

"Certainly you may. But not this time, please. Tomorrow Chanda and I shall leave for his ashram. Bharati, Brother writes in his letter that he has discovered a supreme Truth. He says that he will tell me personally. I am most curious and anxious to hear about it."

"You may go, then, but I shall not allow Chanda to go with you. She is a little girl. She won't be able to go through the austerities of ashram life."

"All right. You can keep her with you."

"So it is settled that Chanda will stay with us."

Chanda was silent, but Tandra spoke on her behalf.

"Mother, why don't all of us go and visit my uncle's ashram?"

"That is what we want, dearest Tandra. But we need his permission. I will write to him. Satya really and truly loved me."

"Oh, my uncle's name is Satya?"

"Yes."

That night Chanda had no sleep. She was full of fear. She thought that her mother would not take her to see her father, and she had good reason for her apprehension.

The following morning her Aunt Bharati refused to let her go with her mother.

Mukti tried to persuade Bharati to change her mind.

"I think it will look odd if I don't take Chanda with me. What will her father think of me? She has been eager to see him for a long time."

"I understand all that. I will take her with me when I go to visit Satya with the rest of the family."

Tandra was extremely happy that Chanda was not going. She would be able to learn how to ride a bicycle from her cousin. Mukti was about to depart, and everybody was saying farewell to her.

Brahmamoy said, "Don't forget us, please."

"Impossible! How could I?"

But Chanda was missing. Where had she gone? Mukti was terribly worried and upset. At the last moment all her plans were disrupted. Where had the child disappeared to? Without saying farewell to Chanda, how could Mukti think of leaving?

Everyone was searching high and low for Chanda, but Chanda had made herself comfortable in the car. She would not be deprived of the earliest possible visit to her father. Impatient to begin the journey, she honked the horn. Mukti's tears of anxiety were transformed into tears of joy, and mother and daughter set off together happily.

APPENDIX

NOTES TO THE PRESENT EDITION

Notes to the present edition

Obeying the Author's wish, the present edition follows the typographical style for typesetting drama plays, either in verse or prose, defined by the Imprimerie nationale.
    That includes the introduction of characters' lines, rendering of stage directions, division of plays into acts and scenes, *dramatis personæ*, etc.

Plays in both volumes

Some of these plays were published in more than one book. The exact content and sequence has been preserved, so it will be possible to find a play in both volume I and II of the *Plays*.

Chanda and Tandra

The first edition of *Chanda and Tandra* presented no dramatis personæ and no stage directions. Also, character lines were not preceded by character names.

PREFACE TO FIRST EDITIONS

Editor's preface to the first edition of Sacred fire

This play was written by Sri Chinmoy as a devoted offering to the soul of America on the bicentennial of the founding of this country.

Editor's preface to the first edition of Deshabandhu: Bengal's beloved friend

India won her independence from British rule on 15 August 1947. Sri Chinmoy wrote this imaginative play about India's revolutionary heroes in Bengali, his mother tongue, in 1948 at the age of sixteen. The play celebrates the contributions of three immortal freedom-fighters from Bengal: Deshabandhu, Netaji and Deshapriya. Deshapriya hailed from Sri Chinmoy's own birthplace of Chittagong.

Sri Chinmoy translated this play into English in November 1996 in honour of the forthcoming 50th anniversary of India's Independence and the birth centenary of Netaji Subhas Chandra Bose, the greatest Indian freedom-fighter of all.

The play was first performed by Sri Chinmoy's students in Kagoshima, Japan, on 23 January 1997 – the day of Netaji's birth centenary. It is significant that Netaji's ashes are preserved at the Renko-ji Temple in Japan. Sri Chinmoy made a soulful pilgrimage to this temple on 26 December 1996.

BIBLIOGRAPHY

SRI CHINMOY:

– *The disciple illumines the Master*, New York, Sky Publishers, 1973, [DI].
– *The heart of a holy man*, New York, Sky Publishers, 1973, [HH].
– *Mother, give me the Light of Knowledge*, New York, Sky Publishers, 1973, [LK].
– *Supreme sacrifice*, New York, Sky Publishers, 1973, [SU].
– *The sacred fire*, New York, Agni Press, 1975, [SF].
– *Deshabandhu: Bengal's beloved friend*, New York, Agni Press, 2000, [DF].
– *Chanda and Tandra*, New York, Vishma Press, 1974, [CT].

Note: suggested citation-key in square brackets.

POSTFACE

Publishing principles

This edition of *The works of Sri Chinmoy* aims to obey the Author's wish: scrupulous fidelity to his original words, use of typographical style by him selected, specific spelling choices, end placement of any editorial content (i.e. not written by Sri Chinmoy himself), particular treatment of some personal nouns in special cases, etc.

Textual accuracy

This edition has been checked to ensure faithful accuracy to the originals. Although much effort has been put in proofreading and comparing different versions of the text, this print may still present lingering errors. The Publisher would be grateful to be apprised of any mistypes via postal mail or facsimile, possibly with scan of the original page where the text is different. Please use original books only, specifying the year of publication, as no online version can be considered authoritative.

Ongoing reprints will include any revised text from these errata.

Acknowledgements

The Publisher is very grateful to the late Professor Lambert and his équipe for his invaluable advice. For many decades Prof. Lambert conducted a small publishing house specialising in hand-made prints of philological edition of the classics. The standard of this edition would not have been the same without his scholarly advice.

The Publisher is also grateful to the international team of collaborators that spent countless hours proofreading and checking the current text against the originals.

Our deepest gratitude to Sri Chinmoy. His living presence can be felt breathing throughout his writings. It is a privilege to be involved with his works, in any form.

Citation keys

Citation keys are used throughout *The works of Sri Chinmoy* to allow accurate cross-reference of texts across titles and editions. Examples: EA 13, ST 50000, UPA 7.

Sri Chinmoy Canon

We could not use better words than Professor Lambert's, who kindly offered the name *Sri Chinmoy Canon*:

> «By defining Sri Chinmoy's first editions as *editio princeps* we chose to follow classical scholarship criteria, not because we consider Sri Chinmoy's work antique, but because we believe it is among the few post ‹classical antiquity› works to rightly deserve to be considered a *classicus*, designating by that term *superiority, authority* and *perfection*.
>
> «The monumental work Sri Chinmoy is offering to mankind is awe-inspiring and supremely pre-eminent in proportions and quality. It is manifest that Sri Chinmoy's work — which we feel right to call *The Sri Chinmoy Canon* — will be of profound help and source of enlightenment to anyone seeking a higher wisdom, truth and reality supreme.»

[Translated from French by M. G.S.]

TABLE OF CONTENTS

PART I:

THE DISCIPLE ILLUMINES THE MASTER	3
THE DISCIPLE ILLUMINES THE MASTER	3
MAITREYI	23
SAVITRI	31
KALI AND KRISHNA ARE ONE	45
SUNDA AND UPASUNDA	53
RADHA AND KRISHNA ARE PURE	67
GANAPATI'S MARRIAGE	75
DASHARATHA PROMISES AND RAMA EXECUTES	85
DASHARATHA'S DREAM IS AT LAST FULFILLED	101
WHO IS THE OWNER: THE LIFE-SAVER OR THE LIFE-TAKER?	107
THE BUDDHA AND ANANDA	113
SRIBAS	119
WHOEVER DIES TODAY AT FOUR P.M. WILL GO TO THE HIGHEST HEAVEN	125

PART II:

THE HEART OF A HOLY MAN	147
THE HEART OF A HOLY MAN	147
ARUNI	151
DON'T ENCOURAGE THE UNDESERVING ONES	159
LIGHT IS THE ONLY WEALTH WORTH HAVING	167
SARASWATI	179
THE SAINT AND THE KING	189
THE SEEKER AND THE THIEF	195
GAUTAMI	199
KURU	205
UDPANTIRTHA	209
THE DISCOVERY OF SHOES AND UMBRELLA	219
THE MASTER WITH HIS FOUR DISCIPLES	225

PART III:
MOTHER, GIVE ME THE LIGHT OF KNOWLEDGE 233
MOTHER, GIVE ME
THE LIGHT OF KNOWLEDGE,
THE LIGHT OF DISCRIMINATION
AND THE LIGHT OF RENUNCIATION 233
VISHWAMITRA 239
DHRUVA 249
TWO DIVINE LIARS: ARE THEY REALLY SO? 265
O WORLD-RENOUNCER, BE CAREFUL! 275
JAJATI 281
SIDDHARTHA BECOMES THE BUDDHA 291
SARIPUTRA, YOU ARE A FOOL 301
TWO DISCIPLES 305
AKBAR, TANSEN AND HARIDAS 313
NOT HOW MANY HOURS YOU MEDITATE,
BUT HOW YOU MEDITATE 325
PRAJAPATI AND HIS THREE STUDENTS 331
I AM FALLEN 343

PART IV:
SUPREME SACRIFICE 359
THE SUPREME SACRIFICE OF KING SHIBI 359
BUDDHAM SARANAM GACCHAMI 373
SURYA AND SANJNA 383
HARISH CHANDRA 399
UPAMANYU 419
ONE MUST FOLLOW ONE'S OWN NATURE 435
WHO IS THE GREATEST? 441
HE EATS GRASS BUT CARRIES A NAKED SWORD 455
NOT SO EASY TO CHANGE ONE'S FATE 465
THREE MIRACLES BY A BRAHMIN'S HANDS 475
THE WINNER 481

WHY SHOULD I BE RESPONSIBLE?	489
RAMA FAILS	499
PART V:	
THE SACRED FIRE	509
PART VI:	
DESHABANDHU: BENGAL'S BELOVED FRIEND	567
ADDITIONAL WRITINGS ON DESHABANDHU	581
THREE DRAMATIC SCENES FROM "THE DESCENT OF THE BLUE"	591
SIX STORIES ABOUT CHITTA RANJAN DAS	597
CHITTA RANJAN AND SUBHAS CHANDRA: THE LIGHT-BESTOWER VERSUS THE STRENGTH-PRODUCER	607
BENGAL'S BELOVED FRIEND	611
PART VII:	
CHANDA AND TANDRA	617
APPENDIX	643
NOTES TO THE PRESENT EDITION	645
PREFACE TO FIRST EDITIONS	649
BIBLIOGRAPHY	653
POSTFACE	657

A LYON, LE 13 FÉVRIER LXXXVIII Æ.G.

*Composition typographique par imprimerie
Ab Academia Aoidon, Paris & Lyon.*

*Un grand merci à Prof Knuth pour
l'utilisation avancée de TEX.*

www.ingramcontent.com/pod-product-compliance
Lightning Source LLC
Chambersburg PA
CBHW030110240426
4366ICB00031B/1358/J